MAKING IT TILL FRIDAY

MAKING IT TILL FRIDAY

Your Guide to Effective Classroom Management

◄○►

Fifth Edition

James D. Long
Robert L. Williams

Princeton Book Company, Publishers

Copyright ©1977, 1981, 1985, 1989 and 2005 by Princeton Book Company, Publishers
PO Box 831
Hightstown, New Jersey 08520

Drawings by John McMenamin
Design and composition by Elizabeth Helmetsie
Cover design by John McMenamin and Elizabeth Helmetsie

Library of Congress Cataloging-in-Publication Data
Long, James D., 1942–
    Making it till Friday: your guide to effective classroom management / James D. Long,
  Robert L. Williams—5th ed.
        p.cm.
    Includes bibliographical references.
    ISBN 0–87127–268–7 (alk. paper)
      1. Classroom management.   I. Williams, Robert L. II. Title.
  LB3013.L66 2005
  371.102'4—dc22

                                                              2005048665

8 7 6 5 4 3 2 1

Contents

‒‹o›‒

Preface

The title of our text might initially suggest that it is a survival manual for teachers, a blueprint for coping with the stresses of each work day until the weekend finally comes. Indeed, there are teachers who begin looking forward to the weekend on Monday morning. Besides anticipating the weekend, some are living for the holidays that punctuate their teaching calendar, with summer vacation being the ultimate prize. Some teachers actually mark their calendars and count down the days until the next break from teaching. The problem with focusing on the breaks from teaching is that teachers may miss the sense of fulfillment and enjoyment potentially available in each teaching day.

Although our title is intended to resonate with teachers, our text is not just about survival. Instead, the primary focus of this edition of *Making It Till Friday*, like earlier ones, is to provide teachers with strategies for achieving success each workday. Each chapter contains both ideas that effective teachers have used for years and cutting-edge trends in classroom management research. For example, a new chapter on communication has been added to stress the importance of developing effective ways of communicating with all members of the teacher's school family, that is, students, parents, and co-workers. This chapter also contains ideas presented in earlier editions about the influence of teacher attitudes on interpersonal relationships.

Another new chapter on life outside the classroom discusses the integral relationship between life inside and outside the classroom and offers suggestions for achieving a balance between your personal and professional life. In addition to the new chapters, you will find new information on teachers' beliefs about who is responsible for what happens in the classroom, ways teachers can reconnect with their vision of teaching, planning strategies likely

to contribute to learning gains, ways to support student efforts and achievements without being perceived as manipulative, strategies for extending the benefits of extrinsic rewards, suggestions for dealing with bullying, and a model for managing classroom problems, to name just a few. In brief, we have tried to emphasize that a pleasant journey during the work week makes for a pleasant arrival at the weekend.

Another notable change you will notice is a change in authorship. Dr. Virginia Frye, the co-author of previous editions, has retired from her full-time job as Assistant Professor of Medical Genetics at the University of Tennessee Medical Center, Knoxville and supervising psychologist at the University of Tennessee Developmental and Genetics Center. She continues to work part-time and to serve on the Professional Advisory Board for a local Autism Society. We offer our special thanks to Virginia for her work on previous editions and for her editorial assistance and help with the references for chapter seven.

Although no brief text can include every strategy useful to teachers, we have tried to offer enough strategies to permit all teachers to identify some approaches that will work for them and their students. Because the text is selective rather than inclusive, it should be viewed as a beginning point in your efforts to become an expert on classroom management. Finally, because most of the ideas offered are based on research conducted in actual classroom settings, the book stresses practice rather than theory per se. We hope your study and application of the ideas in *Making It Till Friday* will enhance your life, both in and out of the classroom.

"What's the problem, Liz? You seem a bit anxious."

"I am. You know what tomorrow is, don't you?"

"First day of school. You'll do fine. You always have."

"I know, but I can't help being nervous. I get this way every year a couple of weeks before the summer ends."

"You've never had any problems you couldn't handle. So why worry?"

"It's not problems that concern me, Dan. Teaching is a big responsibility. I'll have new students and parents who will be depending on me. Being able to work with so many people who have different needs isn't easy. And just getting back into the routine takes some doing."

"I know. I sometimes feel anxious myself when taking on a new project. What can I do to help?"

"Being supportive and listening helps a lot. Maybe I can share the highlights of my first day back with you over dinner tomorrow evening."

1

Beginnings
An Introduction

Many teachers, new and veteran, experience feelings similar to those expressed by Liz in the opening dialogue with her confidant. Beginning a new school year is much like starting a new job, even for those who have been teaching for years. There are new students, new parents, new colleagues, and sometimes a new principal. It can be particularly stressful for a teacher who is facing everything for the first time. The beginning of the school year also may bring an abrupt change in how you spend your time. During the summer, you may have had considerable time to call your own and focus on your own needs, but now you must spend much of your time meeting others' needs, especially your students'.

Just the necessity of adjusting one's routine can create anxiety. In addition, having responsibility for the well-being of others can produce legitimate pressure. There really isn't any way of avoiding some tension over the start of a school year. Even skilled actors talk about stage fright. Many say they simply never get used to facing a new audience but they often use their anxiety as motivation for giving a superb performance. When properly managed, your apprehension about the start of school can lead to superior preparation for the school year. In fact, most of the beginning and experienced teachers we know want to do well—which is why they may feel both excited and uneasy about the prospects of a new beginning.

Although tensions associated with beginning the school year are natural, anxiety need not be a continuing facet of your work. Teaching should enrich not only students' lives, but teachers' lives as well. Accepting anything less is an unnecessary compromise. Individuals who are truly committed to teaching are usually able to overcome the initial stresses of a new beginning and bolster their confidence as the school year unfolds.

Teachers can do many things to approach their work with confidence. This is the focus of chapter one. We begin with a short discussion about what to do during the first few days of school, discuss what it means to manage a classroom, look at ways of assessing your commitment to teaching, and then turn to selected teacher beliefs about teaching. We end the chapter by highlighting what you can expect in the remainder of the text.

The First Few Days

All teachers, especially new teachers, have challenging questions to answer at the beginning of a school year. Perhaps the most immediate question is, "What can I do to get the school year off to a good start, particularly during the first few days of school?" It is difficult to overestimate the importance of this question because the beginning of the school year sets the tone for the remainder of the year. Moreover, being adequately prepared for the start of the school year can help you control any initial jitters you may have about addressing the needs of a new group of students. So let's look briefly at your most important priorities at the beginning of the school year.

Arrive Early

Although arriving early at your workplace is fundamental to success on any job, arriving well ahead of time during the first few days of school is especially critical. Parents may be waiting to see you about their children's specific needs; students may already be in the classroom without supervision; or administrative issues may need your attention before the day begins. Indeed, if you arrive just in time for school, you may feel yourself working under a sense of urgency to get things done. Seeing you scurrying about is unlikely to give students a sense of psychological safety or put you in an authoritative light to them.

Allowing yourself extra time before work begins on the first few mornings, perhaps thirty to forty-five minutes, will help you deal with the unexpected and compose yourself for the day. You will also have time to ensure all materials are in place for your students (e.g., required texts on student desks, needed supplies in the classroom). You can then station yourself at the entrance to your classroom to greet students, welcome them to your classroom, direct them to their seats, and instruct them to begin work on an assignment at

AVOIDING IDLE TIME

Once students have been directed to their seats, you want them immediately to begin working on an interesting learning activity while you are still greeting other students. After greeting the student, instruct him or her to find a seat or to go to the seat you have assigned to begin work immediately on the activity at his or her desk. You should avoid a high-intensity group activity that will involve lots of movement and noise the first day of class. Instead, you might have a personal information form, a survey of student interests, a brain teaser, a crossword puzzle, an art activity (for younger students), or an interesting current event article on each student's desk that students can work on independently. If you have an aide or volunteer available, he or she can make sure students are engaged in the learning activity until you are ready to address the whole class. The idea is not just to avoid leaving students on their own, rather to establish right away that the classroom is a productive learning environment.

Set a tradition from the first day that class begins as soon as a student enters the classroom, even before the bell has rung. To maintain this tradition throughout the school year, you should post the assignment every day. Students can immediately see what is to be done that day and begin work right away. Thus, entering the room rather than hearing the bell or the teacher's admonition to get to work will become the cue for starting each day's assignment.

their desk. You will also have time for brief conversations with parents should they accompany their children on the first day. An inviting smile and a "Good morning, I'm (name); welcome to my class" tells students that you are expecting a good day. A warm greeting can also help them get started on a positive note.

Learn Students' Names Quickly
Many people say they have no difficulty remembering faces but are not good at remembering names. It's certainly easier to remember whether you have seen someone than to remember the person's name. Although remembering names need not be a difficult task, it typically takes some practice and repetition. When meeting students and parents, you should make a practice of using their names in conversation. For example, as you greet students, you should give your name and then ask their names if they don't spontaneously identify themselves. You can then repeat their names as you welcome them to your class.

You should also review your class roll before students start arriving. This will allow you to practice saying the names, as well as give you an opportunity to check on the pronunciation of names with which you are unfamiliar. Reviewing your class roll before the first day of class will also help you identify students not on your roll who show up in your classroom; they may have been added to your class or actually might belong in another classroom. If a student who is not on your roll appears, ask for the student's registration form to confirm he or she is in your class. If the student is not in your class, direct him or her to the proper classroom. Posting your name and the class identity (such as grade level and subject area) beside your door will keep some students from entering who are supposed to be elsewhere.

Another strategy you might use to learn students' names is to write each student's name on a five-by-seven index card, fold it, and stand it up on the desk where you want the student to sit initially. You might also want to take pictures of your students sitting behind their name cards. If you use a digital camera, you can then place the pictures on a computer and print them out for you to review several times during the first week of school. You can also take a group picture of the class, which you can display for students to view.

Quickly learning your students' names is important for many reasons. Students who feel anonymous may be more inclined to misbehave than students who recognize that you know who they are. More important, learning their names lets students know you

CHECKING THE ROLL

One task you will have the first day of class and every other day of the school year is taking the roll. For a variety of reasons (e.g., students' safety, school funding), it is very important to know who is present in your class each school day. Because you will probably not know many of your students at the beginning of the school year, you cannot readily check the roll by simply scanning the classroom. However, if you have assigned seats, you may be able to check attendance by scanning the matches between name cards and students in those seats. Or, you can put a check mark by the names on your roster as students enter the first day of class.

Despite its importance, taking the roll is not your first priority the first day of class or any other day in the school year. Getting students to work immediately is your first priority (Wong and Wong, 1998). Roll should be taken unobtrusively as students are working on their assignments. The only reason ever to call the roll is when you are using the activity for get-acquainted or instructional purposes. For instance, on certain days, you might have students respond to the roll call with specific information about themselves (e.g., favorite leisure activity, best-liked activity at school, vocational aspiration). Or you might ask students to answer the roll call with a question about the day's assignment.

are interested in them because you have taken the time to learn who they are. Few things are more precious to students than the sound of their own names, especially when it is connected to positive comments the teacher makes about them.

Write Home

If you have not done so before school starts, one of your early tasks will be to send a letter home to your students' parents. A welcoming letter to parents can take a variety of forms, but essentially you want to let them know you are eager to work with them in meeting their children's educational needs. You can find a sample letter home and sample newsletter for parents in chapter six, a chapter devoted exclusively to strategies for working with parents. Our point here is that early positive contact with parents, especially young students' parents, can be an important contributor to beginning the school year successfully. Parents are more likely to provide input you request and to follow through with your suggestions for working with their children if they have a personal sense of who you are and how you will be helping their children.

Spell Out Your Expectations

Students need to know from the first day what you generally expect of them both socially and academically. You do not want, however, to create stress for students by laying out details for every assignment you are going to make. Instead, your aim should be giving students the *big picture* of what your class is all about, how classes will be conducted, how much homework they can expect, what materials they will need to bring to class, and what achievement you expect from them.

You might also give students some preliminary ideas about their first unit of study and about any special tasks or programs they will be completing. For example, if they will be using computer programs to help them develop better writing skills, you can demonstrate how to use the program, give them an opportunity to try the program, and indicate how much time will be devoted to that learning activity. Similarly, if students will be completing a research project, you might provide examples of successful projects and indicate how you will assist them in developing their projects.

Develop Rules and Procedures

Details for establishing rules (those related to being respectful of others, participating in class discussions, and so on) and procedures (e.g., what students should do upon entering the classroom, how to line up for leaving the room, and how to use the restroom properly) are described in chapter three. It is best for you to begin the school year with your basic rules and procedures already in place and prominently posted in the classroom. Later you may wish to invite student input in refining those rules, possibly dropping some and adding

Spell out expectations

others. Early on, however, you should emphasize your rules and procedures, periodically review the rules, and let younger students practice any procedures that are new to them.

You may also want to tell students how you plan to respond to them—that is, discuss rules you have established for yourself, such as listening when students raise questions, asking students for their input on critical issues, and responding politely to them. In essence, you will practice the golden rule by treating your students as you want them to treat you. The main idea to convey to them is that your rules and procedures will create a positive environment where everyone can learn and be comfortable.

Determine Academic Functioning and Personal Interests
Before you can begin your instructional program, you need to know your students' levels of entering skills. You can begin by reviewing their past achievement records, which will give you a general notion of where to begin. But you can still conduct additional assessments to determine how much review your students need. For example, if you are teaching Algebra II, you want to know how much of Algebra I students have retained over the summer months and whether some students would benefit from a review of key Algebra I concepts. Similarly, if you are a kindergarten teacher, you will want to know what skills (e.g., knowledge of colors, recognition of letters, reading readiness) students possess.

You may opt to give a general test over prerequisite concepts for your first unit. Your school may have pretests in place that you can use or you may develop your own supplemental tests. The students should be informed that the tests would not be used to grade them, but rather to determine the best place to begin, to help them succeed with the first unit of study. Depending on the length of the pretests, they can be given the first or second day of class. Obviously, the format of the tests should be such that you can score them quickly and determine which prerequisite concepts may need to be reviewed. Ideally, you should begin that review the day after students take the pretest.

Don't forget to include a variety of preassessment procedures and topics. Too much paper-and-pencil assessment can dull student enthusiasm. For example, you can have discussions with students about their academic knowledge and personal interests. You can learn a great deal about their needs by asking them to tell you some of their customs and neighborhood activities. Details for addressing student needs and interests are described in chapter three. The point here is that you should not start an instructional program before determining students' academic skills and their major areas of interest in school.

Determine Any Special Needs
In addition to considering overall needs (which will help you develop strategies for making instruction practical for all students), you should determine whether you have students in your class with previously identified disabilities. Review of your class roster and student records will likely highlight students who have already been identified as having special needs and will provide information regarding the accommodations they need to progress in the general education curriculum. Chapter seven offers more details about working with special-needs students and clarifies your explicit responsibilities as a regular education teacher to students with special needs.

Early contact with parents also may help you identify any students who need referral. Later on you may recognize the need to make additional referrals for students who present problems you have been unable to address adequately. Your objective at the beginning of the school year is to be prepared to work effectively with all students and to make all of them welcome members of your class.

Challenge Misbehavior Immediately
Although greeting your students in a warm and friendly fashion may defuse some students' motivation to misbehave the first day of class, some may have an image to protect that transcends your kind treatment. In fact, they might interpret your cordial behavior as a sign you will be a soft touch. A cue that these students might be inclined to give you trouble can often be seen in how they enter the room on the first day of class. If they enter with a style likely to attract others' attention, watch out! If they make unnecessary noise, meander

around the room instead of taking their seats, and push another student or two as they make their rounds, ask them to come back to the door where they entered. Describe how they entered and specify the appropriate procedure for entering the room. Then ask them to find their seats in the manner you have specified (Wong and Wong, 1998).

You may think that confronting misbehavior when a student first enters a classroom is a bit early to challenge a student's misconduct. Remember, students are looking for any early sign as to what you will tolerate. Some are testing you from the time they enter the classroom. It is never too early to be firm in articulating and enforcing your expectations for appropriate conduct. Dealing later with a misbehavior that has established momentum will be far more difficult than dealing with it when it is first manifested. In their book *How to Be an Effective Teacher: The First Days of School*, Wong and Wong assert that "student achievement at the end of the year is directly related to the degree to which the teacher establishes good control of the classroom procedures in the very first week of the school year" (1998 p. 4). They further emphasize that "it is urgent also that your students know that you know what you are doing" (p. 4).

Challenge misbehavior

Review

Getting off to a good start involves knowing what you want to accomplish during the first few days of school. Being enthusiastic is always positive, but you can also take a number of logistical steps that help to make your entire school year a good one. The following actions increase the chances of your getting your school year off to a good start:

- Put in writing the kind of relationships you want to build with your school family (chapter two deals with building relationships through the use of effective communication skills);

- Arrive at school early to allow yourself time to get composed, make any needed preparation for the day, and avoid acting out of a sense of urgency should unexpected events arise;

- Greet students and parents at the entrance to your classroom;

- Have an initial assignment on students' desk that they are to begin upon taking their seats;

- Establish a plan for quickly learning your students' names;

- Make early contact with parents, such as sending an introductory letter home;

- Spell out on the first day of class the expectations and priorities you have for your students;

- Post rules and procedures for your classroom before the first day of class and devote considerable time the first day and first week of class to reviewing rules and practicing procedures (especially if you are teaching students in the early grades);

- Conduct preassessments so you know the best place to begin your instructional program;

- Determine whether you have students with special needs in your class and identify what accommodations they require to progress in the general curriculum;

- Confront misbehaviors when they first occur, and demonstrate appropriate responses in those situations.

We turn now to an examination of some of the more global issues of teaching that can impact your success as a teacher, focusing largely on the beliefs teachers bring with them into the classroom.

Beyond a Conventional View
of Classroom Management

A common perception, especially among the general public, is that stronger discipline is needed in managing American classrooms. Obedience and respect for authority are seen as the principal goals of discipline. And discipline problems are perceived primarily as inappropriate acts, such as those that undermine order or challenge authority. Further, many regard punishment as the most useful means for achieving discipline. However, we take the view that classroom management greatly transcends disciplinary issues.

A Positive View of Classroom Management

Classroom management and management problems are sometimes viewed as the equivalent of discipline and discipline problems, respectively. When Dan tried to reassure Liz in our opening dialogue, he was probably thinking of classroom problems involving misbehavior. Liz was quick to emphasize she was not concerned with problems per se. She appeared to be more concerned with her overall responsibilities in promoting student development, a perspective likely to be more useful in gaining control over her anxiety than simply equating success with freedom from classroom problems. Enjoyment comes from the contributions one makes, not from what one can escape or avoid.

In essence, classroom management consists of a diversity of strategies to facilitate teaching and learning. Even when you are trying to reduce undesirable student behavior, the underlying purpose should be to facilitate the development of desired behaviors. In other words, classroom management isn't just about diminishing what you don't want; it is far more about instilling what you do want—those things that will enhance the classroom experience for both you and your students. Developing positive behaviors is the first and most essential element of managing a classroom effectively.

A Broader View of Classroom Problems

Developing a broader view of classroom management also includes having a broader view of what constitutes a problem. Problems are not limited to situations where students disrupt learning activities; it is also a problem when students do not have the academic and social skills needed to be successful in and out of the classroom. Of course, teachers should set limits on the behaviors that students can exhibit, but teachers should be concerned primarily about deficiencies in student skills. If a student fails to interact with others, withdraws, or doesn't turn in assigned work, that student's behavior is a problem the teacher needs to address. Although such behaviors may not be disruptive to classroom proceedings, they may constitute even bigger impediments to long-term student development. Plus, upgrading students' skills is a principal means of reducing disruptive behavior.

Construing a management problem as a need for the student to learn important skills involves asking the question, "What is the best way I can help this student learn important subject matter and develop both a love of learning and skill in interacting effectively with others?" This perspective should lessen any tendency you may have to make accusations or to feel sorry for yourself about a management problem. It should also help you to perceive students who present problems as persons needing assistance in learning helpful content and skills rather than as troublemakers.

Assessing Your Commitment

Your commitment to your job can greatly affect your ability to deal with the stresses of work. If you have a passion for teaching, you will be less likely to retreat in the face of adversity. Your sense of what you want to achieve and experience in your life transcends the difficulty of the moment. In other words, commitment provides the motivation to confront the obstacles that can discourage the pursuit of your dreams, whether those obstacles are just jitters over beginning the school year or deeper disappointment later on.

Whenever you feel your enthusiasm for teaching is waning, you might reflect on your original reasons for pursuing teaching as a career. Remembering your desire to work with young people and to make a difference in their lives should help rekindle your interests.

A passion for teaching

Entering teaching to please others or merely to improve your chances of getting a job will engender little enthusiasm. Lasting commitment to teaching is more likely to be associated with enjoying what you do and believing that your work makes a difference. We believe that teaching is among the most important of all professions and have spent most of our adult lives as teachers. The following questions may help you assess whether you see a similar role for teaching in your life:

- What initially motivated you to be a teacher?
- What is it about a teacher's work that is more appealing to you than the work in other professions you considered?
- Do you have a passion for working with a particular group of students, such as those with disabilities or those from disadvantaged backgrounds?
- Do you have a love for a particular subject you want to share with others?
- Do you see teaching as a major way to contribute to young people's development and improve the quality of society?

If you have difficulty reconnecting with your original vision of teaching, talk with other teachers who are enthusiastic about their work and ask them about their initial aspirations. For example, you might ask, "Can you share with me some of the reasons you chose teaching as a career?" or "Tell me how you maintain your commitment to teaching when problems accumulate with students." Their responses might give you a new insight into teaching or renew a dormant desire. Also, if you are in a preservice or in-service program as you read our book, perhaps the book will help you chart a course of professional development that will bolster your dream of becoming a master teacher.

Identifying Your Current Sources of Job Satisfaction

"Remembering when" can be useful in reconnecting with your professional dreams, but you can also benefit from considering current sources of job satisfaction. Being satisfied with what you do, however, may depend on your focus: people tend to see what they are looking for. How many positives can you identify in teaching? If you are still preparing to be a teacher, you can look at studies examining the "perks" of teaching. For example, in a study conducted with experienced high school teachers in a California school district, Brunetti (2001) found teachers were motivated to remain in teaching for a number of different reasons, including:

- Having the opportunity to interact with students

- Seeing young people learn and grow

- Helping those students with difficulties to develop academically and socially

- Sharing their passion for certain subject areas

- Enjoying the excitement of working in the emotional and intellectual climate of teaching

- Having autonomy in making choices related to the management of their classes

- Serving society

Although some of the teachers in Brunetti's (2001) study reported being motivated by the practical benefits of teaching, such as having time off in the summer and job security, they felt that the professional aspects of teaching, such as working with students and seeing them learn, were the most satisfying. Overall, the teachers were highly satisfied with their jobs. Obviously, the more sources of job satisfaction in teaching, the more likely you are to persist in your chosen career.

Believing in Yourself

To overcome anxieties about working with students and others in your professional network, you must believe you are capable of meeting the challenges of managing a classroom. Teachers who don't believe they can control events in their classrooms are going to approach their role much differently than those who believe they can affect much of what happens in the classroom. To get a more precise sense of how much influence you have over your class, compare your perceived influence with that of others (e.g., parents, students, counselors, principal) who may have some control over conditions in your classroom. For example, who do you believe has the most control over the following classroom conditions?

- Instructional materials

- Class size

- Room configuration (e.g., seating arrangements)

- Student achievement

- Student conduct

- Group activities

COUNTING YOUR BLESSINGS

Is there any validity to the conventional wisdom that counting your blessings is good for you? Philosophers have long thought so, and researchers are now beginning to confirm this claim. For example, in a series of three studies, Emmons and McCullough (2003) found that keeping a list of one's blessings positively affected various measures of well-being. In study one, college students who listed the things they were grateful for (once each week over a ten-week period) reported more enjoyment of life and more hope about the upcoming week than did students in two other groups who listed either hassles or neutral events. The group who listed their blessings also reported getting more exercise and having fewer symptoms of health problems.

In study two, college students who kept daily records of their blessings over a two-week period indicated on a rating scale that they had experienced feeling "determined," "energetic," "interested" and "joyful" to a greater extent than did those who recorded hassles. There were no significant differences in positive affect for either the blessings or the hassles group when compared with a third group who recorded ways they believed they were better off than others. However, those recording blessings reported offering emotional support to others more often than students in either of the other two groups. There were no significant differences in reported health benefits over the shorter time period in study two.

Finally, in a third study (involving individuals suffering with neuromuscular disease), one group made daily recordings of blessings over a three-week period, whereas a control group responded only to rating scales and research questions. The gratitude group showed higher levels of positive emotional affect (i.e., feeling happy, excited, and inspired), less negative affect (i.e., feeling bitter, sad, and afraid), more satisfaction with life as a whole, more connection to others, and more optimism than individuals in the control group. The gratitude group also appeared to have improved sleep patterns (in terms of quality and quantity of sleep), but there were no other measurable health benefits.

You can add other conditions to this list and then assess who has the most control over each item. After your list is completed, assign a percentage value to each person's *over-all* contribution to a classroom where students are academically productive. For example, if you believe the teacher has slightly more than half the responsibility for the conditions that make for a successfully managed class, you might assign yourself a weighting of 55 percent. Then assign a weighting to each person on your list who can help you manage your class effectively. Given that you are trying to identify all the contributors to a well-managed classroom, the total value for all your sources of influence should equal 100 percent. Then construct a formula that summarizes the relative influence of various contributors to a successfully managed classroom (SMC). Your formula might look like the following:

SMC = *f* teacher (55%) + parents (15%) + students (15%) + principal (10%) + other (5%)

(where SMC is a function of the sum of all the factors you have listed.)

If you perceive yourself as having considerable influence over a condition needing to be changed, you should mobilize that influence irrespective of who might have originally created the condition. A child who does not get enough sleep at night to do his or her in-class assignments, for example, is not a problem you have created unless he or she is staying up to do an inordinate amount of homework. But you can still initiate contacts with others (the student, parents, or school social worker) who can help with the problem. In brief, if you see yourself as being an important player in producing classroom outcomes, you should be more willing to be proactive in improving the learning climate in your classroom than someone who perceives him or herself as having little influence.

Even if you did not initially assign a high value to your influence, you can change that perception. Sadowski, Blackwell, and Willard (1985) suggest that a greater sense of personal control might be achieved by learning new techniques to influence student behavior. Controllability is almost always a function of skill level. We are often surprised when surgeons talk about enjoying surgery. Nothing seems more intimidating to the two of us than cutting on the human body with someone's life at stake. But a person with the proper training and experience can approach even intricate surgery with a sense of confidence and

COMPARING YOUR ASSESSMENT WITH THAT OF OTHERS

One study (Long, Biggs, and Hinson 1999) dealing with teacher influence found that prospective teachers attributed only 41 percent of the responsibility for a well-managed classroom to the teacher, with the remaining 59 percent attributed to other involved groups: 25 percent to the students, 12 percent to the parents, and 22 percent to a range of other factors. Experienced teachers in the same study attributed 49 percent of the responsibility to the teacher, 13 percent to the parents, 12 percent to the students, 12 percent to administrators, and the remainder to other factors.

Both groups of participants believed the teacher was the most influential factor, but they still indicated that an accumulation of other factors was more influential than the teacher alone. In another study (Long, Long, and Gaynor 2000) dealing with the same topic, 100 out of 198 participants (teachers, student teachers, and education majors) listed the parents as having the single greatest influence on how a student behaves at school. How might this perception of parental influence affect the way teachers approach responsibility for classroom management?

accomplishment. So it is with teaching. Perhaps one of the following activities will extend your professional skills and comfort in teaching:

- Expanding your knowledge in a teaching specialty,
- Learning new strategies to enhance student motivation,
- Becoming involved in a professional organization that promotes teachers' well-being,
- Identifying ways to involve parents in classroom activities,
- Developing procedures to help students be more accountable for their own behavior,
- Working more closely with other school personnel,
- Visiting other schools or classrooms to observe what works well there.

Unfortunately, even if you see yourself as largely responsible for conditions in your classroom, you might still question whether you have the wherewithal to change those conditions. Individuals who don't believe they can execute the behaviors necessary to reach their goals are said to be low in self-efficacy. Beliefs regarding the ability to perform particular actions tend to be fairly stable because people often interpret events in ways that support their existing views. But change is possible nonetheless. Albert Bandura (1989, 1997), the foremost researcher on self-efficacy, suggests that a number of behaviors are associated with a strong sense of personal efficacy:

- Setting challenging goals,
- Visualizing yourself succeeding in your undertakings,
- Trying alternative strategies when you are confronted with obstacles to goal attainment,
- Believing you can ultimately succeed even when you initially fail to reach your goal,

- Placing yourself in challenging situations (e.g., meeting new people, learning new ideas) where you can use your talents,

- Preparing yourself for success by planning and pursuing activities to reach your goals,

- Monitoring your actions so you can make necessary adjustments to reach your goals.

Doing the things listed here will help you develop increased confidence in your teaching skills and your increased self-efficacy can have an important impact on others. Henson's (2001) review of studies on teacher self-efficacy reports a number of positive outcomes associated with teachers' confidence in their abilities, including higher self-efficacy and achievement among their students. Seeing improvement in your students' performance will boost your confidence even more.

COMBINING PERCEPTIONS OF COMMITMENT, CONTROL, AND JOB CHALLENGE

One of our former teachers used to say, "'Can't' never could do anything." She didn't accept "I can't" from any of her students and likely not from herself either. She realized you have to believe in yourself to have any chance of success. Indeed, various ways of thinking about yourself and your teaching serve as seeds for success or failure.

Suzanne Kobasa's (1979) research with business executives showed how their thinking about work influenced their health. Her research focused on the personality structures of 161 business executives whose scores on a stress scale predicted whether they would become ill during high-stress periods in their professional lives. Among those executives, approximately half (75) subsequently reported becoming ill following stressful events, whereas the others (86) with high stress scores remained healthy. Kobasa noted that the executives who remained healthy had greater perceptions of *control* over

what happened to them, had a higher *commitment* to resolving their work-related problems, and viewed the stressful events in their lives as *challenges* rather than as threats to their well-being. She referred to the combination of these three C's as "hardiness" and reasoned that their combined presence kept these hardy executives from succumbing to stress.

A study by Thomson and Wendt (1995) shows that student teachers are among other professionals who can benefit from a hardy personality. Thomson and Wendt found that hardy student teachers expressed fewer feelings of alienation (e.g., feelings of powerlessness and lack of involvement), even in a nonsupportive school climate, than did their less-hardy counterparts. The hardy student teachers seemingly had a set of beliefs that served as buffers to the stressful conditions of student teaching; they saw themselves as being able to influence and improve their student-teaching experience.

Believing in Your Students' Potential

The beliefs you hold about students are just as important as the beliefs you hold about yourself. In fact, the two are probably inseparable. You may occasionally find yourself regarding certain students very negatively, especially when they are highly disruptive. Just remember that even these students also exhibit desirable behaviors. The caring teacher's goal is to see beyond these students' faults to their commendable behaviors. As noted earlier, you should not see the student as the problem. Instead, you should focus on environmental events that may be creating the problem and seek to correct those conditions (see chapters three and four).

Even when focusing on changing environmental events to alter troublesome behaviors, you may still need to make a concerted effort to see the good in all your students. To help you focus on the positive things about students, try talking informally with each of them. Desirable times for personal conversations may be during lunch hours, before or after school, or at school social functions. These settings offer unique opportunities for getting to know more about students' interests, special talents, and needs. Informal conversations may produce more positive attitudes toward students than can be acquired through classroom discussions alone.

We do have a word of caution about establishing rapport with students. A few students may resist your initial overtures to get to know them better. More than one try may be needed to convince them of your genuine interest in them. But if you persist in your efforts to converse informally with them, you will likely find them to have positive qualities not readily

See the good in all students

apparent in the classroom. You can then use those special characteristics as windows of opportunity for connecting with these students academically.

Attaching negative labels to students who misbehave can obscure your perceptions of their positive qualities. Labeling any student as a troublemaker invariably obstructs seeing his or her virtues. Simply substituting a positive label for a negative one may increase your awareness of students' good qualities. Referring to students as *"tenacious"* instead of as *"bullheaded"* or *"stubborn"* can give you an entirely different opinion of them. Trying to find some redeeming value in a student tendency can help you see both that tendency and that student more favorably. For example, you can try regarding students who question everything you recommend as "having a mind of their own" rather than as "being oppositional."

You might also try giving students something to live up to. We recently heard a father tell his son, "Don't be so slow." His mother interjected, "Tell him to hurry." Although the latter directive was only slightly different from the first, it conveyed a totally different message—one that wouldn't cause the son to think negatively of himself. Finally, envisioning what students might become under caring guidance, from a person such as you, can be helpful in sustaining positive beliefs about students. In our own teaching experience, some students who evidenced less than a sterling performance in the classroom eventually became eminently successful in their professions.

Dealing with Unrealistic Job Expectations

In a popular book devoted to helping people live more effectively, Arnold Lazarus and Allen Fay (1975) describe a number of mistaken beliefs that are sources of unhappiness in people's lives. Included in their list are the notions that *(a)* you should strive to be good at everything, *(b)* work at pleasing everybody, *(c)* not take chances, and *(d)* try to become totally independent of others. Their approach for helping people avoid and change mistaken beliefs consists of instructions on how to rethink the beliefs and how to engage in corrective behaviors.

As with views about life in general, the expectations you have about teaching can contribute to how happy you will be with your job and your life. Many teachers enter their first job with very idealistic views about teaching. There is nothing wrong with wanting to contribute to a better world or to inspire young minds, but you can become disillusioned very quickly when you find that many students appear indifferent to what you have to offer. Rather than give up your ideals, you have to evaluate whether you are expecting too much too quickly from your students.

Although positive beliefs about yourself and others can have a profound effect on how you approach your job, the expectations you have about your job are also important.

Some surprises are a part of every job, but many of the "disconcerting" surprises that result from unrealistic expectations can be avoided. One of the things you can do is to examine your own perceptions about teaching and assess whether the views you hold have a strong factual basis. Such an evaluation can begin by exploring your expectations as to how others will treat you and what responsibilities will occupy most of your time. Then you can ask yourself *(a)* whether your beliefs can be verified from research literature on classroom management or from experienced teachers' accounts, *(b)* whether you are open to other views that might be more valid, and *(c)* whether your beliefs will be helpful or hurtful if you act on them.

The idea is not to lower expectations for yourself or for others, but rather to confront the realities of teaching so you can better deal with whatever challenges you face. Inasmuch as no one holds a monopoly on truth, you are the one who must distinguish between fact and fiction in your teaching experience. In the next sections, we describe some ideas that reflect misconceptions about teaching. We refer to these ideas as *myths* and suggest ways to avoid each one.

Myth: Teaching Is Easy

Have you ever heard anyone say or imply that teaching is easy? It is not uncommon for people outside of teaching to think teaching is an easy job. Labaree (2000), however, notes that this perception is endemic even among prospective teachers. He reasons that this mistaken view might be based on prospective teachers' initial observation of experienced teachers. If an observer merely looks at what a veteran teacher does, without understanding the preparation underlying the teacher's actions, teaching will of course appear much easier than is really the case. Labaree also notes that the skills and knowledge taught in the schools become generic when education is effective, adding to the notion that what teachers know is ordinary. In reality, the development of general knowledge often involves diligent teaching and learning.

Gaining more exposure to teaching, even before student teaching, by observing and doing projects in a variety of school settings, by talking with teachers about why they take particular actions, by asking teachers about their planning strategies, and by discussing professional goals with experienced teachers can help prospective teachers have a more realistic view of what teaching involves. We are not suggesting you view your job as more difficult than other professions, only that you should not succumb to the idea that just anyone can do what you do. To do your job well requires preparation and effort comparable to that of the most demanding professions.

Myth: Love for Children Is All You Need

Love is certainly a good starting place for working with others, but love *alone* is hardly sufficient for teaching skills to others or in knowing how to manage a classroom effectively.

PONDERING THE MEANING OF LOVE

Even figuring out the meaning of love can be a challenge. For instance, does having love for students mean you like each of them equally? Many students behave in ways that make it easy to like them, but a few behave in ways that make liking them more difficult. Every teacher has different feelings toward different students. But recognizing that you don't feel the same way toward every student can cause some cognitive dissonance if you perceive yourself as accepting all students. You can experience considerable distress when your feelings don't match your egalitarian beliefs.

The philosopher-scholar C. S. Lewis (1952) made a useful distinction between liking and loving. For Lewis, *liking is an emotion* that is difficult to control; whereas, *love is an action* that can be voluntarily demonstrated. In fact, Lewis believed this distinction makes it possible to love even your enemies. You don't have to be fond of them to wish them well or to behave positively toward them. If you are having difficulty liking all your students, try Lewis's approach: love them. That is, behave positively toward them. Once your actions demonstrate you care for your students, liking them should become easier. Daily acts of kindness, words of encouragement, positive comments on papers, help with class work when they experience difficulty, and periodic smiles are among the most direct ways of showing you care.

Competence in your subject matter is also critical. Rather than presuming that love is enough or that knowledge of subject matter is enough, you should realize the two are typically combined in effective teaching. You can temper your overemphasis on either one by remembering the teachers who most helped you learn. Did these teachers take a purely intellectual approach, or did they combine knowledge with loving, supportive treatment?

In a study where adolescents were asked to describe a caring teacher, many students identified helping with and explaining schoolwork as the hallmarks of a caring teacher (Ferreira 2000). In other words, concern for students was demonstrated in teachers' regular instructional activities. Knowing your subject and offering support can be reflected in almost every interaction with students. You can't give learning to students, and you can't make students learn, but informed and considerate instruction can amplify their opportunities for learning.

Myth: Good Teachers Don't Have Problems with Students

The notion that good teachers don't have problems is based on the assumption that these teachers have control over all student behaviors. Unfortunately, student difficulties at home, problems with peers, and mood changes can generate difficulties for even the best teachers. As a teacher corrects one situation, another challenge can surface. Everyday inter-actions occur between teachers and students that can lead to conflict, making it impossible for anyone to escape occasional discord. Some teachers keep their problems to themselves, hoping others will view them as highly effective, which may also contribute to the myth that good teachers are problem-free.

When confronted with a classroom problem, the teacher who believes good teachers don't have problems inevitably concludes, "I am simply not a good teacher." Teachers who subscribe to this myth might be inclined to give up, thinking they don't have what it takes to be a successful teacher. Conversely, recognizing that every teacher encounters some problems in working with students can prevent disillusionment with teaching. Excellence in teaching often results from experiencing and overcoming difficult situations. The kernel of truth in this myth is that good teachers do develop strategies for managing their problems more effectively, thus making their classroom less problem-ridden. However, this doesn't mean they are able to anticipate and prevent all problems in their classes.

Recognizing that all teachers have problems also suggests a need to solicit help from others in finding solutions. No one can handle *all* problems alone. Some teachers, however, have difficulty accepting their limits. They regard help from others as a sign of personal failure. Although teachers do have the principal responsibility for what occurs in their classes, no teacher can be the sole problem solver. One important resource for improving classroom behavior is input from students. Students can be involved, for example, in establishing classroom rules and procedures, in identifying rewards for desirable behaviors, and in monitoring and changing their own behaviors. Professionals such as the school psychologist, counselor, nurse, and social worker can help with a variety of academic, behavioral, and personal problems. Parents, too, can engage in many volunteer activities that strengthen classroom programs.

Myth: Teachers Can't Be Effective Without Parental Support

Because of problems at home, not all children come to school behaving the way teachers would like. Many parents have significant problems just trying to earn a living, and may seldom attend school functions or respond to teacher overtures. This can easily be misin-terpreted as lack of concern about their children's education. Even experienced teachers have been heard to say, "With his home background, there is little I can do to change things," which suggests the teacher is powerless if the parents (or other caregivers) don't intervene to change the child's behavior.

A student's home, community, and peer group certainly contribute to how the student initially behaves at school. Nonetheless, if other environmental forces can influence a student, why not the teacher? Whether or not a student *continues* to exhibit behaviors in the classroom that were learned elsewhere is largely under the teacher's control. Also, a child who does not have the prerequisite skills for learning a task can be taught those skills. Efficacious teachers will continue to seek workable alternatives even when past efforts have repeatedly failed. Moreover, many parents who initially seem uninterested in their children's learning, in actuality work hard to provide for their children's needs and will work with the school, if given comfortable opportunities. (We'll have more to say in chapter six about working with parents to enhance the learning of all students.)

One of the best ways of debunking the notion that teachers are powerless to improve classroom conditions without parental support is to review effective classroom-management systems. For example, behavior-modification programs provide an array of useful strategies for regular and special classrooms. Another popular approach emphasizes student choices and advocates helping students take responsibility for their own behavior (Glasser 1987, 1997). In chapter three, we highlight specific classroom-management strategies that are useful in initiating desirable social and academic student behaviors for all children, with or without parental support.

Myth: All Students Should Be Treated the Same

Parents occasionally complain, "My child was singled out for punishment no one else received." To avoid such accusations of unfairness, the teacher may attempt to treat all students alike. Admittedly, infractions for certain school policies may warrant standardized punishment. However, the need to show impartiality in implementing school policies should not take precedence in all circumstances. For example, suppose most students own home computers, but a few do not. Those who do not own computers will need more training and extra attention than those who do. Obviously, these students cannot be treated "equally." The desire for equality is really more a desire for justice than for sameness. Justice requires that students be given equal opportunity rather than identical treatment.

Those who fear that treating students differently will lead to charges of unfairness should ask themselves whether failing to provide additional assistance to students with clear-cut disadvantages constitutes equitable treatment of those students. Moreover, students have different preferences and are unlikely to feel slighted when their needs are met in different ways. It is only when the needs of a few are being met to the exclusion of others that students sense injustice. Try providing students with choices on certain assignments or offering different reward options. You will find that students are pleased to have more choices. Further, you might try maintaining a log of students who receive any specific attention from you and whether the attention given is positive or negative. For example, you can keep track of who gets called on most often (males, females, the academically talented, those with special learning needs) and whether students who occasionally (or frequently) misbehave receive supportive comments when they engage in desirable behaviors. You might learn that the students least in need of attention receive the most support.

Developing Guiding Principles

Thus far we have focused on how the beliefs you hold affect what you do in the classroom (and beyond, for that matter). You may apply your beliefs inconsistently, however, if you have no overriding code or core value to guide your day-to-day interactions. A few years ago the popular song "Teach Your Children Well" (Crosby, Stills, and Nash) encouraged parents to give their children "a code that they can live by." Giving children a "code to hold their dreams on" is good advice not only for children, but for everyone. All of us need a code to live by, something to hold our beliefs on, as we face the myriad demands of each teaching day.

A guiding principle represents a code of conduct; it helps you be aware of how you want to act toward others. For example, if showing respect for others is one of your guiding principles, you can act upon this principle by serving as a model for the way to treat others. Furthermore, if a student teases a classmate, you have a basis for choosing an appropriate response. Anything not in keeping with your guiding principle, such as ridiculing the offender, should be ruled out. A more appropriate response might be to have a private conversation with the offender to explore desirable ways of interacting with classmates. In brief, a guiding principle or principles (you will probably want to develop more than one) will help you maintain consistency in your actions. They help you become the kind of person you want to be.

There are several ways to decide what principles should guide your teaching. If you are also a parent, consider how you want your own children to be treated. Being a parent probably creates our greatest sensitivity to students' needs. If you are not a parent, consider what your students' parents want for their children. Most, if not all, want their children to be treated fairly, to be shown love and respect, and to be valued as individuals. Parents also expect teachers to help their children develop academic competencies, get along well with others, make wise choices, and become responsible adults. Any of these parental desires can qualify as a guiding principle for a teacher.

Many teachers rely heavily on the Golden Rule, striving to treat others as they would like to be treated. Some develop principles to guide them in their work preparation. For instance, many teachers strive to be responsible in their work commitments. They wouldn't think of coming to work unprepared because that would violate their idea of being responsible. For your daily strategies to be effective, you have to act in accordance with what you value. Consequently, you might want to make a list of your guiding principles and keep them close at hand to review them from time to time.

Maintaining a Balance

Although a strong commitment to teaching is fundamental to sticking with your job through good times and bad, you should not neglect other important aspects of your life. From our experience as teachers, we have concluded (Williams and Long 1991) that a balance between work, health, social, and leisure activities is essential to any teacher's personal and professional development. Too much or too little attention to any one area can undermine other important areas. For instance, working day and night on school assignments can destroy family life and important relationships. We have devoted chapter nine to helping you nurture the quality of your personal life outside the classroom, which will aid you in maintaining balance.

In order to achieve greater balance in your life, you first have to decide on the relative importance of the personal and professional aspects of your life and then make sure your daily use of time mirrors the relative importance of those areas. Westhorp (2001) proposed that you give prime consideration to the health implications of how you are spending time and energy. She affirmed that decisions be made within the framework of the balance required for healthy living. Achieving balance among the things important to you does not not mean you have to spend equal time in all the areas you value. Simply relaxing a while each day can have beneficial effects, but relaxing need not occupy the same amount of time as your job.

BEING SUCCESSFUL AND HAVING A PERSONAL LIFE TOO

You don't have to sacrifice your personal life in order to be successful on your job. In fact, people who occupy multiple roles often report being very satisfied with their work without having to make personal sacrifices outside of work. In a ten-year follow-up of top high school graduates, many of whom held professional jobs, Peronne (1999–2000) found that married persons were more likely than unmarried persons to report they had not made any sacrifices in personal life roles in order to achieve career happiness and success. Participants who had children also were more likely to report not having made personal sacrifices (i.e., sacrifices related to health, finances, relationships) to attain career happiness and success than were nonparents. In other words, having multiple roles does not have to be a liability.

In Review

Love of teaching is probably one of the most powerful reasons for embarking on a teaching career, but sustaining a love for teaching may not come easily. Teachers, understandably, get frustrated when things don't go well. In this chapter, we have offered a number of suggestions we think are useful in meeting the challenges of teaching. The following were our key points:

- Classroom management is more about fostering students' intellectual and personal development than simply reducing unwanted student behaviors.

- A strong commitment to your job increases the chances you can weather difficult periods to achieve a sense of job fulfillment.

- Job commitment may be enhanced by recalling your initial vision of teaching as a career, by identifying current sources of job satisfaction, and by keeping a record of uplifting experiences in teaching.

- The perspective that you have a significant influence over what happens in your classroom (i.e., a sense of personal control) contributes to your willingness to undertake needed improvements in classroom management.

- Your sense of control may be enhanced by establishing goals related to improving your classroom-management skills, which seem fundamental to comfort in teaching.

- The belief that you can attain your goals (self-efficacy) may be strengthened by engaging in behaviors associated with a sense of strong personal efficacy (e.g., placing yourself in situations where you can use your talents).

- Unrealistic expectations about teaching can lead to disillusionment with teaching.

- You can develop more realistic views of teaching by examining whether the beliefs are verified by research evidence or the recommendations of experts, prove more valid than alternative beliefs, and can be helpful or harmful if followed.

- Teachers often find it beneficial to develop codes of conduct for themselves that can serve as guides in their daily interactions with others. An example would be a code to treat others with the same respect you desire from others.

⌣ Personal fulfillment can best be achieved by balancing your work schedule with other experiences you deem important and healthy.

What Lies Ahead

The remaining chapters of this book describe classroom-management techniques that are appropriate for elementary and secondary teachers. They indicate when a technique is more appropriate for one group than for another. The way a technique is applied can be adapted across different types and ages of students. The information we offer is aimed toward helping you determine your responsibility in managing various classroom activities, develop effective communications skills, plan your daily work activities, expand your knowledge of ways to motivate students and to deal with excessive behaviors, work effectively with others in your professional network, and move students toward being more independent and personally responsible for their own behavior. We also look at life beyond the workplace to help you explore ways of achieving greater personal satisfaction both in and outside of school.

The final chapter in our book presents a model for classroom management that can help you integrate information from earlier chapters to solve classroom management problems. We use the first letter of the key concept in each of the first eight chapters to form the acronym BRIGHTER. From the final chapter, we use all the letters of DAY to complete the acronym BRIGHTER DAY.

We suggest that, as you read each chapter, you think about how the major concept in that chapter can contribute to having a brighter day (problem solving). For example, chapter one focuses largely on how a teacher's *beliefs* (the B in BRIGHTER) can influence events in the classroom. Chapter two deals with using communication skills to build *relationships* (R) with others; chapter three with *initiating* (I) desired student behaviors; chapter four with sustaining *good* (G) student behaviors; chapter five with being *helpful* (H) to students in overcoming troublesome behaviors; and chapter six with working *together* (T) with parents. Chapter seven is concerned with meeting the needs of *everyone* (E), including students with special needs; chapter eight with helping students develop *responsibility* (R) for their own behaviors; and chapter nine with helping teachers address their own well being each *day* (DAY).

Once you have completed the first nine chapters, we give you an opportunity to see how the model can be applied to specific problems—and to solve a number of different problems on your own. You need not wait until the end of the book to use the model, however. You can begin now. What beliefs do you hold that can be put into practice to positively influence classroom behavior? As you progress through the text, consider ways you can combine each new concept to develop more problem solving skills.

Concluding Comments

Your destiny is largely controlled by the choices you make. As you begin a school year, you may have doubts and anxieties, but you cannot permit negative thoughts to permeate your thinking. No one has more control over your thoughts and actions than you do. You can approach your job either with enthusiasm or with continued doubts. These two perspectives will likely produce different results. Believing you can do something or believing you cannot is likely to set the stage for the results you will get. More than anyone else, you have control over what you choose to believe and the amount of responsibility you take. We are not claiming that assuming responsibility for your teaching experience will *always* work out well, but trusting your fate to chance or to others offers far less assurance of success.

References

Bandura, A. (1989). Human agency in social cognitive theory. *American Psychologist* 44: 1175–184.

_____ (1997). *Self-efficacy: The Exercise of Control.* New York: W. H. Freeman.

Brunetti, G. J. (2001). Why do they teach? A study of job satisfaction among long-term high school teachers. *Teacher Education Quarterly* 28 (3): 49–74.

Emmons, R. A., and M. E. McCullough (2003). Counting blessings versus burdens: An experimental investigation of gratitude and subjective well-being in daily life. *Journal of Personality and Social Psychology* 84: 377–89.

Ferreira, M. M. (2000). *Caring Teachers: Adolescents' Perspectives.* ERIC DOC, ED 441 682. Washington, D.C.: Office of Educational Research and Improvement

Glasser, W. (1987). *Control Theory in the Classroom.* New York: Harper Collins.

_____ (1997). "Choice theory" and student success. *Education Digest* 63 November 16–21.

Henson, R. K. (2001). Teacher self-efficacy: Substantive implications and measurement dilemmas. Paper presented at the annual meeting of the Educational Research Exchange, Texas A&M University, College Station, January.

Kobasa, S. O. (1979). Stressful life events, personality, and health: An inquiry into hardiness. *Journal of Personality and Social Psychology* 37: 1–11.

Labaree, D. F. (2000). On the nature of teaching and teacher education: Difficult practices that look easy. *Journal of Teacher Education* 51: 228–33.

Lazarus, A., and A. Fay (1975). *I Can If I Want To.* New York: William Morrow

Lewis, C. S. (1952). *Mere Christianity.* New York: Macmillan.

Long, J. D., J. C. Biggs, and J. T. Hinson (1999). Perceptions of education majors and experienced teachers regarding factors that contribute to successful classroom management. *Journal of Instructional Psychology* 26(2): 105–10.

Long, J. D., E. W. Long, and P. Gaynor (2000). Attributions about classroom management. Paper presented at the Lilly South Conference on College Teaching, University of Georgia, Athens.

Peronne, K. M. (1999–2000). Balancing life roles to achieve career happiness and life satisfaction. *Career Planning and Adult Development Journal* winter: 49–58.

Sadowski, C. J., M. Blackwell, J. L. Willard (1985). Locus of control and student teacher performance. *Education* 105: 391–93.

Thomson, W. C., and J. C. Wendt (1995). Contribution of hardiness and school climate to alienation experienced by student teachers. *Journal of Educational Research* 88: 269–76.

Westhorp, P. (2001). Balance in all things: A formula for wellbeing in adult education. *New Zealand Journal of Adult Learning* 29 (1): 30–49.

Williams, R. L., and Long (1991). *Manage Your Life.* 4th ed. Boston: Houghton Mifflin.

Wong, H. K., and R. T. Wong (1998). *How to Be an Effective Teacher: The First Days of School.* Mountain View, Calif: Harry K. Wong Publications.

Libby, you have such a good class. You get along so well with your students. What's your secret?"

"Thanks for the compliment, but there's no magic in what I do. Getting along well with students has not come easy for me. When I began teaching, I had some students I didn't particularly like and who didn't especially like me.

Come to think of it, I have some students now who don't warm my heart. Believe me; I have had to work at developing better relationships with some students."

"What did you do that improved your rapport with students?"

"Well, it was many things. But primarily I worked on how I communicated my concerns to students. Even when conveying disapproval, I tried to put the criticism in a positive framework. Learning to be more positive in how I relate to others has changed how I feel about school and even about life in general."

"You've got my attention. Tell me more."

2

◄◦►

Building Relationships

Teacher Communication

Chapter one emphasized how teacher beliefs can influence teacher behaviors, whether those beliefs are realistic or erroneous, positive or negative. Obviously, teaching can be more enjoyable and productive if founded on realistic, positive views about yourself and others. Unfortunately, not all teachers successfully act upon their positive beliefs. They sometimes unintentionally act in ways that cause others to respond negatively to them. At other times, they simply don't realize that they are turning others off, or perhaps they don't know what to do to have a more positive impact.

Whether you are trying to act on a positive belief, teach a lesson, control a discipline problem, or simply be supportive of others, an essential contributor to attaining your goals is effective communication. Your beliefs about yourself and others influence how you communicate, which in turn affects how you view teaching. If you get along well with others at school, you likely will look forward to your school day. In contrast, expected conflict with others can create uneasiness even before you step in the school building. Indeed, probably no skill is more basic to good feelings about teaching than efficiency and effectiveness in communicating.

In working both with individuals currently teaching and individuals preparing to teach, we have observed that the primary difference between successful and unsuccessful teachers may not lie in their intellectual skills. Some teachers who are both brilliant and

A positive view of yourself

scholarly experience so much difficulty in teaching that they eventually leave the profession. In contrast, others with more moderate intellectual skills find teaching to be their lifelong calling. Although superior intellectual and academic skills certainly contribute to success in teaching, your ability to communicate might be even more important.

Effects of Teacher Communication

Teacher communication skills ultimately determine the nature of interpersonal relationships, most especially with students, but also with parents, colleagues, and administrators. Research across a variety of professions indicates that relationships contribute to job advancement as least as much as technical expertise (Clarke and Hammer 1995; Moskal 1995; Weiss 1994). Relationship-building skills are important in most professions, but they are vital in teaching. Probably no profession involves more face-to-face interaction, with such far-reaching effects, than teaching. An individual who is uncomfortable or unskilled in interacting with others is unlikely to be successful or satisfied in teaching, not to mention being a poor example for how students should relate to one another.

Experiencing interpersonal problems at school is a major contributor to on-the-job stress. In fact, conflicts with students rank among the leading causes of teacher stress. Even though some individuals within the school setting can make school life less than pleasant, your communication skills can promote workable relationships even with difficult individuals. We are not suggesting that you take responsibility for others' mistreating you, but rather that you seek constructive ways of responding to hurtful behavior. If you get into an attack and counterattack mode, whether with a student or a supervisor, you may find yourself the ultimate loser.

Sometimes you can pressure another individual to do what you want. Forced compliance hardly settles the issue. You can count on resistance and possibly subversive reactions from the compliant individual. The relationship will likely be laden with tension, which can be chronically disconcerting to you. You may have difficulty getting the conflict off your mind, diluting your focus on important tasks and diminishing your joy in teaching. In contrast, influencing others through supportive communication can spare you an immense amount of stress (Chan 2002; Hemmings and Hockley 2002).

Your School Family

Relationships in your personal life can profoundly affect your satisfaction with teaching and your job effectiveness. Trouble at home with a spouse, children, or parents can take a heavy toll on what you bring to the classroom or derive from the classroom experience. Although you will find personal applications for some suggestions in this chapter, our emphasis here is on interpersonal relationships within your *school family*. *School family* refers to all the individuals with whom you routinely, or at least periodically, interact in your professional activities. A later chapter (chapter six) suggests possibilities for strengthening relationships on the home front.

The most important persons in your school family are your students. They are the ones you are most responsible for helping and with whom you spend the most time. Other important persons in your school family are the students' parents or caregivers, your colleagues, and your administrative supervisors. Developing a good relationship with each person in your school family is important—first, because of that person's inherent value and, second, because that relationship can affect your interactions with other members of the school family. For example, your relationship with a student may profoundly affect your relationship with the student's parents.

Establishing good relationships in your school network requires multiple channels of communication, including face-to-face conversations, comments on papers, notes or letters, phone calls, and e-mail messages. When trying to decide which channel is best for a particular situation, you may have to choose between efficiency and personal closeness. Teaching is such a busy profession that you will always be looking for more efficient ways to communicate within your school family. The concept of efficiency pertains to the amount of time required to send and receive messages. An e-mail message is often the most efficient way to communicate a quasi-formal message (e.g., ask a question, respond to a question, offer a compliment), but some situations require a more personal touch to be effective (e.g., clarify a misunderstanding, apologize for an offensive comment).

If you are experiencing recurring problems with someone in your school family, a private conversation may be in order. Face-to-face interaction not only entails more complete communication and includes the nonverbal as well as the verbal, but also contributes better to building relationships than other modes of communication (such as phone calls, notes, and e-mail messages). If a message can be communicated with equal efficiency through various channels, you should opt for the most personable channel. But whatever mode of communication you select, your messages should convey a spirit of goodwill (at least a desire to get along with the other person). Finally, given that people will make judgments about your teaching skills from your written communications, make certain that your e-mail messages, notes, and comments on papers reflect correct grammar and spelling.

Relationship with Students

A beginning point in examining your relationships with your students is to evaluate how you feel toward particular students and how they may perceive your demeanor. Students at all ages can quickly "sense" your feelings toward them and subsequently will behave in keeping with their impressions. It takes a very short time (maybe no more than two weeks) for most students to learn what they can and cannot do in your classroom and to assess whether you are a supportive, aloof, or critical individual. They do this by reading your verbal and nonverbal messages, which they assume reflect your feelings (or beliefs) about yourself and others. Psychologists often use the term *attitude* to describe the outward expression of feelings.

Carl Rogers (1969), one of the twentieth century's most prominent humanistic psychologists, has long claimed that teacher attitudes are major influences on student learning. Rogers and his followers contend that three teacher attitudes in particular free students to raise questions, seek answers, and become more self-directive: (1) realness or genuineness, (2) acceptance, and (3) empathic understanding. Each of these attitudes embodies important verbal and nonverbal behaviors that reflect your feelings toward students.

Realness or Genuineness. Rogers describes *real* or *genuine* teachers as persons who generally are aware of their feelings and behave consistently with those feelings. Such persons do not pretend to feel differently toward others than is actually the case. Although realness requires that teachers periodically acknowledge that they are angry, bored, or frustrated, expression of unpleasant emotions is not a license to blame others. For example,

Smoldering resentment

the honest teacher is more apt to say, "I am frustrated with how our lesson is going today" than "You students don't know how to behave." Realness means that individuals also recognize personal feelings as their own—not directly caused by someone else. "I am angry" is more accurate than "You have made me mad." Letting students know you are a real person may involve other types of personal disclosure. They might be surprised, and pleased, to learn that you shop for groceries, mow the lawn, attend movies, and enjoy rap music.

If you choke at the prospect of expressing your true feelings, please consider the alternatives. Trying to keep your feelings under wrap may result in passive-aggressive responses toward others. You don't tell them how you really feel, but rather find ways to make life more difficult for them. You don't attack them; you just refuse to cooperate. In deciding whether to express your feelings at a given time, you might ask: "How am I going to feel if I do not express my feelings?" and "Will expressing my feelings improve the situation?" A common consequence of not expressing your feelings is resentment on your part and continued bad behavior on the offender's part.

Acceptance. For Rogers, the attitude of *acceptance* (sometimes referred to as *prizing* and *trusting*) means that the teacher values the student's feelings, opinions, and personhood. This attitude reflects an unconditional positive regard even when a student is not academically gifted, handsome, or well behaved. Teachers who demonstrate this attitude see each student as a person of worth. They appreciate individual differences among students, accepting differences of opinion and behavior. Accepting teachers realize that they are dealing with imperfect human beings having a diversity of feelings and abilities. It may be easier to prize some students if you focus on what they can become rather than on how they are currently behaving.

Acceptance should not be interpreted as meaning you must be tolerant of every student behavior. Every classroom needs standards of conduct that the teacher consistently enforces. However, teachers can tell students that a certain behavior is unacceptable without rejecting or shaming them. Saying "Enrique, raise your hand to be recognized" conveys a totally different message than "Enrique, don't you have any manners?!" The first comment is directed at behavior, whereas the second implies that something is wrong with the person. When your comment condemns, the attitude of prizing is lost.

Empathic Understanding. Rogers describes *empathic understanding* as sensitive awareness of how the student views education and learning. The teacher looks at the learning experience from the student's perspective rather than focusing strictly on his or her own perspective. The empathic teacher stands in another's shoes, so to speak, and views the world from that person's position. Empathy involves showing that you understand and appreciate a student's feelings, permitting you to respond to the student's actual feelings rather than to how you think the student should feel.

The empathic teacher's sensitivity contrasts with the harshness of teachers who block honest emotional expressions from students. The latter teachers may comment, "I am surprised at you" or "Don't you dare say that again." Such statements tend to cut off communication. The empathic teacher increases communication by responding to the feelings behind the student's words. For example, this teacher may comment, "Susan, you feel like you have been mistreated," "Bill, you found the discussion upsetting," "Hank, you're not seeing the purpose of what I am asking you to do," or "Isabel, you act as though you would rather be working on another project." Empathic comments increase open communication between the

Cutting off communication

teacher and student, correct teacher misperceptions of student actions, and help students examine their feelings about academic experiences.

A Note of Clarification. The attitudes described here are sometimes difficult to display. (We have more to say in this chapter about specific verbal and nonverbal skills that underscore positive attitudes toward others.) It is questionable whether anyone can ever be completely genuine, accepting, and empathic all the time. For example, some student comments (e.g., "Teacher, why don't you get lost," "You're the worst teacher I have ever had") can make it difficult to respond empathically ("I can see that you're upset with me"). Nonetheless, being genuine, accepting, and empathic are desirable in most relationships. Students who feel accepted have less need to defend themselves, which perhaps allows them to explore more constructive ways of behaving. As students' feelings are understood, they also may become more understanding of others' feelings.

SIMPLE STRATEGIES FOR IMPROVING TEACHER-STUDENT RELATIONSHIPS

Thedrick Pigford, once a junior high teacher and now a college professor, proposed that the teacher-student relationship is the most important contributor to classroom learning. If you agree, you should examine Pigford's (2001) recommendations for getting to know individual students and establishing positive rapport with them. Although Pigford provides a list of fifteen strategies for improving your relationships with students, the following ten appear most manageable to us:

1. Regularly eat lunch with your students and share personal interests.
2. Greet students individually as they enter your classroom and say something of personal relevance to them.
3. Challenge selected students to friendly competition in an area of mutual interest (e.g., shooting foul shots in basketball, doing pushups, drawing a picture of a famous person, or doing a popular dance step).
4. Participate occasionally in playground activity with students.
5. Provide a box in which students can place suggestions for classroom activities.
6. Allow students to interview you about your personal interests.
7. Periodically attend activities in which your students participate (e.g., plays, concerts, ball games).
8. Provide each student a personal card for his or her birthday.
9. Write a personal letter to each student at the beginning of the school year.
10. Be alert to students who may be struggling personally or academically, letting them know you are there to help.

The application of Pigford's suggestions takes time. However, the time and energy saved in dealing with the misbehavior of students with whom you have minimal rapport will make Pigford's suggestions well worth your time.

Relationships with Caregivers

It is especially important for teachers of the kindergarten and primary grades to have periodic contact with their students' caregivers (typically parents, grandparents, or relatives) through conferences, home visits, telephone calls, and notes home. (From this point on, we refer to all caregivers or surrogate parents as parents.) At this stage of the child's development, the teacher-parent relationship is best construed as a partnership for nurturing the child's academic and personal development. As students progress to the high school years, parents may be replaced by peers in providing much of a student's out-of-class support for academic work and personal development. Nevertheless, even at that point a teacher-parent partnership might help a struggling high school student get back on track emotionally and academically. At any grade level, you can help both students and parents stay informed as to what is happening in your class either by posting the course syllabus, schedule, assignments, and grading standards at a course web site, by transmitting this information via take-home documents, or by doing both.

Although the teacher should take the initiative in communicating with parents, the interaction should become increasingly bilateral. Teachers and parents should regularly exchange information that might be helpful in working with a struggling child. You can learn how best to relate to a student by getting parents' input regarding the child's likes and dislikes as well as the child's psychological vulnerabilities. Teachers can learn what buttons to push or not push. For example, a child may like to read but cringe at the prospect of reading in front of the class.

Teachers also need to enlist parents' help in creating conditions at home that are conducive to performance in school. Adequate sleep,

Keep parents well informed regarding their child's performance.

a time and place for homework, and the use of home-based rewards for good schoolwork can affect how a child performs in the classroom. Bear in mind that your actions also can affect conditions in the child's home. If you require an inordinate amount of homework, you may undermine the child's potential for rest and create considerable stress for both the parents and the child.

Teachers and parents have traditionally kept their distance from each other. On the one hand, teachers may fear the prospect of being called on the carpet by an irate parent. On the other hand, notes home often bring bad news to parents. If you want the parents' help in difficult times, you must establish a tradition of supportive communication in better times. That means communicating with parents when the child is improving or performing well. Just keeping parents well informed regarding their child's performance, highlighting the most promising news, will maintain a partnership spirit for dealing with difficult times. In chapter six, we say much more about the specifics of the teacher-parent partnership.

Relationships with Colleagues

If you prefer to work in virtual isolation from your colleagues, teaching is not for you. A variety of planning and management responsibilities often require teachers to work together. Plus, there will be times when you need your colleagues' professional and personal support, which they are far more likely to offer if you have shown interest in their own teaching experiences. However, the major reason for staying in touch with your colleagues is not to bank support for difficult times, but rather to enhance your teaching effectiveness mutually (Gable and Manning 1997). Most of us tend to be a bit myopic about the way we do things. We continue with our routine as long as it's working relatively well. Sometimes a slight twist in the way another teacher structures a learning activity can substantially enhance its effectiveness. Regularly exchanging teaching ideas with colleagues enriches both your teaching and your relationships with fellow teachers.

Some educators characterize idea exchange between teachers as a form of teacher collaboration. Gable and Manning (1997) refer to informal sharing of ideas as indirect collaboration, in contrast to direct collaboration in which teachers formally share responsibility for teaching a group of students. Indirect collaboration is a voluntary exchange of ideas, usually taking place before or after school or during mutual planning periods. You want to be sure that your informal collaboration includes teachers at both the high end and the low end of instructional effectiveness. You can ask those recognized as superlative teachers questions about their instructional procedures and compare notes on instructional possibilities with those struggling with their students. In the first case, you are hoping to learn, and in the second you are trying to teach. You will increase the effectiveness in these interchanges with fellow teachers by observing these guidelines:

1. Do more questioning than telling ("What are your thoughts about this possibility?" rather than "My position is that we shouldn't proceed").

2. Provide supportive input wherever legitimate ("You've invested considerable time on this project").

3. Offer suggestions tentatively ("Might this work in your situation?").

4. Avoid highly opinionated statements ("Multiple-choice tests are stupid") that would stymie future communication.

Some teachers are fortunate enough to have paraprofessionals in their classroom, ranging from full-time teacher assistants to part-time community volunteers. Because these classroom helpers typically live in the community where the school is located, they may have greater longevity in the school than some teachers. Paraprofessionals can be especially helpful in working with students needing individual or small-group guidance, allowing you to address the needs of more students. Because your helpers are invaluable, developing supportive relationships with them is important. Palma (1994) has suggested several guidelines for strengthening those relationships: show respect for your assistants at all times, capitalize on their talents and work habits, give credit for their accomplishments (especially work done behind the scenes), involve them in planning and decision making, give instructions in terms of *we* or *us* rather than *you*, and provide an array of supportive verbal and nonverbal feedback.

Relationships with Administrators

A category of relationships that may concern teachers even more than their standing with students is their relationship with administrators. What your principal thinks of your teaching may ultimately affect your professional status more than how your students regard you. Although relationships with students perhaps should count most, teachers are not hired and fired by students. Good relationships with your students may not guarantee the job security and the professional advancement you deserve. Von Bergen, Soper, and Licata contend, however, that "your effectiveness as an educator may be no better than your relationship with your administrator" (2002, p. 73).

Input to Your Principal. Even though you may assume that it's your administrator's job to be well informed about all the accomplishments in your classroom, that may not be the case for a variety of legitimate reasons. For example, your principal may be dealing with a host of school problems (such as budget crises, transportation breakdowns, and parental complaints) having nothing to do with your classroom. The principal's inattention to your teaching may relate more to other pressing priorities than to lack of concern about your professional effectiveness.

Your principal may be dealing with a number of problems

It is probably true that some administrators operate on the premise that "no news is good news." If you aren't sending a steady stream of students to the principal for disciplinary action, he or she may regard you as doing your job well. However, it is not wise for you to allow the communication to remain at this level; you need to keep your principal apprised of what is happening in your class just in case others voice objections to your teaching. You don't want your principal to be caught off guard when a parent complains about a new instructional approach or grading standard in your classroom. You want your principal to have precise information about your grading standards when Ms. Jones calls about Jere's making less than his usual A in your course.

Keeping your principal well informed about events in your classroom may elevate your status from the *acceptable* to the *invaluable*. However, you walk a fine line in sharing classroom accomplishments with your principal: you don't want to come across as a self-serving braggart. In informal interchanges with your principal, you may have occasion to allude to activities in your classroom without labeling them as the "best ever." In sharing accounts of superlative accomplishments, you should always acknowledge how others have contributed to those accomplishments. If your students are doing exceptional work, highlight their responses to your new instructional procedures rather than your astute judgment in designing and initiating those procedures.

There are several formal channels for making the principal aware of your contributions to the school. On occasion, the principal will need faculty members to serve on school committees (such as curriculum revision, faculty retreats, accreditation planning). Volunteering to serve on important committees may provide a natural forum for demonstrating your expertise and for sharing the workload in the school. Your school also may require annual reports regarding instructional achievements, thus providing another natural outlet for you to document what you have accomplished. In listing your achievements, again be sure to acknowledge others' contributions to those accomplishments. For example, if any element of teamwork has been involved in the achievement, underscore the contribution of that teamwork. By elevating others in your comments, these persons will want to see you succeed and will try to help you do that.

Support for Your Principal. Seek natural opportunities to converse cordially with your principal (not necessarily about your classroom) and to pass on compliments about his or her work in the school. Be brief, specific, and tempered in your positive feedback. You want your principal to know that he or she has your goodwill, respect, and support, but you don't want to leave the impression that you are trying to gain an advantage with him or her. Natural, low-key feedback works better than demonstrative back-scratching. Von Bergen, Soper, and Licata contend that "the best way to get along with your administrator is to start by identifying his or her strengths" (2002, p. 73). Your quietly-stated affirmations may help your principal feel better about his or her work in the school and see the best in your teaching.

Just as you may not be the perfect teacher, your principal probably will not be the perfect administrator. In addition to affirming the principal's strengths, you may need to help compensate for some of his or her weaknesses. That means volunteering assistance in areas where the principal may be having difficulty. For example, suppose Ms. Hunter is a well-intentioned principal with many thoughtful ideas for improving the school. However, her interpersonal style may work against her accomplishing these valued goals. She may not be assertive enough or may be overly aggressive (laying down the law) in presenting her ideas to teachers.

Maybe you can smooth out some of Ms. Hunter's rough edges by reinterpreting her messages in more palatable and compelling terms. This reinterpretation can often be accomplished by your posing reflective questions to the principal that give her an opportunity to express her message more effectively. Suppose Ms. Hunter has described somewhat awkwardly a new planning procedure she wants to implement with the faculty. You might facilitate the acceptability of her presentation by posing questions such as, "Are you saying that if we adopt this planning procedure, we can free up more time in our school day for

A NOTE OF APPRECIATION

Because both you and the principal may have a rigorous schedule, finding a convenient time to chat about school life can be challenging. What may work better is periodically to send the principal a note or e-mail message regarding her good work in the school. The message need not be copious or comprehensive—rather, just a note of appreciation about some specific contribution the principal has made to the school:

"Your presentation to the faculty yesterday was well received. I particularly appreciated your comments about faculty renewal." Your principal has feelings like anyone else: criticism hurts and compliments help. Instead of becoming preoccupied with whether your principal is adequately supporting you, why not be sure that she or he knows you are supporting her or him.

planning?" or "You're saying you will give us the time to do the planning required in the proposal described?"

The payoffs for helping rather than simply criticizing can be significant. Dodson and Dodson (2000) claim that helping with the principal's weaknesses means that you will get more of what you need and deserve, thus benefiting yourself, your students, and the principal. Nonetheless, you should avoid being viewed as the front person for a thoroughly disliked principal or as getting undue benefits because you are playing up to the principal. If you happen to be working with a principal whom the staff views as largely incompetent and unqualified for the position, you might better use your time by concentrating on your own teaching rather than by trying to bolster the principal's standing. An equally ill-advised tactic is for you to become the informal leader of a "dump the principal" movement.

Reduction of Relationship Problems

Never is the expression "an ounce of prevention is worth a pound of cure" truer than in dealing with relationship problems in your professional network. Nonetheless, being on your best behavior will not prevent all such problems given that some of those problems go well beyond your actions. You will deal with individuals in your school family (just as you do in your own extended family) who are prone to get their feelings hurt and to misinterpret others' actions. These individuals may have unrealistic expectations of how you should treat them and may read sinister motives into your most benign comments. You may find that their treatment of you changes drastically from one day to the next for reasons unknown to you. But even in those cases, reestablishing workable rapport may be feasible. Our point is that even if you did nothing to cause the problem, you can take actions to reduce the fallout from the current bad feelings.

The guidelines for preventing relationship problems are somewhat different from those for dealing with relationships characterized by estrangement or perpetual conflict. What might be very helpful in maintaining good relationships may be misinterpreted in a seriously strained relationship. For example, although a smile and compliment are viewed as expressions of goodwill in most cases, someone negatively disposed toward you may see them as manipulative. Good relationships usually can be established and maintained by simply practicing good social skills, but heart-to-heart discussions may be necessary to reestablish a positive working relationship with an associate antagonistic toward you.

Heart-to-Heart Conversation
Given that our emphasis in this chapter is on establishing and maintaining good relationships within your school family, we comment only briefly here on how you might deal with

a seriously strained professional relationship. First, you need to take the initiative for arranging a time to talk with your antagonist, the sooner the better. When you become aware that your colleague is responding negatively to you, suggest that the two of you meet to discuss how best to work together. Such a meeting can only be requested, not forced. Make it clear that you desire to have good rapport and are seeking ways to improve that rapport.

Be prepared to listen more than talk when the two of you get together. You might begin with your impression of sensitive areas in the relationship and then invite your associate to share his or her impressions of the same areas. For example, "I notice that when we meet in the hallways, you don't return my greeting. Have you been offended by something I have done?" After bringing up potentially sensitive areas, listen closely to your associate's perspective of those areas. Don't arrange the discussion with the intent of telling your associate how he or she needs to change, but rather with the goal of identifying what changes both of you might make to improve the rapport. This is not to suggest that you have been doing anything wrong, but rather that you can still take actions that will help your colleague feel comfortable with you again.

Response to Hurtful Treatment

There may be times when an associate responds very inappropriately to you (such as making a belligerent or sexist comment). In this case, you either should protest on the spot or ask for a meeting (in which you will identify desired changes in your associate's behavior). For example, "I am offended by your comment about my competency level, and I don't want you to refer to me that way again," or "I have some concerns about the way you characterized my competency and would like to meet with you privately to discuss those concerns." If you are enraged by an associate's action, it might be wise to ask for a follow-up meeting rather than respond on the spot. Otherwise, you may make some statements you will later regret.

Unless your associate's action is unequivocally and blatantly offensive, a good first step in dealing with the incident is to seek clarification of what the associate intended. You want to be sure that you understand the intent of your associate's action before asking for behavior change: "Did you really mean that I'm out of touch with students, or were you poking fun at the amount of time I spend with students?" Once you have stated your interpretation or asked for clarification of the action, you can then express how you feel about the incident. Be sure to lead with "I" rather than "you" in clarifying your feelings: "I felt hurt when you . . ." rather than "you hurt my feelings when you. . . ." Although expressing your feelings is an important part of the interchange, your major objective is to get your associate to respond differently to you in the future. Thus, your bottom-line request is that your associate not repeat the offensive action toward you.

Actions for Building and Maintaining Good Professional Relationships

Our intent in this section is to identify behaviors that will help you have good relationships with all members of your school family: students, parents, colleagues, and administrators. In attempting to establish and maintain good relationships, you probably should avoid being identified with any clique in the school. Make it clear in all your interactions that you are your own person. Although most of your input to others should be supportive, there will be times when you will disagree. Disagreement should be based on what was said rather than who said it.

Establishing and maintaining rapport are influenced by two broad categories of behavior: nonverbal and verbal. Although the specifics of a message often are more evident in verbal communication, the tone of the message may be more apparent in your nonverbal responses. Nonverbal behaviors may convey your feelings even more powerfully than what you say. For example, a compliment given while looking for a missing item on your desk may be less believable than one given when you are maintaining solid eye contact with the recipient. For communication to be effective, the nonverbal and the verbal must convey the same message.

Nonverbal communication

Nonverbal Behaviors

What we say here about nonverbal behaviors may sound simplistic, but the message is seldom applied to its fullest potential. Even with limited verbal affirmations, nonverbal behaviors can convey significant warmth and respect for others. The overall intent of nonverbal communication is first to acknowledge others' presence and then to convey goodwill toward them. Consistently doing those two things will prevent most relationship problems.

The beauty of nonverbal behaviors is that they can occur in the most fleeting or extended interaction, ranging from the loosely informal to the highly formal. For example, consider the incidental interactions that occur at the beginning of your teaching day. On the way to your classroom in the morning, you see several colleagues and students, but you are anxious to get to your room and make sure that the physical environment is set for the first activities of the day. The last thing you need is an extended conversation with a colleague or student. You can solve your dilemma simply with a nonverbal gesture that communicates a "pleasant good morning." In a crowded hallway, making eye contact, smiling, and waving as you pass is usually sufficient. These simple nonverbal behaviors brighten another's day as well as your own.

Smiles. Perhaps the most underused nonverbal behavior, yet one of the most powerful, is periodic smiling during your interactions. Smiling shows that you appreciate others and what they have to say, whereas a neutral expression provides little sense of connection. Research shows that smiling contributes more to others' positive feelings than does greeting them with bland expressions (Kleinke and Walton 1982). Unless others indicate that you smile a great deal or others smile frequently at you, most likely you are operating on the thin side of smiling. That being the case, one of the most powerful ways to enhance your communication within your school family would be to smile more frequently at more people in more situations.

An essential step in learning to smile more often is to identify specific people who deserve a smile and then specific situations in which you think a smile would be appropriate (that is, in which you wouldn't feel artificial about smiling). If you are unaccustomed to smiling, you may have to remind yourself to smile in the company of these individuals. Planned and practiced smiling is not synonymous with artificial smiling. Even in sports, actions that appear natural and spontaneous may have been meticulously orchestrated through years of practice. So it can be with smiling. You may initially feel awkward as you practice smiling, but eventually smiling will come naturally.

Laughter. A response closely akin to smiling is laughing. In fact, the more you smile, the easier it will be to laugh; and the more you laugh, the more inclined you will be to smile. You can brighten everyone's day by periods of laughter. Your laughter can turn an embarrassing *faux pas* into an episode of good humor. Several years ago one of us discovered during his presentation at a departmental meeting that his fly was unzipped. In retrospect,

Laugh at your own mistakes.

his deep purple blush might have been averted had he thought to say something like "my mother always told me to wear clean underwear." The very best subject matters for laughter are your own foibles. If you can turn your own limitations and mistakes into moments of levity, those mistakes won't seem so embarrassing, and students will see you as more human. The most relaxing classes we can recall from our days as students were those in which our teachers laughed often, especially at their own mistakes, which helped us be less anxious about the possibility of our making mistakes, too.

There are, of course, limits to the infusion of laughter into the classroom. Your laughter should never be directed toward students, even though some students' mistakes will strike you as so funny you want to roll on the floor with laughter. Perhaps you can release the pressure of the moment by sharing one of your own mistakes and redirecting the laughter toward your miscues. A final caution about laughter is that it should never be used as a substitute for promoting academic skills. A teacher who spends the day telling jokes is not a good teacher, but a teacher who finds humor in ordinary events will probably be viewed as both intelligent and relaxed.

Head Nods. A relatively unobtrusive way to show how you are responding to another's message is through head nods. Others want and deserve at least some indication that you

CLOSING THE GAP

Although Mr. Fulmer was a competent and well-intentioned high school teacher, his relationship with students could hardly be characterized as warm and comfortable. As the students gathered for class, they seldom made eye contact with Mr. Fulmer and virtually never engaged in casual conversation with him. The irony of this situation was that Mr. Fulmer wanted to have better rapport with his students, and they may have wanted to feel more comfortable in his presence.

A supervisor's observation of Mr. Fulmer's class revealed that his class periods were fully devoted to academic matters. He obviously knew his subject matter well, but his students may not have fully understood or appreciated his explanations. They seldom asked questions or volunteered answers to his questions. The supervisor judged the class climate as businesslike but cold.

In the times that the supervisor had observed in Mr. Fulmer's class, she had never seen him smile. He was always deadly serious. The supervisor suggested that Mr. Fulmer deliberately attempt to build smiling into his social repertoire. At first, he was very uncomfortable with the idea and thought that attempting to smile would make him seem artificial. A "suddenly smiling" Mr. Fulmer might even have made students suspicious that he was on some type of drug.

The supervisor suggested that Mr. Fulmer begin with low-profile smiling. He customarily began class with a comment such as "Okay, let's get started." The supervisor suggested that he soften the tone of the comment just a bit to "All right, shall we get started?" and that he smile slightly when he made the comment. The game plan was for Mr. Fulmer to include some understated smiling early in the class period.

Mr. Fulmer eventually became comfortable with smiling at his students, and his students began to reciprocate in kind. His classes still are not fun and games, but he now smiles periodically, and the tone of his comments has actually become friendlier. He has yet to win the "friendliest faculty member" award, but students describe him less often as bland, stiff, or aloof.

are following what they are saying, if not necessarily agreeing with their message. Although effective communication begins with eye contact while you're speaking or listening, eye contact per se provides little indication of how you are reacting to others' comments. Slight head nods suggest that you are tracking and understanding what is being said, and emphatic head nods typically convey strong agreement with what is being said. You may want to refrain from shaking your head as others are speaking because it shows disagreement with what is being said and thus may unnerve the speaker. If you feel that slight head nods might be misconstrued as agreement, simply maintain good eye contact while others are speaking and then voice your disagreement when it's your turn to talk.

Physical Touches. One of the most powerful modes of nonverbal communication is physical touching. Unfortunately, it also has powerful potential for misinterpretation, so you may need to be cautious in physically expressing your affection to members of your school family. There are times when hugging is appropriate, especially with young children, but the current sensitivity about sexual overtures makes hugging more questionable for older children. Even with young children, hugging them might be objectionable to some educators and parents. Before launching a hugging campaign with your students, be sure to check the school's guidelines with respect to touching. What you intend as a pure expression of affection might be perceived differently by someone else. A form of touching that is acceptable for most any age and context is a gentle touch on the shoulder—not a lingering touch, but rather a touch that simply conveys a supportive connection.

To sum up, your nonverbal messages should convey respect and goodwill and credibility regarding what others are saying. Before a word is spoken, your nonverbal behaviors show how you are responding to another's presence and communication. They also create both receptivity and believability with respect to your own verbal messages. If there is inconsistency between your verbal and nonverbal communication, the nonverbal will usually be regarded as more believable.

Verbal Communication

Though nonverbal behaviors often set the tone of your communication, verbal language transmits most of the specifics. Our analysis of verbal communication begins with active listening and then extends to such possibilities as asking questions, achieving focus and precision in conversation, disagreeing without being disagreeable, and offering supportive comments. We address these issues in the interest of both improving your instructional skills and enhancing relationships within your professional network.

Active Listening. The effectiveness of your verbal communication begins with the way you listen, which on the surface sounds more nonverbal than verbal. However, the con-

cept of active listening embodies more than simply maintaining eye contact and occasionally nodding your head while another is talking. Active listening entails verbal feedback, indicating that you are understanding or attempting to understand what another is saying. Thus, active listening sometimes is expressed more as a question than as a

STUDENT LISTENING

An important issue in our analysis of effective teacher listening is its potential effect on student listening. From the time children begin school until they graduate with advanced degrees, listening is what they do most in the classroom (Wolvin and Coakley 2000). In most class-rooms, students are expected to listen for as much as 50 percent of the time (Wolvin and Coakley 1988). Yet research (Hunsaker 1990) shows that students fail to assimilate oral infor-mation approximately 75 percent of the time, either because they are distracted or simply fail to understand the explanations given. In fact, some research at the college level (Conaway 1982) suggests that deficient listening is a stronger contributor to student failure than is limited reading skills or academic ability. Despite listening deficiencies, individuals typically obtain approximately 80 percent of their knowledge through listening (Hunsaker 1990). Thus, improving students' listening skills can significantly increase how much they learn.

statement. The purpose of questioning is to make sure that you have understood what the other person has just said. Communication often becomes diluted and confused because one person is responding to a misinterpretation of another's comment.

Suppose a colleague relates to you that Taylor is a poor student. What exactly is your colleague saying about Taylor? Your attempt to clarify the message might be reflected in any of the following questions: "Can you be more specific?" "In what ways is Taylor a poor student—is he off-task a great deal, does he have limited intellectual skills, or does he disrupt other students' work?" The answers to these questions will sharpen your under-standing of what your fellow teacher is trying to convey. Usually an active-listening response is briefer and more to the point than the message you are attempting to acknowl-edge or clarify. Nonetheless, time devoted to active listening is typically well spent because of the time saved in unraveling a web of misunderstood interchanges.

Listening is a two-way street: If you want your students to listen to you, you must be willing to listen to them. How students listen to you may be greatly influenced by how you listen to them. We are referring to both modeling and reciprocity. The best way for you to teach active listening is to model it in your interactions with students. Jalongo concludes that we teachers "can do a better job of teaching children to listen by examining our own effectiveness as listeners, appreciating the connection between active listening and learning" (1995, p. 18). Regarding reciprocity, we believe that students are more likely to care about what you have to say if you demonstrate that you care about what they have to say.

On the surface, it might appear that listening is the easiest part of teaching. After acknowledging the rewards of effective listening, Floyd concludes that "it is only fair to emphasize, however, that improving listening abilities is difficult, demanding, and challenging" (1985, p. 2). Speaking requires considerable concentration on what you are saying, but you can go through the motions of listening when your thoughts are elsewhere. You want your teaching messages to be precisely and accurately connected to what students say. Nothing less than vigilant attention to student comments will accomplish this precise connection. Despite the challenge of becoming an astute listener, few skills are more crucial to your professional effectiveness and to your students' academic success than active listening. As Calvin Coolidge once observed, "No man ever listened himself out of a job."

Teacher Questions. Although considerable classroom time is devoted to explanations, good teachers ask more questions than give answers. If a concept warrants a precise definition (which you or a student may initially provide), you can best determine how well students understand the definition by asking questions. In other words, you can confirm students' understanding by inviting them to share their understanding of what you explained. This is especially important if another student has provided the initial explanation. Other students may not listen as well when a peer gives the explanation as when you explain the concept. Thus, you may want to ask Alicia to give her understanding of what Carlos has just said regarding the concept under discussion. Your intent is to develop a discussion climate in which students listen closely to one another.

After an initial clarification of a concept or procedure, you should anchor students' understanding by asking follow-up questions. Although such questions come in many forms, the following types are among the most productive:

- *Requesting examples of the concept:* "Have you experienced or observed an event recently that is consistent with this concept?" Here you want students to draw from their own experiences in illustrating the target concept. If students can describe personal experiences that reflect a concept or procedure, you can be sure that they have grasped the concept.

- *Comparing or contrasting the concept with other recently learned concepts:* "How is this concept like [blank], which we studied yesterday?" "How is this concept different from [blank], which we studied yesterday/last week/in the previous unit?" "What does this concept remind you of that we studied yesterday/last week/in the previous unit?" "Give me an example of an event that reflects this concept and one that counters the concept."

- *Asking for inferences and predictions regarding the application of the concept:* "Given this principle, what would you expect to happen if . . .?" Here the student is being asked to use a previously learned principle in predicting what would happen under particular circumstances. This line of questioning is consistent with the notion of critical thinking, a widely emphasized concept in contemporary educational circles.

A focused teacher

  Whether giving explanations or asking questions, teacher comments should be concise and focused. Brief comments are better than lengthy proclamations. Make a practice of using the fewest words possible in representing an idea. One sentence is better than a paragraph, and one word is better than one sentence. In the interest of brevity, come right to the point rather circuitously drifting toward the main point. By the time you provide all the peripheral information, you may have lost your audience. At the other end, once you've made your point, don't continue to restate or amplify it. In so doing, you may cloud students' initial understanding of the concept or dull their interest in the concept.

  Questions and explanations vary in their level of precision. An explanation may reflect a general understanding of a concept but may not represent the full expanse or the critical limits of the concept. In the first instance the explanation is too limited and in the second instance too broad. If a colleague describes positive reinforcement as the use of praise, that explanation is both too limited and too general: many other events besides praise can be reinforcing, and praise doesn't always function as a positive reinforcer. Precision tends to beget precision, whereas broad explanations leave issues open to misinterpretation. Two individuals can be using the same term (such as *critical thinking* or *creativity*), but meaning something quite different when the term is discussed only in general terms.

Disagreement with Others. Inevitably, you and other members of your school family will see some issues differently. When those differences relate to valued beliefs and actions, disagreement can be taken very personally. If students don't like your style, that comes very close to not liking you. If a colleague objects to your use of class time, this objection might suggest you are wasting that time. Although others may disagree with you in potentially crass ways, you can learn how to express your disagreement with respectful diplomacy.

It is usually beneficial to let others know when you truly disagree with what they're saying or with the direction that a discussion is taking, rather than sitting quietly by and then complaining later about the discussion. Please consider the following guidelines for expressing helpful disagreement:

1. Make sure you understand another's comment before voicing your disagreement ("Are you saying that we should completely disband faculty meetings?").

2. Pinpoint your disagreement in the context of what you find acceptable ("I generally concur with your plan to restructure faculty meetings, but I wonder if we shouldn't get input from all the faculty before implementing the change").

3. Underscore that your disagreement represents only your view ("I see this issue somewhat differently from you").

4. Acknowledge that your disagreement doesn't necessarily represent the final word ("This is the way I currently see our problem, but I might be off target").

5. Recognize others' support for the view you're questioning ("Most people seem to feel as you do about faculty meetings").

6. Nonverbally convey goodwill as you express your disagreement (lean closer and periodically smile at the person with whom you are disagreeing).

Supportive Comments. Affirmative input is a major means of letting others know that you care about their development and success. Your comments, whether positive or negative, help set the tone for your relationships with others. You might assume that complimenting others is a straightforward, noncontroversial procedure, but it actually is among the most hotly debated issues in contemporary education. Some educators contend that praise is often given in a fashion detrimental to others' development. However, we strongly believe that compliments, when *wisely* given, can be good for both the giver and the recipient. Consequently, in chapter four we offer a detailed analysis of how best to praise and encourage other members of your school family, especially students.

Concluding Comments

You probably view your role as a teacher in a variety of ways, all of which have some validity. You may view yourself as a scholar, a strategist, a technician, and possibly an artist. Certainly, there is no substitute for knowing your subject matter well, for designing effective problem-solving strategies or for using proven instructional techniques. And how you put all of this together may require an artistic touch. Your integration of knowledge, problem-solving strategies, and instructional techniques may be quite different from that

Students of a good communicator

of a colleague who is equally capable in all these areas. Each of you has constructed a combination that reflects your own synthesis, style, and flow.

Perhaps most fundamental to teacher identity is his or her status as a communicator. Communication skills can compensate to some degree for limitations in other areas, but strength in these other areas can be negated almost totally by poor communication skills. If you communicate caring and understanding to your students, you may be a very successful teacher with less than world-class scholarship. In contrast, your cutting-edge scholarship can be rendered virtually useless to students if you cannot communicate your message understandably. Of course, the optimal combination is high-level scholarship and superb communication skills!

In the final analysis, students will probably remember their relationship with you more than the subject matter you taught them. If you develop a respectful and cordial style of relating within your school family, everyone will benefit. Such profound results can begin with a wave or a smile as you pass a student or colleague in the hallway at the start of a busy day.

References

Chan, D. W. (2002). Stress, self-efficacy, social support, and psychological distress among prospective Chinese teachers in Hong Kong. *Educational Psychology* 22: 557–69.

Clarke, C., and M. R. Hammer. (1995). Predictors of Japanese and American managers' job success, personal adjustment, and intercultural interaction effectiveness. *Management International Review* 35: 153–70.

Conaway, M. S. (1982). Listening: Learning tool and retention agent. In *Improving Reading and Study Skills*, edited by A. S. Algier and K. W. Algier, 51–63. San Francisco: Jossey-Bass.

Dodson, M., and D. S. Dodson. (2000). *Managing Up*. New York: American Management Association.

Floyd, J. J. (1985). *Listening: A Practical Approach*. Glenview, Ill.: Scott, Foresman.

Gable, R. A, and M. L. Manning. (1997). The role of teacher collaboration in school reform. *Childhood Education* (73, summer): 219–23.

Hemmings, B., and T. Hockley. (2002). Student teacher stress and coping mechanisms. Education in Rural Australia 12(3): 25–35.

Hunsaker, R. A. (1990). *Understanding and Developing the Skills of Oral Communication: Speaking and Listening*. 2d ed. Englewood, Colo.: Morton.

Jalongo, M. R. (1995). Promoting active listening in the classroom. *Childhood Education* (72, fall): 12–18.

Kleinke, C., and J. Walton. (1982). Influence of reinforced smiling on affective responses in an interview. *Journal of Personality and Social Psychology* 42: 278–82.

Moskal, B. S. (1995). Promotions: Who gets them and why. *Industry Week* 244: 44–47.

Palma, G. M. (1994). Toward a positive and effective teacher and paraprofessional relationship. *Rural Special Education Quarterly* 13(4): 46–48.

Pigford, T. (2001). Improving teacher-student relationships: What's up with that? *Clearing House* 74(6): 1–4.

Rogers, C. R. (1969). *Freedom to Learn.* Columbus, Ohio: Charles E. Merrill.

Von Bergen, C. W., B. Soper, and J. W. Licata. (2002). Managing your administrator. *Educational Forum* 67: 70–80.

Weiss, W. H. (1994). Handling communication problems. *Supervision* 55: 17–94.

Wolvin, A. D., and C. G. Coakley. (1988). *Listening.* Rev. ed. Daybook, La.: Williams C. Brown.

———. (2000). Listening education in the 21st century. *International Journal of Listening* 14: 143–52.

"I think the most basic challenge for a teacher is to get students involved in productive behaviors. Wouldn't you agree, Bill?"

"I'm not so sure that I do. Isn't controlling discipline problems even more basic?"

"I agree that discipline problems can undermine learning, but couldn't we eliminate many discipline problems by first concentrating on what students should do rather than on what they are not supposed to do?"

3

◄○►

Getting What's Best

Promoting Desired Behaviors

Some teachers contend that you must control discipline problems before you can do any teaching. This may be Bill's contention. This position appears to hinge on the premise that student problems always precede what the teacher does, which often is not the case.

Although students bring some problems into the classroom, many problems arise from conditions in the classroom. If you can get students engaged in productive academic and social behaviors, many of the problems that otherwise might occur can be prevented. Thus, the focus here is on being proactive in promoting desired student behaviors and student success. Problems that might still arise despite your best efforts are addressed in chapter five.

As the previous chapter suggested, your communication skills are basic to establishing effective relationships with students, but such skills cannot be separated from most classroom activities. This chapter describes the classroom management and instructional strategies in which your communication skills can be applied. A number of specific strategies for promoting productive student behaviors are discussed under the following broad headings:

- Planning for Success
- Developing Class Rules
- Developing Logistical Procedures
- Enhancing the Learning Environment
- Modeling Productive Behaviors
- Monitoring Student Progress

Although not exhausting the list of important strategies for promoting learning and appropriate classroom conduct, the recommendations posed in this chapter do set the stage for classroom learning to occur. They do not provide the complete prescription for effective teaching, but their absence will severely impede student learning. This chapter, in combination with chapters two, four and five, provide most of the basic guidelines for relating well to your students and for promoting their learning.

Planning for Success

Teacher planning can be approached in a variety of ways. Some teachers prefer to arrive at school an hour or so early to get organized for the day. Others prefer to stay an hour or so after school to plan for the next day. Still others prefer doing both, reserving their time at home for family activities. Whether you are a "morning" or an "evening" person may dictate when you do your daily planning.

With respect to long-term planning, many teachers formulate their overall plans for the entire academic year before beginning the school year. Others prefer planning ahead for a semester or at least a month. Few, if any, successful teachers restrict their planning to the current day's activities. Trying to provide adequate instruction by staying a page ahead of students or simply "playing it by ear" will put any teacher under constant pressure. We have seen numerous teachers become physically and emotionally drained because their planning does not match the complexities of their job.

Getting Started

Although effective teachers vary in their preferred time frames for planning, successful comprehensive planning cannot occur overnight. Thus, you need to set aside time to reflect on what you want to teach and how you want to teach. Perhaps the best time to make your long-range plans is well before the school year starts and other demands on your time begin. Perhaps you can devote part of your summer to planning for the coming school year. Teachers differ as to whether they prefer to do all their planning in one block of time (a

DEVELOPING A PACING CALENDAR

As you consider your state's required course of study and think about additions you wish to make, you may want to develop a long-range calendar that lists your daily teaching activities. You can use a month-by-month calendar with large boxes and begin by blocking in standard activities such as lunch, recess, library sessions, and planning time. You also should list before-school and after-school duties, club sponsorships, faculty meetings, and the like. Be sure to include any atypical events scheduled for the school year: senior-class trips, assembly programs, and schoolwide events.

The most important item on your pacing calendar is your teaching schedule. Because your commitments will vary somewhat from day-to-day, you may want to construct a detailed schedule for the first couple of weeks. From that point on, you may be able to operate from memory until you encounter a major scheduling change. However, you should pencil in the unit topics and then circle the dates when you will begin and complete each unit. Your calendar is essentially your guide for letting you know what needs to be done at a given time. It can serve also as a motivational tool. People who write down what they must do at particular times are more likely to stay on task and on schedule than those who do not.

two-week period), spend a day now and then, or devote some portion of several days to planning for the school year. Whether you concentrate your planning in one block of time or spread the planning over several weeks, you need to devote the equivalent of a few weeks (perhaps two to four weeks) to getting ready for the coming school year.

Once you have committed yourself to long-range planning, you need to think about an approach that will yield the best results for you and your students. You want your daily plans to flow from a comprehensive instructional program. You might begin by looking at instructional development models. Gustafson and Branch (1997) review four models (Gerlach and Ely 1980; Heinich et al. 1996; Kemp, Morrison, and Ross 1994; and Reiser and Dick 1996) that have applications in a variety of teaching settings. Although exhibiting some differences, all four models emphasize the importance of goals or objectives, learner characteristics (e.g., readiness, entering behaviors), selection of resources, assessment procedures, and reviews or revisions based on student performance. This chapter reflects those common themes in our recommendations for your long-term and short-term planning.

Defining Goals and Objectives

One good starting place in establishing your goals and objectives is to use the Internet to determine the standards set by your state department of education. Because we live and teach in North Carolina and Tennessee, we refer to the web resources for teachers in these states. The Tennessee Department of Education provides the *Teacher's Guide to the Tennessee Curriculum*, which lists the standards (goals) and skills (objectives) for each grade and subject in the Tennessee curriculum. Each skill is labeled to show whether it is something to be introduced, has already been developed at the previous grade, and is something assessed in the state's criterion-referenced testing program. Similarly, in North Carolina, the State Department of Public Instruction provides a standard course of study for each grade level. Your state also has a list of standards and resources to help meet those standards. Thus, teachers who begin their planning with goals and objectives have important standards already defined for them. Using this resource, they can also easily identify skills introduced and assessed at lower levels.

Whether you are using state goals and objectives or ones you have developed or modified for your class, you need to be sure that the attainment of such goals can be unequivocally determined. Locke and Latham's (2002) analysis of goal setting in business and industrial settings indicates that specific goals are superior to "do your best" goals. Applying their notions to classroom learning suggests that student goals and objectives should be stated in measurable terms. This is typically the case with objectives provided by state education departments and with those in teacher materials accompanying textbooks. You also need to ensure that any goals and objectives you develop or adopt from various sources are measurable.

For example, the objective of helping Lucille "become a better speller" can be made measurable by restating the desired outcome as "spelling correctly nineteen of twenty words on the next spelling test." Similarly, a measurable objective for a language arts teacher might be that students be able to identify the topic sentence for each paragraph in the assigned reading. The clearer a goal is stated, the better students will understand what to do. And their knowing what to do increases the probability of their staying on task. When a student is off-task, possibly engaged in disruptive behavior, you can ask, "What should you be doing?" rather than "What are you doing?"

Locke and Latham (2002) also suggest that goal attainment be enhanced by stressing the importance of a goal and by helping individuals believe they can reach the goal. You can identify how the student can benefit (in ways important to him or her) from attaining a particular goal and outline a strategy likely to produce achievement of the goal. Even if a student clearly understands a goal, he or she is unlikely to work hard to attain a goal he or she regards as unimportant. But even if a student perceives a goal as important, he or she may not pursue the goal unless he or she expects to be able to reach the goal. Providing instruction that will help students see the personal value of a particular goal and the strategies they can use to reach the goal should increase the probability of their performing well on goal-related tasks.

Identifying Student Needs

Besides identifying specific goals and objectives you wish to accomplish, you should consider your students' special needs. For instance, what kinds of cultural and economic backgrounds are represented among your students? What types of skills will these students need to cope better with experiences outside the classroom? What types of social and academic skills will your students need to develop this year to progress comfortably to the next academic year? What types of skills will the students need to develop now to increase their chances of a promising future beyond the school years? What skills will the students bring with them to your classroom, and what will you need to do to maintain those skills?

The critical criterion for identifying important student needs is *practicality*. You can make your instructions more practical by focusing on what will help your students cope better in the world beyond the classroom. For example, how important will it be for them to know how to use a computer, to be able to express their views accurately and concisely, to learn respect for others' rights and feelings, or to know the practices basic to physical health? We suggest that you develop some priorities as to which student needs will receive the most attention in your classroom. Obviously, in identifying the outcome skills students will need, you should consider the outcomes your school and state deem critical in the school experience. But even with those outcomes considered, you will still have some latitude in how you plan and present your lessons. For example, state and local school systems are not always at the cutting edge with respect to the promotion of personal health habits, though such habits should be among the most important targets of schooling.

Collecting Relevant Resources

At some point, the sooner the better, you need to begin gathering materials to be used in your instructional program. An enterprising teacher will accumulate an array of instructional activities over a period of several years. Many teachers begin by filing instructional activities developed during their teacher-training program. When you go to workshops or interact with colleagues, collect examples of instructional activities as you might collect food recipes. If you are just beginning to teach, you should use Internet resources. As noted earlier, you can visit the website of your state department of education. Most states provide an array of resources for teachers.

North Carolina's web site, for example, offers lesson plans and provides the names of other sites containing useful lesson plans on various topics. Included among these sites are Apple Learning Interchange, Ask ERIC Lesson Plans, Eisenhower National Clearinghouse, the Lesson Plan Page, Learn NC's Lesson Plan Directory, and Tried "N" True Lesson Plans. Your state likely has similar lists of resources.

In addition to looking at external sources of help, you can examine what is available at your school. You would be wise to identify another teacher whose teaching responsibili-

Collect resources

ties are similar to yours. This person should be someone you know reasonably well (or someone you can get to know well) and whose commitment to teaching is similar to yours. Open your files to each other. The interaction between the two of you is likely to stimulate more productivity from each of you. Also, media specialists and instructional supervisors can be very helpful in preparing lists of instructional materials they have for a specific topic. If you are building your instructional system around objectives, you should develop and collect brief tests to evaluate whether your instructional activities have been effective in helping students meet the stated objectives.

Orchestrating Day-to-Day Activities

Although most of your planning is for the long term, it still needs to include how to make each day run smoothly. First, each child should be informed about what is expected of him or her on that day. Ideally, the child should have a printed indication of the work to be done at any given point in the day. If you are using extensive sets of instructional objectives, your daily planning should specify which objectives the student is to work on that day. You might operate from a card file so that each student can simply move through the file to select a new objective as each assignment is completed. Or you can prepare handouts containing the objective(s), and the students can give their responses to assigned tasks on the handout sheet. Elementary teachers may prefer writing daily objectives and assignments on the board. Some teachers are using student planners where students record objectives, assignments, and notes to parents.

In your long-term planning, you already have identified and possibly collected most of your instructional resources. Your daily planning thus will simply involve making sure that you know which instructional resources are to be used the following day and that those resources are ready for use. You most likely will need to prepare copies, pick up technical resources, and place instructional resources in the appropriate locations in the classroom for each day's activities.

We suggest you attempt to do most of your short-term planning during the school day. Most teachers have at least some free time to get school-related work done at school, thus freeing their evenings for personal pursuits. Other ways to salvage planning time during the school day include arranging for some self-directed learning activities and providing personal reading time for students. Even a few minutes of planning and evaluation at school can avert gathering up and carting papers home.

Finally, on certain days you will have special activities—for instance, assemblies, guest speakers, or field trips. Although we strongly favor such expanding activities, we also recommend always having contingency plans. Assemblies may be cancelled, computers may go down, speakers may not show up, and transportation may prove unavailable. If you are absolutely counting on your special plans, you may become very frustrated and waste valuable time. Always have some conventional activities ready should your special plans not materialize. Having productive activities immediately available is critical to maintaining effective use of class time.

DEVELOPING A FILING SYSTEM

Collecting resources necessitates a filing system to prevent cluttering of your work environments, to protect materials for reuse, and to permit quick retrieval of desired materials. For most teachers, materials not currently in use should be out of sight. You need a relatively clean workspace that allows you to focus your attention on the task at hand. Plus, materials placed within a file are less likely to be lost or mangled than those moved around from stack to stack on your desk or in your classroom. The major point of filing is to be able to find what you need when you want it.

Having an efficient filing system requires that your classification system be very transparent, permitting the filing of materials under obviously logical headings. Try not to outsmart yourself by creating esoteric categories you will not be able to remember in the future. The principal conceptual categories to include in your filing system are instructional objectives, instructional activities, and evaluation tools. In this highly technical era, much of your filing can be housed in computer files. We suggest you always back up your files within the various computer drives and even print and file hard copies of your most critical documents.

PLANNING FOR A SUBSTITUTE TEACHER

There will be days when you must be away from school for illness or other reasons. When you return to school, you may learn students have behaved inappropriately during your absence, and you end up having to deal with "yesterday's problems." You can save yourself considerable grief by highlighting your expectations for student conduct prior to your absence. Among other things, you can review what is expected behavior during your absence, what students can do when they have completed their assignments (e.g., working on any special projects, getting ahead on homework, reading a library book), and what the consequences will be for appropriate and inappropriate behavior.

You also should have a plan available for the substitute. Review sheets of important concepts or review sheets for an upcoming test can be kept in your desk and be readily accessible for the substitute. You may not want new material presented in your absence, given that the substitute may not be adequately informed regarding that material. If you must be away for an extended period, you should make your long-range plans available to the substitute. You can expect most students to follow your wishes when expectations are known in advance and when you anticipate the kinds of activities that will keep them engaged during your absence.

Thinking Small in the Beginning

You may be overwhelmed by the prospect of long-term and highly specific planning, so we advise you to *think small in the beginning* rather than concentrate on grandiose accomplishments. For example, many teachers aspire to have an academic program that is individualized with respect to both student interest and skill level. Although a noble intention, such a goal needs to be approached gradually, especially by new teachers. For instance, if you want to use learning centers as a part of your instructional program, begin with *one* learning center. You can then add other learning centers after you have one operating smoothly. Also, divide any large task you want to accomplish into a series of smaller tasks. Then arrange these tasks in order of priority, dealing with the most important small task first— not the entire large task. You can always add to your small successes, but don't build failure into your teaching by initially trying to do more than can be managed. Perhaps the old adage "big oaks from little acorns grow" aptly represents the possibility of large outcomes from small beginnings in the classroom.

Reviewing Your Planning Activities

Although instructional planning might follow a variety of formats, we have offered suggestions useful to most teachers. You can use the checklist provided here to review what you have already done and what remains to be done with respect to planning. Just check the items you already have addressed and place an asterisk by items that merit further consideration. Which of the following have you done?

- Set aside a block of time for long-term planning;

- Considered the required program of study prescribed in your state and the established goals and objectives consistent with state standards;

- Ensured that all your goals and objectives are stated in measurable terms;

- Developed a long-term calendar, mapping out your schedule for the first several weeks and noting how you will pace yourself through the curriculum;

- Identified important student needs, such as those related to students' cultural backgrounds and future job aspirations and opportunities;

- Begun collecting resources to use in meeting instructional goals and objectives;

- Developed a filing system for your instructional materials;

- Identified others who can assist you in obtaining instructional materials and who can work with you in implementing instructional activities;

- Determined how to inform students about what is expected of them on a daily basis;

- Prepared or arranged for instructional materials to be ready on the days they are needed;

- Established a set time each day when you can do some short-term planning;

- Developed a backup plan to cover unexpected events, such as speakers not arriving as scheduled and equipment break-down.

Developing Class Rules

Although the rules you develop depend somewhat on your students' ages and needs, some guidelines for developing rules are applicable at all grade levels. First, rules should not exist just to keep order; they should reflect what is helpful to students. For example, if you want students to be responsible, the rule to do their homework each night reflects personal responsibility. Second, you should involve students in setting rules, not only to gain their commitment, but also to clarify reasons for those rules. Third, in order to avoid setting a negative tone in the classroom, state rules positively. You should develop rules related to what should be done, rather than stressing what students are to avoid doing.

Underscoring the Purpose of Rules

Rules should not be viewed as a mere vehicle for maintaining order. Even very young students will quickly figure out whether you are trying to control them through rules or whether your classroom rules serve a higher purpose, such as making life better for them both in the classroom and elsewhere. Much of their insight probably evolves from how rules are developed and implemented. Ideally, you want to convey through your words and actions that there is a relationship between the quality of school life and your class rules. Your rules should reflect the important priorities and goals for your class ("Make Sure Class Rules Reflect Learning Goals" 2000). Some of your goals, of course, are academically oriented, whereas others focus on social skills students need for getting along with others. Whatever the case, rules should be tied to the important lessons you want students to learn rather than being mere instruments of control.

Consequences are the principal consideration for many students in following the rules. Will I experience a positive outcome for observing the rules and what will happen if I break the rules? Rademacher, Callahan, and Pederson-Seelye (1998) suggest that teachers use logical positive and negative consequences for rule compliance. Examples of positive consequences include extrinsic rewards (such as complimentary notes home and free time) and intrinsic benefits (such as getting more work done and developing new skills). They suggest that giving up some earned free time to complete an assignment might be a logical negative consequence for not completing the assignments on time. The point is that rule compliance should benefit the students in extrinsic or intrinsic ways or both.

Involving Students in Developing Rules

How might you establish rules for your classroom? A class discussion early in the school year is a logical starting point for developing class rules. Involving students in the decision-making lets them know they have a stake in how the classroom operates. Even very young students can provide some ideas as to what makes a good or bad class. A modified form of the strategies presented by Taba (1966) for teaching cognitive skills can be used for conducting a class discussion to generate workable ideas for classroom rules. The procedure initially involves giving students a *focus* question (e.g., "What do you consider to be appropriate or inappropriate behavior in the classroom?")

After a student has suggested a behavior that should be considered appropriate or inappropriate, ask follow-up questions that probe for the rationale behind the suggestion (e.g., "Why do you feel that listening when others are speaking is important in the classroom?"). Students should be encouraged to explain and support their statements. For example, the teacher might say, "Juan, you state that we do not need a rule about coming to class on time. Give me some reasons why you think the class would operate better if we did not have such a rule." Ask students to predict what kind of classroom behavior will result if suggested ideas were implemented. The discussion should lead to rules acceptable to both you and your students.

Examining School Rules

In addition to classroom rules, it is important for students to know school regulations and policies that have a direct bearing on their conduct. Are certain schoolrooms off limits at certain times during the day? Are certain messages on clothing prohibited? Is there a dress code? How many absences or times tardy are allowed before an attendance official is consulted? Questions of school policy are especially important for secondary school students. Discuss established regulations with students and post a copy in the classroom for continued reference. Stressing the positive aspects of school policies increases the probability that students will function within the rules. A discussion period also allows students to vent any frustrations they might have toward certain restrictions. In cases where rules are viewed as unfair or unnecessary, help students work within the school structure to create change.

APPLYING THE RULES

A compelling application of rules for helping students learn useful behaviors is presented in the best-selling book *The Essential 55* by Ron Clark (2003). For example, rule 2, "make eye contact," represents an important skill that everyone should practice when engaged in conversation. Similarly, some of his other rules, such as "show respect for other students' comments, opinions, and ideas" (rule 4) and "say 'Thank you' when I give you something" (rule 9) are matters of courtesy having important significance in and out of school. However, rule 52, "accept that you are going to make mistakes," lets his students know they do not have to be perfect. In all, Clark eventually developed fifty-five rules he believed to be essential for working with his students, first in rural North Carolina and later in the Harlem section of New York City. Besides teaching important life skills, his rules gave students a sense of control over their lives—he asked for nothing that could not be learned and mastered with practice. In fact, he provided many opportunities through class discussions, field trips, and social outings to put the rules into effect.

Emphasizing Positive Behaviors

In addition to the specificity of class rules, the overall tone of those rules is critically important. Your ten basic rules may be stated clearly and specifically, but still adversely affect your classroom climate if stated negatively. A combination of negatively stated rules (e.g., "don't come to class late, don't talk to your classmates when the teacher is talking, don't turn in your work late") underscores that your class is a place where a student can get into trouble. The same issues are better stated positively (e.g., "arrive at class early, listen closely when the teacher is talking, and turn in your work on time"), suggesting to the student ways to magnify his or her success in the classroom.

Developing Logistical Procedures

You also need to establish procedures to keep classroom activities moving smoothly. These procedures should indicate how students are to perform each activity and move from one activity to the next. In determining necessary procedures, make a list of what students will be doing while they are under your supervision. Your list may include such things as turning in assignments, working independently and in groups, seeking your assistance and that of peers, working at computer stations or learning centers, exiting the classroom for a variety of reasons, and performing such routine tasks as sharpening pencils and using supplies and work materials. Any student activity that may affect your classroom management should be included on your list. As with rules, discussions are a good way to develop and clarify how students are to perform different tasks. You can start with discussions related to the most routine and prevalent activities, with the option for further discussion prior to introducing new activities.

Besides clarifying procedures through discussions, you also should ensure that students know how to meet your expectations. Evertson, Emmer, and Worsham (2000), who have done extensive research on classroom rules and procedures, suggest that elementary teachers use three processes in teaching procedures to students. First, teachers should describe and demonstrate the expected behaviors. For example, if you are teaching students how to use a "quiet voice" at a learning center, you can describe what you mean and give a demonstration. Second, you should permit students to rehearse procedures so they can get a feel for what you are asking of them. Third, you should provide feedback regarding how well your students are implementing the desired procedures. If some students are having difficulty with the procedures, you may need to ask them to describe what they are to do and then give additional practice opportunities. Emmer and colleagues' (1997) text for secondary teachers includes details for establishing rules and procedures at that level. Among their recommendations, they suggest that teachers begin with less-complex procedures, such as those related to whole-class activities and seat work.

WHAT DID YOU SAY TO DO?

Whether you are specifying a rule, a classroom procedure, or academic instructions, you need to be precise. The following examples may help you distinguish between clear and unclear instructions.

Unclear Instructions	*Clear Instructions*
Come in early in the morning and finish your chemistry test.	Come in at 7:45 and finish your chemistry test.
Show more team spirit.	Cooperate with team members by allowing other players to score rather than always attempting to run the ball. Show you are a team member by cheering others on.
Show you have some manners during lunch.	Use your napkin. Chew your food with your mouth closed.
Don't take too long in the restroom.	You have five minutes to go to the restroom before you board the bus.
Don't be so immature.	Don't pass notes.
Don't get too far from the building during recess.	Stay on the asphalt area during recess.

Enhancing the Learning Environment

Desirable and undesirable student behaviors are greatly influenced by the classroom environment. Thus, in addition to thorough instructional planning and the establishment of guidelines regarding student behavior, you should give careful consideration to creating a classroom environment conducive to learning. You can begin by answering two important questions: "How can I relate classroom learning to student interests?" and "How can I arrange a physical environment conducive to student learning?"

Assessing Student Interests

Any number of individual factors influence interests, such as students' cultural background, their learning history (e.g., previous success or failure in a given area), their perception of

There are several strategies to determine
how to keep student interest.

their own competence in a skill area, their perception of the relevance of an activity for achieving a desired goal, and their background knowledge in a subject (Bergin 1999). Such factors should be considered as you plan lessons to broaden learning activities for students. Connecting learning activities to valued and successful background experiences is a prime way to make current learning activities valued and successful.

Interviewing Students. Several strategies are available for determining what is appealing to students. For example, you may wish to conduct brief interviews with each student. You can use the interviews to identify learning activities students enjoy, what they do in their free time, what aspirations they have for the future, and what difficulties they are experiencing in and out of school. You also can use interviews to assess the mental processes students use in academic activities (Carr 2002). In the latter case, you need to pose questions that permit them to reveal what processes they use in approaching and completing a task (i.e., how they think their way through a task). The idea of an interview, of course, is to learn more about students—their current interests, their perception of their competence, and their cognitive skills.

Administering Questionnaires. You may prefer to use a questionnaire, especially with older students, to assess student interests. As with interviews, you can use a questionnaire to identify a range of interests, or you can focus on a specific academic area, such as reading. For example, a reading questionnaire will probably reveal some highly individual interests as well as some topics everyone seems to enjoy. McKenna (1986) reports that young students tend to be interested in a variety of topics and notes considerable differences in the reading preferences of boys and girls. In contrast, *all* remedial junior high and high school students seemed to be interested in certain topics. The students, for instance, shared an interest in "strange" topics. They liked weird but true stories as well as stories about ghosts, magic, and the unknown. (The current interest in the Harry Potter books by J. K. Rowling certainly supports McKenna's earlier findings.) McKenna speculated that books about oddities in science or a book of unusual math puzzles might encourage more reading in science and math. Similarly, reading about unusual events in any subject area may heighten interest in that subject.

Rather than focusing on unusual events, you may want to use information gleaned from a questionnaire to engage students in another subject area. Urso and Welchman (1999), for example, used information about the types of books (fiction and nonfiction) students reported reading in order to teach math skills. The students completed data cards about their books and worked in groups to sort the data cards, to make predictions about reading preferences, and to present data in different forms, such as graphs, tables, and pie charts. The students also were asked to draw conclusions based on their findings and to make suggestions about what kinds of literature would be needed for an imaginary class library.

You also might include items in a questionnaire about what television programs students watch. Although you might prefer that they watch less television and study more, television viewing can be integrated into an occasional lesson. There are many good educational programs you can recommend, as well as television movies based on popular books that might be interesting to students. Such shows might be triggers for class discussions and reaction papers. Letting students know you share some of their interests outside of school can be an important means of establishing some common ground with them inside the classroom.

Conducting Class Meetings. The class meeting is a process recommended by William Glasser (1969, 1998) for getting involved with students and helping them learn more about themselves and others. The teacher typically facilitates class meetings, ensuring that students are respectful of one another and that all have a chance to voice their opinions. A class meeting does not have to be teacher led, however. Leachman and Victor (2003), for example, found that student-led meetings not only enhanced students' interests and participation, but also fostered empathy and responsibility in their students. They noted that class meetings give students a safe venue to be heard, to listen to other points of view, and to make effective group decisions. Although class meetings are more prevalent in the elementary grades, they can be used at any grade level to deal with issues ranging from goal setting to interacting effectively with others.

Observing Student Involvement. If you don't like the prospect of interviews, question-naires, or class meetings, other strategies are available for assessing student interests. You can observe student involvement and reactions to lessons you present. No set of materials or single teaching approach is likely to be sufficient for holding students' interests indefinitely. Thus, you need to be alert to clues from students that signal a desire for some variety. As a matter of fact, prospective and experienced teachers have perceived variation in lessons, flexibility in the way lessons are presented, and creative teaching ideas to be among the most important approaches teachers can take in creating a productive class (Long, Biggs, and Hinson 1999). The use of films, discussion groups, academic games, and group competition serve as both breaks from the routine and useful learning activities. Being attentive to what students talk about during casual conversations is yet another possibility for assessing their interests, as is observing what they do during their free time. Whatever method you choose, learning more about students' interests will help you plan better for individual students and help them feel they are an important part of the learning environment.

Making the Physical Setting Conducive to Learning

Physical surroundings can have a substantial impact on students' behavior, enjoyment of school, and ability to learn. Something as simple as variation in lighting can influence students differently because they don't all have the same preferences. Rayneri, Gerber, and Wiley (2003), for example, found that almost all of a group of sixth-, seventh-, and eighth-grade gifted students preferred dim lighting; however, more of the higher-achieving gifted students preferred bright lighting than did lower-achieving gifted students. The researchers suggested that student preferences be accommodated as long as they are productive. Teachers can alter lighting by using bookcases, screens, plants, and other techniques. Lights can be turned off over learning centers and computer centers, and lamps can be used so that students can select the lighting they prefer. Of course, students should not remain in dim light to the point that their eyes become fatigued, and you should be sure each student can see the board and screens when visual information is provided.

Adjusting the Seating Arrangement. Student behaviors sometimes can be improved simply by rearranging chairs and tables in the classroom. How you arrange the seating in your classroom depends largely on what the students will be doing. As Weinstein (2003) noted, having desks in clusters promotes social contact. This arrangement may be useful if you want students to collaborate. However, when students are engaged in individual work, sitting in clusters or around tables may promote more social interaction than is desirable. Hastings and Schwieso (1995) found that having students sit in rows for indi-vidual seatwork promotes more on-task behavior than having students sit at tables or in

A LITTLE ELBOW ROOM, PLEASE!

Is it a good idea to bring students close together for demonstrations, reading sessions, and the like? That depends on how close the students come to one another. Teachers have long observed that placing students in crowded conditions generates pushing, shoving, and hitting. However, the desire to have students see materials often leads teachers to ask students to "huddle around a little closer." Unfortunately, research indicates that crowding students not only increases aggressiveness, but also markedly reduces attention to the teacher and the material. Krantz and Risley (1977), for example, found that asking kindergarten students to crowd around a teacher for a demonstration resulted in far less attention to the teacher and much more disruptiveness. Perhaps students become too preoccupied with their "personal space" to be attentive to lessons. Therefore, make sure that students have sufficient elbow room when you bring them close together for a lesson.

clusters. Furthermore, the increase in on-task behavior promoted by having students sit in rows was greatest for students who otherwise typically engaged in high levels of off-task behavior.

Although the students in Hastings and Schwieso's (1995) research indicated a preference for group seating and a belief that they were more productive in group seating, the data did not support the students' views. The seating arrangement students prefer and the seating arrangement most conducive to productive behavior can be quite different. You have to determine what students are to do and whether a particular seating arrangement will be consistent with that task. Seats can usually be moved to accommodate different types of student activities (e.g., group discussions, joint projects, individual seat work), and you can teach students the procedures required to change seating arrangements efficiently.

In making decisions about seating arrangements, you also should consider the best location for audio-visual media (and where these items will be stored when not in use) so all students can see equally well. Computer stations and learning centers need to be located so as to minimize disruption for students not engaged in those activities. In addition, if you have students with special physical needs, you need to be sure they sit in locations conducive to their assimilation of important academic and social input.

Sequencing Learning Activities. The way activities are sequenced or the time of the day when they occur also can influence how students behave. For example, students who have just come in from recess need time to calm down before they are ready to take a test. Students also can be too exhausted near the end of a class to concentrate on a new concept. You can observe how students are acting and how you feel to determine whether you need to make adjustments in what you want students to do at any given time. You may find it useful to save less-demanding tasks for the end of class or the end of the day, to give students occasional breaks from a tedious task, or to extend the time for finishing a difficult assignment. You also can use time at the end of the day to do routine chores, such as collecting money for various materials and school functions, making announcements, and handing out information to be taken home to parents. Most important, you want to match the most difficult tasks with times during the day when students are most alert and energetic. For many students, that time is early in the school day.

Making the Classroom More Attractive. Given that you and your students will be spending a major portion of each day in school, you want to make your classroom physically inviting. The addition of pictures, rugs, plants, some informal furniture, possibly a change in the paint colors, an aquarium, and so on can be helpful. You can involve parents and students in making desired changes (perhaps in acquiring needed items). Most especially, you don't want to short-change student involvement. Their involvement helps create a sense of "joint ownership." You will find that students behave more responsibly in a classroom that they have helped to create and partly "own."

Answering the following questions may help you think about possible ways to create a more pleasant classroom setting:

- Is the temperature of the room generally comfortable?

- Would changing the color of the walls make the room more attractive and appealing to you and your students?

- Are the walls decorated in a manner that generates student interest in learning activities?

- Do students have sufficient personal space? (Do some furnishings need to be removed?)

- Is the room kept relatively clean and orderly?

- Have you asked the students what can be done to improve the physical environment, and have they been involved in implementing whatever changes have been suggested?

Modeling Productive Behaviors

Another way to promote appropriate student behavior is for you to model appropriate behavior. You can demonstrate through your own actions the behaviors you expect from students, or you can draw attention to students who are exhibiting desirable behaviors. The central idea of modeling is that students learn by first observing and then imitating the behavior of another person (the model). Although you can use modeling to help teach almost any desirable behavior, modeling is especially useful for demonstrating appropriate academic responses. You are the expert in your subject area, and you can expect most students to follow your lead. Furthermore, when students learn effective ways for approaching academic tasks, they are less likely to misbehave in order to avoid those tasks.

Emphasizing Process

Modeling *processes* rather than *products* is especially important in strengthening academic responses. For example, posting teacher and student awards provides little information as to how to achieve those awards. You may post examples of outstanding work (e.g., term papers, drawings), but you also need to model the steps involved in constructing those papers and drawings. For example, outstanding papers may involve a multitude of steps that begin with the choice of a topic and proceed with the retrieval of related information and conclude with pinpointing exactly what word best fits in a key sentence. Also important is demonstrating that you enjoy what you do. Enthusiasm for the process may initially be more critical than the work produced. Some risk taking and willingness to accept less-than-perfect products may encourage students to take risks and try activities in which they have had little prior success.

Promoting Class Participation

Teachers typically do most of the talking in classroom settings. When students engage in discussion, they usually are responding to questions posed by the teacher. Developing student inquisitiveness, however, requires that students also be able to ask appropriate questions. Gordon (2003) suggests that teachers use modeling to help students frame productive questions. For example, a teacher might begin by modeling how to ask who, what, when, where, how, and why questions, and then use flash cards to cue and reinforce students for asking similar questions after they have read a story. The teacher can then move to the modeling of "deeper" questions, such as those that require reflecting on the importance and personal meaning of what has been read.

You also need to develop ground rules for listening to others, taking turns speaking, agreeing and disagreeing, and building on others' ideas. Increasingly, you want students to interact directly with one another rather than channel their comments through you. Gordon (2003) notes that having students form their own questions following a reading assignment gives them an opportunity to respond directly to questions posed by their classmates. We would add that you should demonstrate conciseness in responding to questions, taking care to avoid rambling and lengthy responses. You want to promote balance in participation rather than a situation in which some students talk all the time and others never talk.

Developing an Interactive Approach to Reading

Modeling can be an especially useful tool in establishing a more interactive approach to reading. Combs (1987) reports that poor readers often think of reading as a matter of identifying and calling words, whereas good readers view reading as a process of interacting with the text and constructing meaning from it. To determine whether role modeling would be effective in helping kindergarten students learn that reading is a thought process as well as a visual process, Combs compared role modeling with a more traditional approach of reading aloud to the students. When using the traditional approach, teachers introduced books by telling stories about the title and making a brief comment about the content of the story. They held the books in such a manner that students could see the picture and the print. The teachers read with few pauses and followed the reading with questions about the contents.

In contrast to this traditional approach, teachers using Combs's (1987) modeling approach offered several opportunities for interaction in the course of reading a story. They began by reading from books with enlarged print. They introduced each modeled book by asking students to think about the story before it was read. For example, students were asked to speculate what might happen if they were the character in the story. Teachers paused during the reading to "think aloud" about certain parts of the story, and they paused to let students confirm or disconfirm their earlier ideas.

At the end of each story, students were asked to recall important parts of the story and to tell why those parts were important. The teachers often reread portions of the story to model how readers can confirm their ideas or make changes in them. This method of teaching reading models an interactive and reflective approach for considering the meaning and implications of what one is reading. Combs's (1987) study reveals that comprehension and recall are much higher with the modeled approach than with the traditional approach. Students also show more enthusiasm for texts that are modeled.

Broadening the Range of Academic Skills

Modeling, of course, can be used to demonstrate a diversity of academic skills, ranging from solving math problems, to identifying the main idea of a paragraph, to exhibiting effective study strategies. The key often lies in thinking out loud to reveal to students the appropriate way(s) of approaching a task. Modeling can be used to show students that you "practice what you preach." You can't expect students to work hard, stay on task, or respect others unless you are behaving in ways consistent with what you ask of them. You need not rely solely on your own actions; you can use symbolic models (e.g., real or fictional characters) in films and videos. Symbolic models are especially useful in teaching social skills, such as those related to developing friendships and appropriate behaviors toward others. Guest speakers also can be used as a means of exposing students to successful role models in their community.

Monitoring Student Progress

You should periodically evaluate the techniques you use in managing your classroom with respect to their effectiveness. Student behavior is essentially the bottom-line criterion of your instructional effectiveness. On a daily basis, you need to be certain that students remain on task; otherwise, they will make little progress. Arranging student desks or your own desk so that you can see all students, frequently glancing around the room and periodically moving about the room, can improve your knowledge of what students are doing. Teacher behavior that communicates to students the teacher's awareness of what's going on at all times has been referred to as *withitness* (Kounin 1970), and, according to this same source, being "withit" reduces student misbehavior. Beyond your daily classroom vigilance, you will find other types of evidence helpful in assessing long-term student progress, including feedback from students and parents, the results of teacher-made tests, and the results of standardized tests.

Soliciting Verbal Feedback from Students

Verbal feedback from individual students often alerts you to how well they are progressing. Do students feel that they are mastering the main ideas in the targeted areas? Do they feel you give them enough time to practice the skills you are teaching? Do they feel they have been given sufficient opportunity to ask questions about material they don't understand? The students' perceptions, accurate or not, are very important. Students with a history of failure may perceive themselves as making little progress when objective data suggest otherwise. Therefore, you may need to identify their erroneous perceptions and then work toward altering them. Sometimes, however, students may have a far more detailed, accurate picture of their progress than you do. They can point to events happening behind the scenes that more conventional modes of evaluation may not detect. If you are teaching skills that have applications outside the classroom, parents also may be able to verify whether their child is acquiring those skills and what you can do differently to promote those skills.

Assessing Student Progress

Once you have identified skill areas that will truly enhance students' lives outside of school and that legitimately fall within your teaching domain, you need to determine your students'

A SUGGESTION BOX FOR STUDENTS

Suggestion boxes are not often seen in public schools. However, in a classroom that maximizes student opportunities and responsibilities, a vehicle for achieving regular student input is imperative. End-of-the-semester evaluations, like those used in college courses, do not change instructional conditions for those currently enrolled in a course. But an old-fashioned suggestion box permits students to give input while they can still benefit from it. You can invite students to suggest activities they would like to do at school, resources they would like to have available to them, and support they would like to have from the teacher, or to inform you of aspects about school that are distressing to them. To make a suggestion system work, you must be willing to protect student anonymity and implement some of the students' suggestions. A failure on either count will quickly erode the credibility of your system.

progress in the targeted skill areas. Ideally, you will have pre-assessment and post-assessment for the important goals students are to attain. Of course, you can examine what standards should have been met the previous year, but you cannot assume all your students will be functioning at that level when they enter your class. Anecdotal records, students' cumulative subject area charts, and prior standardized test results may provide more accurate information regarding students' performance level when they enter your class. However, you may need to plan for additional observation and testing at the beginning of the school year to establish more precisely what your students can or cannot do relative to the identified skills areas.

Probably the most systematic way of monitoring students' academic growth is with teacher-made tests and standardized tests. Criterion-referenced tests usually are preferable to norm-referenced tests. *Criterion-referenced* means that the student is attempting to reach a predefined mastery criterion as opposed to competing against other students (norm-referenced tests). The students' progress over the course of the year is often assessed by standardized achievement tests administered in the school. Although we do not favor the use of these tests as the primary means of monitoring student progress, others (such as school board members and superintendent) may view standardized test scores as critical evidence of student advancement. Consequently, you cannot ignore the results of these tests.

However, a variety of factors can detract from the instructional value of standardized test scores: the tests typically do not give feedback regarding specific academic skills. The tests may not adequately represent the skills taught in your class, some students may experience debilitating test anxiety during the tests, and other students have special learning problems that transcend the procedures for administering the test. We advise you to use such tests as global indices of student progress and to begin incorporating tested skills (e.g., writing a complete sentence, constructing a paragraph, and doing long division) into your instructional program.

Concluding Comments

Planning is fundamental to getting more of what you want from your students. Although there is no guarantee your plans will produce the desired student progress, you can be certain that lack of planning will not produce good results. In large measure, what you receive from your students depends on what you invest in them. One of the major distinctions between highly successful and less successful teachers is the degree to which they anticipate and arrange for what they want to happen in the classroom. By defining in advance what they want to occur, successful teachers are able to minimize off-task behavior and help students develop skills that lead to greater success inside and outside the classroom.

This chapter has recommended that you can encourage desired student behavior by *(a)* developing comprehensive long-term and short-term instructional plans, *(b)* developing class rules, *(c)* specifying logistical procedures, *(d)* establishing an environment that facilitates learning, *(e)* modeling important skills, and *(f)* monitoring student progress. Of course, the suggestions in this chapter represent only seeds for promoting desired student outcomes. The seeds need to be nourished by much thought on your part to produce outstanding results over the long run.

References

Bergin, D. A. (1999). Influences on classroom interest. *Educational Psychologist* 34(2): 87–98.

Carr, S. C. (2002). Assessing learning processes. *Intervention in School and Clinic* 37(3): 156–62.

Clark, R. (2003). *The Essential 55.* New York: Hyperion.

Combs, M. (1987). Modeling the reading process with enlarged texts. *The Reading Teacher* 40(4): 422–26.

Emmer, E. T., C. M. Evertson, B. S. Clements, and M. E. Worsham. (1997). *Classroom Management for Secondary Teachers.* 4th ed. Boston: Allyn and Bacon.

Evertson, C. M., E. T. Emmer, and M. E. Worsham. (2000). *Classroom Management for Elementary Teachers.* 5th ed. Boston: Allyn and Bacon.

Gerlach, V. S., and D. P. Ely. (1980). *Teaching and Media: A Systematic approach.* 2d ed. Englewood Cliffs, N.J.: Prentice-Hall.

Glasser, W. (1969). *Schools Without Failure.* New York: Harper and Row.

———. (1998). *The Quality School Teacher.* New York: HarperCollins.

Gordon, K. (2003). Practical ways to use inquiry approaches in the classroom. *Primary and Middle Years Educator* 1(2): 15–20.

Gustafson, K. L., and R. M. Branch. (1997). *Survey of Instructional Development Models.* 3rd ed. ERIC ED 411 780. Syracuse, N.Y.: Syracuse University, ERIC Clearinghouse on Information and Technology.

Hastings, N., and J. Schwieso. (1995). Tasks and tables: The effects of seating arrangements on task engagement in primary classrooms. *Educational Research* 37(3): 279–91.

Heinich, R., M. Molenda, J. Russell, and S. Smaldino. (1996). *Instructional Media and Technologies for Learning.* 5th ed. New York: Macmillan.

Kemp, J. E., G. R. Morrison, and S. M. Ross. (1994). *Designing Effective Instruction.* New York: Merrill.

Kounin, J. S. (1970). *Discipline and Group Management in Classrooms.* New York: Holt, Rinehart and Winston.

Krantz, P., and T. R. Risley. (1977). Behavioral ecology in the classroom. *In Classroom Management: The Successful Use of Behavior Modification*, 2d ed., edited by K. D. O'Leary and S. G. O'Leary, 349–60. New York: Pergamon Press, 349-66.

Leachman, G., and D. Victor. (2003). Student-led class meetings. *Educational Leadership* 60(6): 64–69.

Locke, E. A., and G. P. Latham. (2002).Building a practically useful theory of goal setting and task motivation: A 35-year odyssey. *American Psychologist* 57(9): 705–17.

Long, J. D., J. C. Biggs, and J. T. Hinson. (1999). Perceptions of education majors and experienced teachers regarding factors that contribute to successful classroom management. *Journal of Instructional Psychology* 26(2): 105–10.

Make sure class rules reflect learning goals. (2000). *Curriculum Review* 40(2): 7.

McKenna, M. C. (1986). Reading interests of remedial secondary school students. *Journal of Reading* 29(4): 346–51.

Rademacher, J. A., K. Callahan, and V. A. Pederson-Seelye. (1998). How do your classroom rules measure up? *Intervention in School and Clinic* 33(5): 284–90.

Rayneri, L. J., B. L. Gerber, and L. P. Wiley. (2003). Gifted achievers and gifted underachievers: The impact of learning style preferences in the classroom. *Journal of Secondary Gifted Education* 144(4): 197–204.

Reiser, R., and W. Dick. (1996). *Instructional Planning: A Guide for Teachers.* 2d ed. Boston: Allyn and Bacon.

Taba, H. (1966). *Teaching Strategies and Cognitive Functioning in Elementary School Children.* Cooperative Research Project no. 2404, U.S. Department of Health, Education, and Welfare. San Francisco: San Francisco State College.

Urso, J., and R. Welchman. (1999). What do you like to read? *Teaching Children Mathematics* 6(1): 34–37.

Weinstein, C. S. (2003). *Secondary Classroom Management, Lessons from Research and Practice.* 2d ed. Boston: McGraw-Hill.

"Ted, I need to speak with you."

"About what, Mr. Solecki?"

"Your math homework. You haven't been turning it in. Why not?"

"I've been having trouble with the assignments."

"Well, you showed a lot of potential in math earlier this term. Let's examine what you've been doing recently in your math assignments, and maybe we can pinpoint the difficulty."

"Okay, I could use some help."

4

Keep Up the Good Work

The Use of Positive Reinforcement

Instead of having a teacher eager to help him, imagine that Ted has no one willing to support his academic efforts. Suppose, for example, that when he turns in assignments, the wrong answers are marked in red, low grades are assigned, and no further acknowledgments are ever made. Imagine also that when Ted shows his work to his parents, they simply look at the papers, hand them back to him without comment, and continue with what they were doing. Consider, too, that Ted has few acquaintances at school, none of whom show any interest in what he is doing academically. In fact, he is never chosen as someone with whom others want to work.

We hope no student is subjected to the fate just described for Ted. But what would happen to a child if this scenario were a reality? Would this child have any interest in school, and would he or she have any sense of self-worth? With no support from others, his or her desired responses would likely soon diminish. And if the student received no attention for good behavior, he or she would probably make his or her presence known through bad behavior. Although support for a student may come from a variety of sources, teachers are in a unique position to strengthen productive behaviors. They may spend more time with a student than the student's parents spend with him or her.

Many students are highly successful in their academic endeavors, deriving much satisfaction from their accomplishments and receiving considerable support from others. But other students encounter difficulties and need teacher encouragement to sustain their efforts. *Indeed, the teacher may be the principal source of academic support for many children.* For these students, you, as the teacher, will need to find ways to help them confront and master tasks difficult for them. Any gains made by prompting them to engage in desired behaviors (see chapter three) can be lost if positive consequences do not follow those behaviors.

This chapter proposes a variety of strategies for positively reinforcing desired student behaviors. Although many of these strategies are typically applied on an individual basis, most can be adapted to reinforce the class as a whole. The chapter is devoted mainly to strategies for reinforcing students when they exhibit productive academic and social behaviors, but the chapter also concludes with brief suggestions for reinforcing your own constructive actions as a teacher.

Defining the Limits of Positive Reinforcement

All human behavior produces consequences. When a student completes and hands in a school assignment, any number of consequences may follow. The student may get a sense of satisfaction in having accomplished the task. The student also may receive positive comments from the teacher, peers, or others for having worked hard or for doing an especially good job. Conversely, the student may be disappointed with his or her work or may be ignored or even criticized. Any of these consequences, whether positive or negative, will have an impact on future behaviors.

Definition of Terms

Consequences that strengthen (i.e., maintain or increase) behaviors immediately preceding those consequences are known as *positive reinforcers*. Such reinforcers may be *internal* (such as satisfaction with what one has done) or *external* (such as a compliment from someone else). To qualify as a positive reinforcer, a consequence must have the effect of strengthening the preceding behavior. For example, if the teacher compliments a student for participating in class and the student subsequently participates less, the compliment does *not* qualify as a positive reinforcer. What the teacher assumes will be a positive reinforcer may not function as such in this case. Also, what is reinforcing to one person may not be reinforcing to someone else. Plus, what is reinforcing at one point may not be reinforcing later even for the same individual.

The process of receiving an internal or external positive reinforcer is known as *positive reinforcement.* Theoretically, there are virtually no limits to what might result from positive reinforcement. For instance, positive reinforcement might lead to increased attention to schoolwork, improved skills with a musical instrument, or considerate treatment of others. Unfortunately, positive reinforcement also can strengthen unwanted behavior. Even consequences negative in tone (such as a teacher reprimand) may function as a positive reinforcer for a student who has just misbehaved (i.e., the student may misbehave more because of the attention reflected in the teacher reprimand).

Delivery of Positive Reinforcers

Initially, positive reinforcers can be used to get students who have little interest in school to work on academic tasks. The ultimate goal in using positive reinforcers, however, is to help students gain satisfaction from their own accomplishments. The way you deliver external consequences can affect the likelihood of students' valuing their work and accomplishments. For example, rewarding quality of performance is more likely to produce self-satisfaction from an accomplishment than rewarding mere participation in an activity (Williams and Stockdale 2004). Rewarding quality of performance helps students develop a sense of competence with respect to their schoolwork. Viewing oneself as competent in performing an activity is a major contributor to deriving satisfaction from the activity (Jacobs et al. 2002).

DID I SAY STAND UP?

Have you ever known a student whose behavior seemed to get worse following criticism? In what has become a classic study, researchers (Madsen et al. 1968) interested in this phenomenon analyzed the reinforcing function of "sit down" commands. They asked teachers who were team teaching forty-eight first graders to triple the frequency of commands to "sit down" to students who were out of their seats, while minimizing attention to students for being in their seats. Although the students usually obeyed immediately, the overall effect was a one-third increase in the time students spent away from their seats. The researchers speculated that students will disobey more often when

that is the only way they can get attention. The story does have a happy ending, however. The teachers were able to reduce standing when they started praising students for staying in their seats.

We are not implying from this example that you should expect your students to remain seated most of the time. Our contention is simply that teachers should be aware of the potentially reinforcing influences of their reprimands. Teachers will find that directing positive attention toward appropriate behavior is more productive than giving repeated negative attention to what is not wanted, which may actually reinforce undesirable behavior.

Giving students a verbal reason for performing a task well, even when you also give an external reward, is likely to increase the value they attach to their performance (Cialdini et al. 1998). Before students perform a task, you might say, "I know you will try to do this activity well because you understand the value of being good at . . . " or "You're the kind of student who understands how valuable it will be to know how to . . ." or something similar. You are basically giving students an intrinsic reason for performing an extrinsically rewarded task. Cialdini and colleagues' research shows that students are more likely to perform better on a target activity in the future if external rewards are accompanied by intrinsic reasons for doing the task well.

The Targets of Positive Reinforcement

In chapter three, we discussed the need for teachers to establish priorities so that they and their students know the most important class goals. The emphasis in this chapter is that teachers need to provide some form of positive reinforcement to keep students working toward those goals. A few students may need external incentives to even get them started on the goals. The teacher's responsibility is essentially to strengthen behaviors that benefit students, especially when those behaviors are not being supported elsewhere or provide little internal satisfaction. Staying on-task, completing academic assignments, and working well with other students are obvious targets of positive reinforcement, but in this section we feature an important academic behavior seldom reinforced and even sometimes punished by teachers.

Promotion of Creativity

One important student behavior that may require extra teacher support is creative responding. By *creativity*, we mean the ability to generate unusual but appropriate problem solutions and products (e.g., paintings, written stories, architectural designs, and pieces of music). Certainly, creative ideas are not the only legitimate targets of positive reinforcement in school, but they are among the most overlooked, undervalued, and even discredited of the important targets. Thus, promoting creative responding may be among the most important challenges for a teacher.

Importance of Creative Responses. An important expression in our time is "thinking outside the box" (i.e., thinking in ways different from the status quo). It appears that the problems to be solved in the twenty-first century will often require solutions that transcend those of the past. Perhaps this is why industry ranks creativity as one of the most valued characteristics of workers who will make a difference in the workplace (Bleedorn 1986). If your students are to become adults who can think in unusual and productive ways, they must have an opportunity to develop those skills in school. An eighteen-year follow-up of high school seniors revealed that creativity was a more powerful predictor of adult success than either IQ scores or grade point average (Milgram and Hong 1993).

Insufficient Support for Creative Responding. Despite the importance of creativity in the adult workplace, we doubt that it is adequately nurtured in school. Our conclusion is based on three lines of evidence: *(a)* much of the reinforcement at school is directed toward conformity; *(b)* creative behavior may be troublesome to some teachers; and *(c)* failure to support creativity undermines many youngsters' comfort in sharing ideas. Teachers who foster creativity permit students to think in ways that are unique and that challenge common perspectives, even those embraced by the teacher.

When students attempt to think beyond the status quo, their efforts may not be welcomed by either teachers or peers. Westby and Dawson (1995) report that elementary teachers rated students who tended to be nonconformist and individualistic (characteristics often associated with creativity) as their least favorite. Dawson and colleagues (1999) assert that past research has shown that teachers generally dislike nonconforming behaviors. Even youngsters sense tension between teachers and creative students. Stone (1980) found that second-grade students who scored highest on creative measures were identified by their peers as the most likely to get into trouble.

Originality and Knowledge Building. Fostering creative responses is often best accomplished in problem-solving activities where imaginative thoughts can be reinforced (as contrasted with question-and-answer sessions where students are reinforced for providing the "right" answer). Just generating unusual or original comments, however, is only a part of the process of creativity. Creative thinking is a principal avenue for improving ideas and building knowledge useful both to the individual and to others (Scardamalia and Bereiter 2003). Scardamalia and Bereiter note that knowledge building involves having students freely share their ideas, which may advance new possibilities and dispel misconceptions about subject matter under study. Thus, a teacher does not have to emphasize giving right answers in order to help students develop a deeper understanding of content in an academic area.

Safe and Supportive Environment. A first step in fostering creativity lies in establishing a safe environment (Vanderslice 1998). An interactive atmosphere conducive to creativity is best achieved when your responses to students are predominantly pleasant. Hardly any teacher behavior so undermines student creativeness as criticism, threat, and intimidation.

In a punitive classroom, students become afraid to express their personal views, afraid to ask questions, afraid to express wild ideas, and most of all afraid of being wrong. In contrast, discussions in which students' unusual ideas are both permissible and desirable should create a climate for increased originality in class.

Some of the threat to creative responding comes from the students themselves. Because creative ideas may sound foolish or funny, they may evoke laughter from a student's classmates. Thus, a strategy is needed to counter the perception that peer laughter reflects ridicule of imaginative ideas. Perhaps some prior discussion about the role of laughter can prevent bruised feelings. An explanation that unusual ideas often result in laughter may dispel discomfort about others' laughter. The intent is to change the connotation of laughter from ridicule to that of delight.

In addition to establishing a setting where ideas can be openly explored, the teacher should provide explicit, supportive feedback for unique responses. The message must be conveyed that novel ideas will be taken seriously—even if they at first sound strange. "That's an unusual idea" may be heard more frequently in such settings than "that's a correct idea." The teacher may initially have to instruct the students that unique ideas are being sought. Glover and Gary (1976) have demonstrated that students can readily exhibit different facets of creativity when instructed to do so. In their study, teachers systematically promoted different aspects of creativity *(fluency, flexibility, elaboration, and originality)* by simply writing one of these terms on the board and letting their students know that they would receive tangible rewards (milk and cookies) for displaying the featured behavior.

Contingent Reinforcement: Behavior Targets

When you are the one providing the reinforcement, whether for creative behavior or for other productive responses, you want to be sure students clearly understand what the reinforcer is actually targeting. In general, positive reinforcers are delivered on a *contingent* basis, which means they are given when the student exhibits a desired behavior. Moreover, in delivering contingent reinforcement, you must be sure that reinforcers do not immediately follow behaviors that might compete with desirable behavior. For example, if you are trying to strengthen "hand raising to be called on," you want to give your attention only when students follow that rule. Calling on students who blurt out responses will quickly erode the necessity of students' raising their hands.

Similarly, if you are trying to strengthen appropriate academic responses, you want to define what is acceptable work and then reinforce work that meets this standard. However, be careful not to establish standards beyond the students' reach; your goal is to produce improvement, not immediate excellence. Reinforcing improvement toward a higher standard prevents students from being overwhelmed by stringent standards in their initial efforts to improve performance.

Noncontingent Reinforcement: Person Targets

If you are thinking that the use of contingent reinforcement sounds a bit too restrictive for how you relate to students, be assured that not all reinforcement has to be delivered on a contingent basis. In fact, there will be ample opportunities for you to offer *noncontingent* reinforcement, especially noncontingent approval. *Noncontingent* means that no conditions are attached to the reinforcement. Noncontingent approval, for example, is offered because you wish to convey respect and warmth to students. To receive noncontingent approval, the student does not have to be well dressed, well behaved, or even a good student. Noncontingent reinforcement exemplifies the unconditional positive regard discussed in chapter two. The student is valued simply as a human being.

The best time to deliver noncontingent reinforcement is when the student is engaging in essentially neutral behavior. You do not want students to equate their behaviors with their personal worth. If you always tie your approval to desired behavior, students may come to think, "I am worthy of support only if I can meet certain standards." Sitting with a student during lunch, talking with students before and after school, and engaging in sports activities with students provide timely opportunities to evidence unconditional goodwill toward your students.

Noncontingent reinforcement is extremely helpful in improving students' self-concept

A teacher should express noncontigent positive regard for his students.

because they can feel good about themselves without the burden of trying to please somebody else or always striving to meet someone else's standard. Such statements as "I enjoy being your teacher," "You have a nice smile," and "You have a good sense of humor" show that the teacher values the student—not just the student's academic performance. Nice gestures given unconditionally can also boost students' sense of personal importance. The teacher who brings a birthday cake to school each month to celebrate birthdays that month is conveying that each student counts.

Identification of Student Preferences for Positive Reinforcers

Once you have identified the targets you wish to strengthen (whether productive behaviors or self concept), you then need to identify reinforcers appropriate for your students. As with most approaches to classroom management, different options are available to help you identify *potential* reinforcers, including articles, books, and web sites on classroom management as well as tips from other teachers about what works in their classes. Perhaps the easiest process, though, is simply to ask your students what they prefer. Even very young students can tell you what they would like for doing a good job.

Class Discussion

For elementary students, you can use a class discussion to identify student preferences. Possible questions for the students to discuss might include: "What are some things that would make school more fun?" "What would be a nice reward for . . ?" and "What are some things that make you feel good about your efforts?" In facilitating this kind of class discussion, you want to be sure not to pass judgment on the acceptability of student ideas too quickly. Your initial goal is to have students freely share possibilities without immediate judgment from you and their peers.

You and your students can later attempt to determine which options will prove most workable in your class. You can list possible reinforcers (e.g., teacher praise, display of student work, more time in a learning center) on the board and have your students discuss the pros and cons of each possibility. Some suggestions may prove a bit too expensive or time consuming, but they should be acknowledged as worthwhile suggestions nonetheless. Finally, students can be invited to vote on or rank the ideas that have been proposed.

Written Questionnaires

With more advanced students, a written questionnaire can be used to find out what they prefer. Published questionnaires are available, but Raschke (1981) suggests that teachers design and administer their own survey, using one of three questionnaire formats: *(a)* open ended, *(b)* multiple choice, and *(c)* rank order. With the open-ended format, students respond to inquiries about their preferences for free-time activities, seating arrangements, learning activities, and compliments and feedback on progress—to name a few possibilities. Inquiries can include the following: "If I had ten minutes free time during this class, I would like most to . . .," "In this class, I feel proudest of myself when . . . ," and so on.

The multiple-choice format elicits much the same information as the open-ended format but has the advantage of including possibilities overlooked in open-ended responding. Certainly, some of the options for the multiple-choice items may come from student responses to open-ended questions, but you can add options you found to be highly reinforcing with previous groups of students. If you have taught for several years, you may have a far better sense of workable reward privileges than most of your students may have.

Finally, the rank-order format requires students to arrange a list of items from high to low according to their desirability. For example, Raschke (1981) says students can rank such consequences as verbal approval, special food treats, free-time activities, stickers, tangible rewards, certificates of achievement, pats on the back, and display of their work. Obviously, you need to put options on the list that are appropriate and manageable for the grade level(s) you teach.

Teacher Experimentation

Students sometimes are not aware of particular consequences that are reinforcing to them, and other times they may think that particular consequences are reinforcing when they actually have little effect on their behaviors. Some experimentation on your part may be required to determine what consequences actually strengthen the behaviors they follow. In some of our early research on this topic, we found that both primary and junior high students were unable to judge very precisely what classroom events would be most reinforcing to them (Adkins and Williams 1972; Runyon and Williams 1972). Therefore, in addition to asking students what they prefer, you might try different types of consequences and see how students respond to them.

You will have to decide what level of complexity you can manage in a reinforcement program. Free time, verbal or nonverbal approval, and feedback tend to be relatively uncomplicated to administer. In general, maximizing attention to good behavior and minimizing attention to bad behavior is a good reinforcement principle to follow. Nonetheless, some teachers like to have an extensive menu of reinforcement possibilities involving a variety of contingencies.

If you wish to launch an intricate reward system, you may want to develop a formal contingency-management plan such as a behavior contract or token economy. Contracts, for example, are written agreements that specify appropriate and inappropriate behaviors and the consequences for each. Both parties (the teacher and the student) typically sign off on the terms of the contract. In token economies, students work on academic and social skills to "earn" tokens (e.g., points, chips, coupons, stickers) that they save until they accumulate enough to purchase backup reinforcers (e.g., small prizes, edibles, or free-time activities). It is usually better to develop a behavior-management system in steps rather than trying to inaugurate a complex system all at once; you may find that some of your initial plans prove less workable than anticipated.

"MAKING FREE TIME LESS FREE"

Although the backup rewards in such behavior-management systems as contracts and token economies can range from certificates to tangibles to free-time activities, it is the latter we have used most frequently in our own applications of contingency-management systems. However, in one of our first attempts to use free time in a junior-high class, we made several miscalculations. First, we set the performance criterion for earning free time only slightly above the baseline level for the target behavior, which in this case was completing the daily assignment. We had projected that students would earn about ten minutes of free-time activities at the end of a fifty-minute class period by efficiently completing their daily assignment. Doing a little better work in forty minutes than what they had been doing in fifty minutes sounded like a fair trade-off to us. Surprisingly, under the free-time contingency, most students began finishing their assignments within ten to fifteen minutes, leaving thirty-five to forty minutes of free time. This is not the kind of ratio between instructional time and free time that most educators would applaud.

Our account is one of those good news/bad news scenarios. Obviously, our free-time privileges had motivated students to work much more diligently than they had done without those privileges, but we had offered free time too cheaply. We could have gotten much more for our free time than we originally projected. Henceforth, we learned to proceed cautiously in setting free-time contingencies by doing some trial runs with free time before formalizing any contingencies. Those trial runs provided a more realistic estimate of what students could do given the promise of free time.

Our second major mistake was failure to restrict access to some of the more valued free-time activities. We had been able to get a local magazine distributor to donate a wide array of comic books for use in this project. During the first few days of the contract, students did little else but read comic books during free time. But after a couple of weeks of overdosing on the comic books, the students abandoned them for the rest of the year. It would have been better for us to provide more restricted access to the comic books to prevent comic book satiation. Providing unlimited access to your most potent reinforcers will preempt their future reinforcement potential.

Interdependent Group-Oriented Reinforcement

Our discussion of reinforcement has so far focused on reinforcing students individually, with the teacher's targeting important behaviors to reinforce, setting appropriate criteria for student performance of those behaviors, selecting consequences that would be reinforcing to individual students, and then applying those consequences when students meet the performance standards. To make this system most effective at an individual level, the target behavior, the criterion of performance, the reward selected, and the delivery of reward could be different for each student. Although this individualized arrangement might be considered ideal, it would be labor intensive for the teacher and potentially unmanageable with a large group of students.

Recent research (Skinner, Williams, and Neddenriep 2004) has considered ways to accommodate some of the individual differences in reinforcement needs by using a system called "interdependent group-oriented reinforcement." With this arrangement, enough randomness is built into the system that all students stand to gain by doing their best work. Possible rewards, target activities, and criteria for reinforcement can be randomized on a group basis.

Reward Selection

As with any reinforcement system, whether individual or group, the payoffs for productive behavior must truly be reinforcing to students to be effective. To accommodate individual student preferences about rewards, you can have students put their suggestions for rewards into a suggestion box in the classroom, and then you can draw a suggestion from the box (Popkin and Skinner 2003). Of course, you need to provide guidelines as to what types of suggestions are permissible (e.g., consistent with school and class rules, comfortable for other students in the room, relatively brief in time duration). After students have submitted their suggestions, you can review them and eliminate those that are inappropriate (especially any activities that might be embarrassing to one or more students). You should be sure that the list of rewards contains some consequences that every student finds highly reinforcing and no consequence that any student finds punishing.

When a group reward is randomly chosen from the suggestion box, any one student may find the selected reward highly reinforcing or not so reinforcing. This outcome translates into a variable reinforcement schedule for any given student (i.e., the student is sometimes reinforced for exhibiting the target behavior when at other times it is not reinforced). This kind of reinforcement schedule usually produces a durable response pattern. In fact, reinforcing a behavior on a variable basis may sustain the behavior better after discontinuation of the reinforcement than reinforcing it every time it occurs.

"DRESSING LIKE A CLOWN"

Choosing rewards to administer to the total class presents greater latitude than selecting rewards for individual students. For example, group rewards can involve games and activities for the total class, whereas individual rewards need to be on the quieter side. With an individual system, some students may be participating in reward activities, while others are continuing to work on their assignments. Any reward involving considerable movement and sound probably will not work in an individual system. In a group-reward system, however, such activities will likely be manageable (as long as your class doesn't disturb nearby classes).

Another type of reward that is more adaptive on a group basis rather than an individual basis is a special class event. Most of the time students suggest these events and enjoy them much more. Skinner, Williams, and Neddenriep (2004) describe such unusual events as teachers' wearing their pajamas to school, dressing like a clown, and singing while standing on their desks as events younger students would work to make happen. A teacher ordinarily may not think of such events as potential rewards for classroom use, but apparently younger students like to see their teachers in unusual roles.

Two other aspects of the group-based reward system that may be reinforcing, especially for students who seldom earn rewards for school achievement, are the social reinforcement derived from helping the group achieve a valued reward, and the suspense surrounding the selection of the group reward (Skinner, Williams, and Neddenriep 2004). Even if a selected reward is not that reinforcing to a particular individual, the student may enjoy participating in the group celebration following the earning of the reward. Also, students may find working for an unknown reward more exciting than working for a previously identified reward (Moore et al. 1994).

Target Activity

A disadvantage of targeting a particular desirable behavior to reinforce is that other desirable behaviors may diminish in frequency for lack of reinforcement (Mace, McCurdy, and Quigley 1990; Skinner, Williams, and Neddenriep 2004). A way to counter students' tendencies to deemphasize academic activities that are reinforced less than other behaviors is to introduce an element of uncertainty about what behaviors will be reinforced. If students do not know which of several different academic behaviors will be reinforced, they will probably engage in all those behaviors (Freeland and Noell 2002).

Popkin and Skinner (2003) integrated this dimension of uncertainty into an interdependent group-reward contingency. In this case, students were rewarded on the basis of class average for performing an academic task. Performance was monitored in three academic areas (grammar, spelling, and mathematics). At designated times, the teacher randomly selected one of these academic areas to reward. The class would receive the reward if the class average met the designated criterion in the randomly selected area. Not knowing which academic area would be chosen for reinforcement, students were more inclined to do their best in all the academic areas.

Criteria for Reinforcement

Almost every classroom reinforcement arrangement entails a criterion for reinforcement. The criterion is usually set at the outset of an activity so that students know exactly how well they must do to earn the reinforcer. Setting the same criterion to apply individually across all students immediately poses one to three problems. A common criterion for all students may be too high for some students and too low for others. In contrast, however, individualizing the performance criterion also makes it difficult to keep track of who has met what criterion. Plus, students with a stringent criterion may be resentful of those having a low criterion.

A group-based reinforcement criterion can obviate all of these complications. A group criterion can be set in at least two ways: specifying the minimum number of students who must meet a certain performance standard for the group to earn the reward or specifying a group average necessary for the group to earn the reward (Skinner, Williams, and Neddenriep 2004). Suppose the teacher uses 80 percent as the criterion level in group-based reinforcement arrangements (e.g., 80 percent of the class must meet the criterion of 80 percent correct, or the class average must be 80 percent of possible correct responses). In either case, it will be advantageous for most students to perform well (at least 80 percent) to maximize their chances for earning the reward. However, in the first case, 80 percent will be too high for some students and too low for other students. The student who cannot perform at the 80 percent level may jeopardize the reward for the total class. Plus, the student who typically performs at or near the 100 percent level cannot help the class qualify for the group reward by performing at a 100 percent rather than at 80 percent.

A way to make sure all students can contribute to earning the group reward by doing their best on a task is to have a variety of criterion levels for the particular academic activity. When students don't know exactly how well they must do to earn a reward, they may try harder to maximize the probability of receiving the reward (Skinner, Williams, and Neddenriep 2004). Although the criterion level that will be applied to a particular activity on a particular day is uncertain, what is certain is that doing one's best will increase the probability of reward both for oneself and the class as a whole.

One teacher determined her criterion levels for spelling performance, a domain in which her students appeared to be underachieving, by first computing a baseline average for spelling (Popkin and Skinner 2003). After determining the baseline level to be 65 percent correct, the teacher wrote different criterion levels on several slips of paper (e.g., 70 percent, 75 percent, and higher levels up to 100 percent) and placed those pieces of paper in a box. Notice that all the criterion levels were above the baseline level. At the designated time following the daily spelling activity, the teacher drew one of the criterion slips from the box and determined whether the class average met that criterion. If the criterion level had been met, students were then given access to a randomly selected reward. The system worked so well that the class average on spelling immediately increased from 65 percent to 95 percent.

Supportive Comments: But Not Without Reservations

Mark Twain once said that he "could live for two months on a good compliment." Supportive comments are also among the most powerful tools for boosting student morale. Praise and encouragement are the major types of supportive comments teachers use in day-to-day interactions with students. You thus might assume that praise and encouragement are virtually synonymous and that both are always appropriate. However, some educational authorities have distinguished between praise and encouragement and have questioned the efficacy of teacher praise (Kohn 1993; Mangin 1998). Although we do not believe that all teacher praise is inappropriate, some of the criticisms of teacher praise do warrant consideration. Certainly, most of us can improve our use of praise in the classroom.

Reservations about Praise

Critics of the widespread use of praise in the classroom contend that teachers use praise too freely, praising everything from completing a masterpiece to picking up one's pencil (Cannella 1986; Katz 1994). It is thought that using praise routinely and indiscriminately cheapens it, eventually eroding the credibility of both the praise and the praiser (i.e., students come to doubt the authenticity of the praise and the trustworthiness of the person giving the praise). Thus, praise needs to be used selectively for student responses that are genuinely praiseworthy. As Samuel Johnson said, "He who praises everybody praises nobody." In their efforts to be supportive, teachers say some very nice things to students: "That's a wonderful paper," "you're a super student," and "I like the way Maria is paying attention." Despite their apparent positive intent, such expressions can create problems for students. First, the statements may send the message that pleasing the teacher is the most important criterion of good behavior. Second, such statements set a standard that may be difficult to live up to in the future. Third, public praise may put students in a bad light among their peers.

Teacher Authority. Many teachers are prone to use common phrases such as "good work" or "very nice" in their efforts to reinforce students' efforts or accomplishments. Schwartz (1996) notes that such phrases may lead children to believe there is always an authority figure who decides what is good or bad. Thus, students look to teachers for the ultimate endorsement of their work. For that reason, Schwartz suggests alternatives to praise in acknowledging students' good work. Instead of saying "that's nice" or "great," a math teacher, for example, might ask the student to explain how he or she arrived at the solution. Schwartz notes that such dialogue can be expanded by inviting the child to identify other types of problems where the solution can be used, or to speculate whether the solution to the problem would have been different given slight modifications in the problem. Thus, the intent is to let students know you recognize their work by having them discuss that work.

Pressure on the Students. One of the most paradoxical effects of praise is the possible pressure it puts on the recipient of the praise. You might think that receiving praise for schoolwork would cause students to feel more confident and relaxed about their work. Certainly, you can minimize pressure by praising easy accomplishments, but then students will question the credibility of the praise. If praise is reserved only for superlative accomplishments, however, students may feel apprehensive about their ability to live up to those high standards. Consequently, they may shrink from "writing a great paper" or "being a super student." They know that the future can bring only disappointment to themselves and their teacher as they fail to live up to the lofty standard reflected in the teacher's praise.

Public Praise. Public praise is viewed as particularly troublesome because it may put the praised student in a bad light with peers. Singling out one person for special recognition may engender resentment from others who perceive themselves as equally or more deserving of the recognition. Also, certain kinds of public praise may be regarded as attempts to manipulate others' behaviors. "I like the way Juan is getting right to work" implies that everyone else should be working like Juan. Even if the public praise is not regarded as unfair or manipulative, it may be a source of embarrassment to a self-conscious student who wants to blend in with the crowd. If you highlight Susan's outstanding paper in class, she may be so embarrassed by the public attention that she never again writes an outstanding paper.

Nature of Encouragement

Critics of praise sometimes distinguish it from encouragement and accordingly view encouragement more favorably. Their major distinction appears to center on the notion of implied judgment. Hitz and Driscoll state that "unlike praise, encouragement does not place judgment on student work or give information regarding its value or implications of student status" (1988, p. 10). In brief, encouragement provides supportive information without putting students under pressure to perform at a high level.

The distinction between praise and encouragement can best be pinpointed in the wording teachers use to provide positive input to students. Hitz and Driscoll (1988) contend that the effectiveness of positive input is judged in terms of specificity, privacy, focus, and tone of voice. A teacher's intent in providing praise or encouragement can be entirely the same, but the distinction between the two can be found in the details.

Specificity. The pronouncement that a paper is "good" gives the student little sense of why it is good and how to write good papers in the future. In contrast, if feedback specifies what aspects of the paper contributed to its quality, then the student will know how to continue writing good papers. For example, feedback might highlight the paper's organizational features, grammatical structure, logical construction, choice of language, inclusion of examples, use of metaphors, compelling content, and extensive documentation. Feedback usually should be given in writing, providing the student a record of exactly what facets of the writing enhanced its quality.

Privacy. Public recognitions are not inherently bad, but a safer way to acknowledge student accomplishments is to give feedback privately (thus diminishing the possibility of embarrassing the child and inviting resentment from other children). Written feedback by nature is usually private, made known to other students only at the recipient's discretion. In contrast, oral feedback can be given publicly or privately. Nonverbal feedback is one way to give support discreetly and avoid embarrassing a student among peers. Smiles, head nods, thumbs up, and pats on the shoulder can convey great support even without much comment. To provide oral input more privately, you might quietly provide feedback to each student as you individually examine the student's work, or you might seek private moments before or after class to share individual input.

Focus. The major focus of supportive input should be student improvement in work habits and performance. This guideline allows all students to be legitimate recipients of supportive feedback, especially if you avoid comparing the student's work to that of other students. You can always look for ways in which the student's work habits and performance are improving: "I noticed you worked longer today than yesterday"; "your paper used more active voice than your previous paper"; "this is the first time you have used metaphors in your papers"; "your writing was more concise and to the point in this paper"; and "your documentation was more extensive in this paper than in the previous one." However, not all aspects of the student's work will reflect improvement. Thus, in combination with supportive input for improved aspects of the student's work, you also can specify ways that future work can be improved. Without this additional input, the student's work might fail to improve.

Instead of focusing students' attention on *your* evaluation of their performance, invite *their* appreciation of their own efforts and accomplishments. Rather than saying, "I feel good about how well you worked on this project," you might say, "You must feel good about how well you worked on this project." Your causal attributions regarding a student's accomplishment should reference both effort and ability. If your feedback targets only effort, older students may assume that they lack ability. In fact, junior and senior high students will go out of their way to avoid attributing their achievements to working hard (McDevitt and Ormrod 2002). Balanced feedback should highlight both ability and work habits: "You can be proud of your skills and timely work in writing this paper." In addition, you want to highlight how the student is likely to benefit from superior work habits and achievements: "Your writing skills can open many career doors," and "many businesses are looking for employees with your work standards."

Tone of Voice. The last of Hitz and Driscoll's (1988) guidelines for giving effective input pertains to tone of voice. Although it is advisable for teachers to be relatively animated in their interactions with students, they need to be cautious about giving

positive input in an exaggerated tone of voice. If your tone of voice conveys a level of excitement atypical for you, the student may wonder if there is something artificial about what you're saying. The safer course may be to speak naturally as you give positive input, but not in a bland, under-stated fashion. Your tone of voice in offering positive input should simply correspond to the level of animation you typically show in your interaction with students.

A Plan of Action

Learning when and how to give supportive input often requires practice. Optimal phrasing of input is certainly different from the "good boys" and "good girls" teachers are accustomed to utter-ing effortlessly. You should exam-ine the stock ways you attempt to support students to determine whether your phrasing meets the guidelines of effective support. If your words are too general, too public, too comparative, or too manipulative in tone, think of ways you can reword input to maximize its benefit to students. You can plan and rehearse how you might word your input rather than waiting for the inspiration of the moment. To make the task easier, however, it's usually safe to comment on student improvement, acknowledge the student's skill and effort, and indicate how the student might benefit from an accomplishment.

There will be many occasions when supportive input comes naturally. When the student has just finished a task and is beaming about his or her accomplishment, it is difficult to overlook that opportunity for sharing in the satisfaction of the moment. If a student is very quiet and easily overlooked, however, you may need to make a special effort to comment on his or her good performance. Some teachers develop a plan for giving supportive input that ensures they don't overlook any student, such as keeping a record of which students received special support each day.

HOW MUCH AND FOR WHAT?

In attempting to offer support to students, you can comment on effort, achievement, and ability. You can also choose to focus on academics or social behavior or both. What should be your focus? How often should you offer encouragement? In a study involving elementary students in grades 3 to 6 in Australia, Burnett (2001) used a questionnaire to investigate how frequently *(often, sometimes, never)* students preferred receiving praise for four different dimensions: good work, good behavior, good effort, or their ability at schoolwork. He also assessed whether the students preferred public or private praise.

He found that the students had similar preferences for how frequently they wanted to be praised for the four dimensions. In all, 91 percent wanted to be praised often or sometimes; only 9 percent did not want to be praised. Most, however, preferred to be praised for trying hard rather than for being smart or clever. No significant differences in the students' praise preferences emerged for academic achievement versus good behavior. The latter finding was in conflict with other cited studies (e.g., Elwell and Tiberio 1994) that showed a much higher preference among high school students for receiving praise for academic achievement than for behavior. Burnett also found most students preferred to be praised quietly or privately rather than publicly.

How often should teachers attempt to praise students? Although we have no absolute answer to this question, teachers need to offer praise frequently enough to strengthen behaviors that might attenuate if left unacknowledged. With the number of students enrolled in most classes, chances are teachers will underuse rather than overuse praise. One thing you certainly want to avoid is singling out a few students for repeated praise and overlooking others who also need support.

A graduate student in one of our recent courses commented on how she was affected by a teacher's comment when she was in elementary school. In returning a paper to this student, her teacher commented that the student had the potential to be a good writer. From that point on, the student began to think of herself as a good writer and to focus on the development of her writing skills. In retrospect, our student commented that she later learned that her elementary school teacher had a system for making sure that every student received some supportive input every week. Our student laughingly recalled that the day she received her "good writer" input was probably just her time on the teacher's approval calendar. Nonetheless, the teacher's comment had an inspirational, long-term effect.

Managing Difficult Situations

What has been said so far works best when students periodically display the behaviors teachers want to strengthen. When the student exhibits one of those target behaviors, the teacher provides a reinforcing response. Unfortunately, not all your students will initially exhibit behaviors you want to reinforce. Minimal progress with academic skills, incomplete assignments, and lack of participation in class are examples of situations where you might have difficulty finding behavior to reinforce positively.

Shaping

A technique known as *shaping* may be helpful in upgrading behaviors that are incompletely performed. This procedure involves reinforcing responses that resemble or approximate the desired response. A student response may initially include only a small component of the desired response. To assist the student in moving toward the desired behavior, you need to reinforce small steps representing movement in the right direction. This process is like the childhood game of telling a playmate, "You're getting hotter," when the person moves closer to a sought after object. Responses that have nothing to do with the final goal are not reinforced and consequently are eliminated.

Consider the possibility of using shaping to change the nature of a student's participation in class. Suppose Mary, an extremely shy student, has never volunteered a single comment in your class. You can tell from her written work that Mary is a bright student and probably has many good ideas to contribute to class discussion. A shaping strategy in this case involves initially acknowledging any sign of her participation in class discussion. If her nonverbal behaviors (e.g., eye contact, head nod) indicate that Mary is paying attention, understanding, or agreeing with what is being said, you can casually recognize her silent engagement in the discussion. Try not to overdo it, though; you don't want to direct class attention to Mary. Just say something such as "I can see that Mary agrees." Then you

The teacher can set the stage for Mary to comfortably speak in class.

can look for brief comments to acknowledge, such as "yes" or "no" responses to questions. By gradually raising the standard for what you will acknowledge, Mary may eventually be able to express herself as well in class as she does in her writing.

Changes in Setting Events and Prompts

Another approach for mobilizing behaviors not in a student's current repertoire is gradually to make the setting more conducive to the target response. For example, you might initially put students in pairs to discuss a particular issue, pairing Mary with her closest acquaintance in the class. Subsequently, you can form slightly larger groups: three students working together, then four, and so on. Again, you want to place Mary with students she knows the best. With a gradual increase in the size of the groups and extension in the level of acquaintance within the groups, Mary should eventually be able to participate in full class discussions.

You may initially have to provide concrete prompts to get a student to exhibit some semblance of the desired response, but you want to make those prompts less conspicuous—fading them out—as you proceed with the teaching process. To promote Mary's participation in class, you can gradually upgrade the complexity of your prompts for her to comment. You might first look at her when you are talking, maintaining eye contact with her as you solicit input on a point of class discussion. A second step might be to ask Mary a question that she can answer with just a head nod or one word. Your giving a nod of approval following her response should be sufficient to help her feel comfortable with her participation. After Mary gets accustomed to giving brief responses, you can ask for a short elaboration of her responses. Then you can engage her in more extended conversation about her class comments by posing follow-up questions. Mary ultimately should be able to provide more elaborate responses without your additional prompts.

Reinforcement is usually a reciprocal process. As shy students like Mary become more outgoing, their behavior becomes reinforcing to others who in turn are more likely to support the shy students' interactive behaviors. The teacher can set the stage for social interaction by arranging activities that require cooperative efforts. Choosing an activity that a shy student can perform well may facilitate this process. If, for example, Mary is proficient in art, her group might be assigned responsibility for advertising a class play. This assignment creates a situation in which Mary can shine among her peers in an area most comfortable to her.

Countering Hyperactivity

In contrast to our example of shy Mary, who needed to develop a behavior pattern she had not exhibited previously, other students' behavior patterns need to be tempered and redirected. Students with hyperactivity often present a challenge to reinforcing constructive behaviors. "He is like a whirlwind," "She never sits still for one minute," or "He's driving me up the wall" are comments often used to describe the child who is constantly talking and on the go in the classroom. Students with hyperactive tendencies *can* sit down and *can* look at books, however, even though such behaviors seem rare. Desired behavior is in these children's repertoire; it is just infrequently performed.

One way to minimize hyperactive behavior is to increase on-task behavior. In a process somewhat similar to the shaping process, you want the student gradually to increase the frequency or duration of a desired behavior. If the final goal is to teach a student to sit without talking and work on an assignment for fifteen minutes, even one minute of the

ADVANCED MATH: ONE TO TEN

Consider one method for teaching a kindergartner addition facts up to ten. The teacher can begin by using concrete objects such as blocks. The teacher initially might place a block on the right side of the table and one on the left side. The child can be asked to count the block on the right (one) and the block on the left (one). After the two blocks are brought closer together, the child can now be asked the sum of the blocks. If need be, the child can count the two blocks. Two blocks on each side can then be used, then three, and so on. Once the child has mastered this process, the teacher might hold up her hands and extend several fingers on each hand (a slightly more difficult arrangement). The child can count the extended fingers on each hand, and the hands can then be brought together for the child to determine the sum. Next, the child might try adding fingers from each of his hands. The teacher might then progress to using pictures with different numbers of drawings of the same shape (e.g., circles or squares) to be added. The child eventually can be asked to add numerals without the aid of concrete representation, the goal being to respond without visible external cues. Nods of approval or smiles should be used at each stage to reinforce appropriate responses.

desired behavior might be too much to require as a first step. Perhaps thirty seconds is more realistic. When the student has learned to sit still for thirty seconds, the length of time required for a reinforcer can gradually be lengthened. Small steps are safer than larger steps. If the behavior deteriorates once you go to the next step, your step is too large.

Reinforcing a hyperactive student for appropriate behavior needs to be carefully orchestrated. First, you have to be sure a consequence is sufficiently reinforcing to command the child's attention. Teacher praise alone may be insufficient reinforcement. Tokens that can later be traded for a small prize may be needed also. To keep other students who are not being reinforced from getting jealous, the targeted student can be asked to share what is earned with the group or to work toward privileges that will be made available to the total group. The timing of reinforcement is critical to a child exhibiting hyperactivity. If a token system is used, tokens should be given immediately following appropriate behavior. Any delay may allow the child to get off task, thus making it more difficult to reward him or her for appropriate behavior.

General Considerations

Regardless of the approach teachers take in strengthening appropriate student behavior, teachers should ensure that their actions are both *practical* and *humane*. A practical program is one that can be incorporated easily into the classroom routine. A humane program is one that does not create unnecessary stress for the teacher or the students. Neither the teacher nor the students should feel under pressure about the use of systematic reinforcement. Programs intended to support desired student behaviors should provide hope and enjoyment. The following questions can serve as a guide in your attempts to offer a suitable plan for your students. Negative answers to any of the questions may suggest a need for further evaluations of and changes in your program.

- Does the program focus on behavior beneficial to the students?
- Does the program provide reinforcement for constructive behaviors that are weak or otherwise might be overlooked?
- Are potential reinforcers available for all students?

- Do students understand what they are to do and not do to earn reinforcers?

- Is the program easy to use? For example, can you or the students or both of you easily maintain whatever records are required?

- Does the program avoid creating dependency on external rewards? That is, have plans been made to help students appreciate their own efforts and not rely solely on the teacher?

- Does the program have enough group and random features to mobilize peer reinforcement and maximize student performance in all academic areas?

- Does the plan encourage improvement in behavior?

- Are students comfortable with what they are doing and the support they are receiving?

Thinking about Yourself

To maintain a positive orientation toward others, you must also receive some reinforcing consequences for your supportive behavior. Generally speaking, you will receive reinforcement to about the same extent you give it, but there is not a one-to-one relationship for all the support you give others. If you expect others always to provide reinforcement for your good behavior, you are apt to be disappointed. When teachers are asked what they appreciate most about teaching, positive feedback from students is likely to be among the first things they mention. The same teachers are also likely to say that one of their major discipline problems is lack of respect from students. In effect, teachers occasionally receive just the opposite of what they desire. Even if most of your students do show appreciation for your positive treatment, just a few negative experiences can have a devastating effect and make it seem as if you are not appreciated at all. Therefore, you need to think about ways in which you receive support for the good things you do without focusing unduly on whether particular students embrace your teaching.

One way to combat a lack of immediate reinforcement from students is to arrange for positive consequences to follow your own goal-oriented behaviors. After working on a new lesson plan or grading a set of papers, you can set aside some time to enjoy music, go to a movie, spend time with the family, or do whatever you find enjoyable. You also can try recalling the good things you have done for students and the eventual benefits students are likely to experience from your actions. You can even say positive things to yourself immediately after you have done something worthwhile for others (e.g., "My lesson today provided a good opportunity for students to learn about the U.S. government," "I set the stage for a good discussion today"). Affirming comments don't have to come from others in order to provide support for your constructive behaviors.

If you still feel a lack of support from others, and most of us do at times, you can take assertive actions to gain additional support. One possibility is to form a discussion group with one or two colleagues who have teaching interests similar to yours. You might plan one afternoon each week when you go out together for coffee. Your group can discuss the week's events and provide encouragement to one another. You need to be certain, though, that your group is devoted to providing support for desirable undertakings as opposed to rehashing everything that went wrong during the week. Another strategy is to invite a colleague to your class to offer supportive feedback and suggestions regarding your interactions with students.

Your hope for changing others has to begin with being able to sustain your own worthy actions. Reciprocity should not dictate what kind of teacher you become. For example, responding to an unkind deed with an unkind consequence often makes matters

worse for both parties. Certainly, an unkind reaction to a student's nasty behavior does not model the type of behavior you want your students to exhibit. One of the greatest challenges of teaching is to remain supportive when others seem indifferent or resistant to what you have to offer. Of course, an occasional frank discussion with your students is not out of the question. You can indicate what you invested in planning the day's activities and then ask for their input as to why they are unresponsive or resistant to those plans.

Concluding Comments

Consequences are a natural component of life and certainly recurring events in the classroom. This chapter has emphasized that you can exercise control over many consequences and thereby have a more positive influence on student behavior. When good things happen to students as a result of desirable behaviors, those behaviors will be strengthened. In contrast, when no support is offered for good behaviors, those behaviors will likely weaken. It is important to focus on what students should do rather than what they should not do. When you support desired behaviors, you will have fewer undesirable behaviors to counteract. Our teacher acquaintances say they are happier when their attention is directed toward the good happening around them. The more good behavior you can reinforce, the keener your vision will be for seeing additional good behaviors.

References

Adkins, J., and R. L. Williams. (1972). The utility of self-report in determining reinforcement priorities of primary school children. *Journal of Educational Research* 65: 324–28.

Beedorn, B. (1986). Creativity: Number one leadership talent for the future. *Journal of Creative Behavior* 20: 276–82.

Burnett, P. C. (2001). Elementary students' preferences for teacher praise. *Journal of Classroom Interaction* 36(1): 16–23.

Cannella, G. S. (1986). Praise and concrete rewards: Concerns for childhood education. *Childhood Education* (March–April): 297–301.

Cialdini, R. B., N. Eisenberg, B. L. Green, K. Rhoads, and R. Bator. (1998). Undermining the undermining effect of reward on sustained interest. *Journal of Applied Social Psychology* 28: 249–63.

Dawson, V. L., T. D'Andrea, R. Affinito, and E. L. Westby. (1999). Predicting creative behavior: A reexamination of the divergence between traditional and teacher-defined concepts of creativity. *Creativity Research Journal* 12: 57–66.

Elwell, W. C., and J. Tiberio. (1994). Teacher praise. *Journal of Instructional Psychology* 21: 322–28.

Freeland, J. T., and G. H. Noell. (2002). Programming for maintenance: An investigation of delayed and intermittent reinforcement and common stimuli to create indiscriminable contingencies. *Journal of Behavioral Education* 11: 5–18.

Glover, J., and A. Gary. (1976). Procedures to increase some aspects of creativity. *Journal of Applied Behavior Analysis* 9: 79–84.

Hitz, R., and A. Driscoll. (1988). Praise or encouragement? New insights into praise: Implications for early childhood teachers. *Young Children* 43(5): 6–13.

Jacobs, J. E., S. Lanza, D. W. Osgood, J. S. Eccles, and A. Wigfield. (2002). Changes in children's self-competence and values: Gender and domain differences across grades one through twelve. *Child Development* 73: 785–98.

Katz, L. G. (1994). All about me. *Principal* 73(5): 9–12.

Kohn, A. (1993). *Punished by Rewards: The Trouble with Gold Stars*, Incentive Plans, A's, and Other Bribes. New York: Houghton-Mifflin.

Mace, F. C., B. McCurdy, and E. A. Quigley. (1990). The collateral effect of reward predicted by matching theory. *Journal of Applied Behavior Analysis* 23: 197–205.

Madsen, C. H., Jr., W. C. Becker, D. R. Thomas, L. Koser, and E. Plager. (1968). An analysis of the reinforcing function of "sit down" commands. In *Readings in Educational Psychology*, edited by R. K. Parker. Boston: Allyn and Bacon, 265-278.

Mangin, M. C. (1998). Praise: What does it accomplish? *Dimensions of Early Childhood* (summer–fall): 12–18.

McDevitt, T. M., and J. E. Ormrod, J. E. (2002). *Child Development and Education: A Custom Edition*. Upper Saddle River, N.J.: Pearson Education.

Milgram, R. M., and E. Hong. (1993). Creative thinking and creative performance in adolescents as predictors of creative attainments in adults: A follow-up study after 18 years. *Roeper Review* 15: 135–39.

Moore, L. A., A. M. Waguespack, K. F. Wickstrom, J. C. Witt, and G. R. Gaydos. (1994). Mystery motivator: An effective and time efficient intervention. *School Psychology Review* 23: 106–18.

Popkin, J., and C. H. Skinner. (2003). Enhancing academic performance in a classroom serving students with serious emotional disturbance: Interdependent group contingencies with randomly selected components. *School Psychology Review* 37: 271–84.

Raschke, D. (1981). Designing reinforcement surveys—let the student choose the reward. *Teaching Exceptional Children* 14(3): 92–96.

Runyon, H. L., and R. L. Williams. (1972). Differentiating reinforcement priorities of junior high students. *Journal of Experimental Education* 40: 76–80.

Scardamalia, M., and C. Bereiter. (2003). Beyond brainstorming: Sustained creative work with ideas. *Education Canada* 43(4): 4–7.

Schwartz, S. L. (1996). Hidden messages in teacher talk: Praise and empowerment. *Teaching Children Mathematics* 2 (March): 396–401.

Skinner, C. H., R. L. Williams, and C. E. Neddenriep. (2004). Using interdependent group-oriented reinforcement to enhance academic performance in general education classes. *School Psychology Review* 33: 383–97.

Stone, B. G. (1980). Relationship between creativity and classroom behavior. *Psychology in the Schools* 17: 106–8.

Vanderslice, R. (1998). Can creativity be taught? Is it? *Delta Kappa Gamma Bulletin* 64(3): 39–43.

Westby, E. L., and V. L. Dawson. (1995). Creativity: Asset or burden in the classroom? *Creativity Research Journal* 8: 1–10.

Williams, R. L., and S. L. Stockdale. (2004). Classroom motivation strategies for prospective teachers. *The Teacher Educator* 39: 212–30.

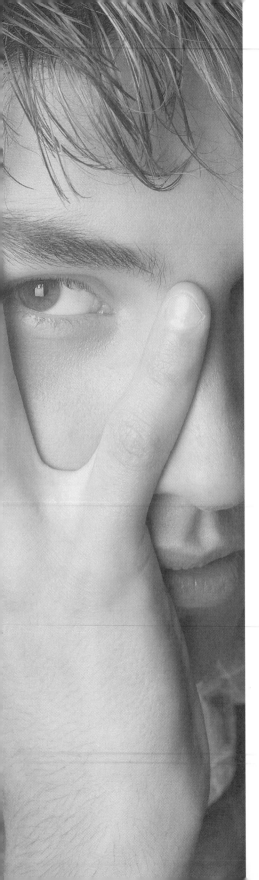

"Tommy, do you know why I asked you to remain behind?"

"I don't know. I didn't do anything."

"I believe you did do something. I heard you saying some very unkind things to Sandra just before the break. You know our rule about being respectful to others."

"I was only teasing."

"Maybe so, but how would you feel if someone said those same things to you?"

"Don't guess I would like it."

"Well, I'm sure Sandra didn't either. What do you think you should do?"

"I don't know."

"Maybe you can tell her you're sorry. Can you think of anything else?"

"I could ask her to be in our group during recess."

"That sounds like a good choice. I'll check with you and Sandra later to see if the problem has been solved. You go join the others."

5

Being Helpful

Managing Unwanted Behaviors

The two preceding chapters suggested that much inappropriate behavior can be prevented simply by promoting appropriate behavior. Ordinarily, a student cannot simultaneously behave and misbehave. Thus, strengthening what is wanted is a principal means of reducing what is not wanted. Nonetheless, some students engage in unacceptable behaviors despite a teacher's best efforts to prevent those behaviors. In fact, some of these behaviors are directed toward the teacher. A student may carelessly or willfully disregard a teacher's instructions, for example. Other students may repeatedly question the teacher's authority in the classroom.

Teachers also need to be alert to inappropriate acts directed toward peers. A student who ridicules a peer may not pose an immediate problem for the teacher, but such behavior is still inappropriate and warrants correction. Realistically, interpersonal problems among students will likely lead to problems that adversely affect classroom learning. The focus of this chapter is helping teachers gain a broad perspective of how to manage troublesome behaviors affecting both them and the students.

Frame of Reference for Reducing Misbehavior

Developing a perspective on managing inappropriate student behavior begins with a clear understanding of why such behavior needs to be changed. Some people might consider teachers successful when they are able to maintain a class where students sit quietly, refrain from talking to their nearby classmates, and raise their hands for permission to speak. On the surface such an environment might seem ideal, but order per se is hardly an adequate measure of effective teaching. That order might reflect little more than mindless conformity to whatever classroom rules are in place.

Even if students can be pressured into conforming to classroom rules, how will they behave in settings that do not have those rules? Helping students learn to behave appropriately across settings involves teaching them that certain behavioral standards are beneficial whatever the situation. The rationale behind your disciplinary procedures is not simply to make your life easier, but rather to teach students standards for useful academic and social behaviors. Your aim is to help students become productive citizens in the classroom culture and the larger society—that is, to help them learn appropriate behaviors that are in their long-term best interests.

Stopping bad behavior is not a singular operation. You need a repertoire of options and a framework for determining what to do, when, for what kind of behavior, by what kind of student. There is no single strategy for responding to all misbehavior under all circumstances. Remaining calm and weighing different options is usually advisable before proceeding with disciplinary actions. In general, the idea of managing disruptions is to make mole hills out of mountains, not the reverse. Most important, teachers should not use any approach that humiliates students.

A general guideline for reducing misbehavior is to use the least intrusive and least aversive procedure that will stop the misbehavior. Your glancing at a student who is misbehaving or moving closer to that student may be sufficient to control minor indiscretions. Also, using a distracted student's name in class discussion may recapture the student's attention. Separating students engaging in side conversation or needling one another may stop those distractions to learning. However, severe acts of misconduct may require private conversations with students, discussions with parents, or referral to other school personnel (e.g., school counselors, school psychologists, principal).

Fortunately, many options are available for managing minor to major acts of misconduct. Some options accentuate the positive, whereas others entail uncomfortable consequences. Whenever possible, teachers should begin with positive interventions, such as differential reinforcement for appropriate behaviors, informative feedback, conversations with students, presentation of logical consequences, and behavior contracts. Nonetheless, some misbehaviors may emerge or persist despite your most positive strategies. Thus, when students do behave badly, you need strategies for efficiently stopping those patterns. These strategies may include verbal reprimands, time-out, response cost, and in-school suspension. Inasmuch as prevention typically is more efficient and effective than remediation, in this chapter we focus first on strategies with the greatest preventive potential—the positive interventions.

Positive Interventions

Both you and your students are likely to benefit from the use of positive interventions. Dealing with misbehaviors through repeated reprimands usually has little more than a temporary effect on those behaviors. Some reprimands may actually serve as reinforcement for the behavior you are attempting to weaken. The reprimanded student stops the behavior temporarily but may get enough attention from the reprimand to try the bad behavior again soon. Plus, the repetition of bad behaviors and your recurring edicts to "stop this and stop that" will likely put you in a rather foul mood by the end of the school day. In contrast, attempting to prevent and reduce bad behaviors through positive strategies will likely be more effective in weakening those behaviors over the long run and will certainly leave you in a better mood by day's end.

Differential Reinforcement Strategies
The winning combination is to reinforce good behavior consistently and to stop reinforcing bad behavior. The latter may be your first action when misbehavior is minor, but the misbehavior is unlikely to be maintained if it is consistently ignored. "Cute" remarks or talking out of turn can fall into this category. A student who speaks without first being recognized, for example, would not be called on for a response. Studies (e.g., Kindall,

Workman, and Williams 1980) suggest, however, that ignoring inappropriate behavior must be combined with positive attention to appropriate behavior to be most effective. Further, teachers may need to gain peers' cooperation in ignoring some disruptive acts, such as cracking jokes at inappropriate times or acting as a class clown. Teachers can develop a standing agreement with their students as to what behaviors everyone should ignore in order to contribute to a productive classroom. If a student's acting out is preventing other students from getting their work done, the student's peers may come to understand that paying attention to that behavior is not in their own best interest.

In addition to the general guideline of maximizing attention to good behavior and minimizing attention to bad behavior, three systematic differential reinforcement arrangements are explained in this section: differential reinforcement of low response rates, differential reinforcement of incompatible behaviors, and differential reinforcement of a particular behavior under different circumstances. You will find these approaches useful to varying degrees across circumstances and perhaps also differentially comfortable for you to apply in various situations.

Differential Reinforcement of Low Response Rates. In this case, instead of reinforcing a student for exhibiting more of a target behavior, you reinforce the student for exhibiting less of that behavior. *Differential reinforcement of low response rates* requires assessing how frequently the target behavior (e.g., talking out, making an offensive comment, hitting other students) is occurring before a systematic attempt is made to reduce it. Then, the general strategy is to reinforce the student for decreasing the rate of this behavior.

Because this approach entails systematic record keeping, you need a standard time for recording the behavior and a way to note when the behavior occurs. If you sense that the behavior is most likely to occur after lunch, you might choose to record it the first thirty minutes after lunch. If you typically teach a lesson during that time, you need an unobtrusive way of keeping track of the target behavior. Some teachers use a counter similar to a golf-score counter that they can hold in their hands and keep a running tally of the target behavior while still teaching.

Once you have identified the behavior you want to decrease in frequency, a time in which to record it, a way to record it, and the baseline level of the behavior, you must establish the contingencies for reinforcement (i.e., how much reduction in the behavior is required for reinforcement). Suppose physically pestering (e.g., poking, pushing, jabbing, tripping) other students has been identified as Jimmy's most problematic behavior, especially upon returning from recess. For a period of several days (the baseline phase), you note how many times you see him physically pestering other students in the first half hour after recess. On the average, he pesters others about ten times per day during this period. Then you approach Jimmy to find out what he might prefer as a reward for reducing his frequency of pestering others.

If Jimmy identifies stickers as something he prefers, a criterion would be set for earning stickers by reducing how often he physically pesters his peers. In the first phase of your behavior-change intervention, you set the requirement for reinforcement slightly below the baseline level (no more than eight instances of pestering rather than the baseline level of ten instances). When Jimmy has brought his level of pestering down to eight instances, you might then reduce the criterion to no more than six instances. You keep lowering the level of pestering required for reinforcement until finally Jimmy can earn his stickers only by totally eliminating his pestering during the target period. Some teachers object to this process because reinforcement is given even while Jimmy is still pestering his peers. We would counter with the view that the reinforcement is not given for pestering, but rather for reducing the pestering.

Differential Reinforcement of Incompatible Behaviors. Reducing a particular inappropriate behavior provides no guarantee students will replace that behavior with an appropriate response. A strategy that might be helpful in accomplishing both a reduction of bad behavior and a concomitant increase in good behavior is *differential reinforcement of incompatible behaviors* (DRI). One behavior is said to be incompatible with another, or to compete with another, when the two cannot occur simultaneously (Kazdin 2001). For example, students cannot be tardy and punctual, talk and listen, or agree and disagree at the same time. Thus, when a teacher is confronted with misconduct, using DRI as a classroom-management tool involves identifying and strengthening the opposite behavior. The strategy, of course, can also be used to strengthen appropriate behavior when the teacher has temporarily halted inappropriate behavior. When the teacher cannot identify an exact opposite behavior to reinforce, he or she may reinforce other positive behaviors that are alternatives to the inappropriate one, a procedure known as *differential reinforcement of alternative behavior* (Kazdin 2001).

Let's suppose you have a student who frequently criticizes classmates. A positive alternative likely to be incompatible with criticizing is cooperating with classmates. Thus, use of DRI in this situation involves reinforcing cooperative behavior. Identifying situations the student enjoys and then reinforcing cooperative acts would be your game plan. Or you and the student can identify alternatives to criticizing, such as finding good points in others' ideas or identifying common interests with them. The student might be paired with peers who exhibit high levels of cooperation, increasing the opportunity to observe and participate in cooperative activities. Even when you use other options to halt the critical commentary, strengthening cooperative behavior still might be the best long-term strategy for countering that behavior.

Teachers who keep students successfully involved in classroom activities are relying on strengthening behaviors incompatible with disruptive actions. A classic study by Ayllon and Roberts (1974) illustrates the potential to reduce misbehavior by promoting academic success. These researchers were interested in reducing negative behavior among five of the most disruptive students in a large fifth-grade reading class (thirty-eight students). The average level of disruptive behavior of these students was 34 percent. Not surprisingly, these students' correct responses on daily reading assignments were below 50 percent. The disruptive behaviors included running in class, walking around the room, loud talking, and making other kinds of noise. Instead of trying to reduce these behaviors though punishment, the experimenters established a token economy that enabled students to earn points for completing academic assignments. The points could be cashed in daily or weekly for a variety of backup reinforcers (e.g., reduced detention, opportunity to be an assistant teacher, and free time to work on the bulletin board).

The results of Ayllon and Roberts's (1974) study are highly encouraging. By the end of the study, the average accuracy rate for academic performance for the five most disruptive students rose to approximately eighty-five percent. Although no direct effort had been made to reduce disruptiveness, the average rate of disruptive behavior fell to around five percent. Teachers don't necessarily have to establish a full-scale token economy to apply the lessons learned from Ayllon and Roberts' study. They may need only to address the inappropriate behaviors of one or two students.

Differential Reinforcement of Target Behaviors across Circumstances. Most behaviors are not unilaterally good or bad. It all depends on the circumstances. As a sacred document proclaims, "There is a time for everything under the sun." Well, perhaps not for everything, but for most things. There is definitely a time to talk to one's classmates and a time to laugh at a classroom event, but there is a time when neither action is appropriate. Learning when to exhibit a particular behavior and when to refrain falls under the category of discretion. If someone you know well has just received devastating news, putting your arms around him or her is considered perfectly natural. In contrast, hugging someone you hardly know just because you like to hug is likely to be considered offensive.

SEARCHING FOR ALTERNATIVES

An appropriate strategy for impeding misconduct is to promote responses that cannot exist simultaneously with poor conduct. Merely reinforcing a desired, but unrelated response isn't likely to control specific problems. For example, reinforcing sharing is unlikely to reduce the use of foul language.

To gain practice in identifying alternatives that are opposite to inappropriate behavior, try working with a colleague. List troublesome misbehavior and then see if the two of you can identify legitimate alternatives. For example, what is the opposite of biting? (*Hint:* Can kindergarten students smile and bite simultaneously?) What about defiance? Lying? Kicking? Laughing at others' mistakes?

With an accumulation of interpersonal experiences, most individuals learn when to hug, when to engage in conversation, and when to laugh, as well as when not to do these things. However, other individuals have behavioral patterns that persist irrespective of what cues others give them. They slap you on the back when you want to be left alone, keep talking to you when you are trying to exit the conversation, and laugh at you when your feelings are hurt. They are overlooking cues from you that these behaviors are not welcomed.

In helping students determine when to exhibit or not exhibit a particular behavior, teachers provide cues that signal appropriateness or inappropriateness. After students enter a class, a bell is typically used as a signal to stop talking to their friends. Students may have been engaging in a lively conversation, but the bell signals that such behavior is no longer appropriate.

For every classroom behavior that is sometimes appropriate and other times inappropriate, you need to provide definitive cues as to which condition prevails. Teachers often convey these cues through nonverbal behaviors, such as a stare, a head nod, a headshake, a smile, or some other response that signals "keep going" or "stop immediately." For these cues to influence student behaviors, teachers must consistently differentiate how they respond to a particular behavior after giving a "green flag" or a "red flag" cue. If you laugh at a student's prank after you've issued a red flag for such behavior, that student will not learn when it is in poor taste to pull a prank.

Informative Feedback

Although feedback is often used to inform students of their progress in meeting an academic goal, it also can help students recognize and reduce problematic tendencies. Somewhat similar to the situational appropriateness of a behavior, some behaviors are appropriate at one level of frequency but not at another level. Virtually all teachers want students to participate in class discussion, but some students participate excessively. They immediately raise their hand or orally respond to practically every question. To create more awareness of this pattern, Zack might be asked to record how many times he raises his hand to respond to a question or fails to raise his hand before speaking out. In this case, the student's own record keeping will provide feedback that will help him see the need for behavior change. Also, this kind of feedback will be more precise and palatable than your telling Zack he is talking too much.

Some students are largely oblivious to how others perceive their behaviors. For instance, students who tend to oppose others' ideas might not realize they are viewed as

A student's first reaction to your feedback may not represent the
way he or she will react after having time to think about what you have said.

argumentative. They may regard their oppositional comments simply as stimulating conversation, certainly not a source of irritation to others. Offering informative feedback about how others interpret their behaviors can help students reexamine their actions. "Darlene, do you realize that when you typically disagree with what others say, they may find the conversation somewhat uncomfortable? How would you feel about trying to find more points of agreement with others' comments?"

Be forewarned that giving this kind of feedback to students may initially evoke resistance. If students refuse to accept your feedback (e.g., "I am not that way," "You're always criticizing me," "You just don't like me"), remain calm and keep the door open to further communication ("Maybe we can talk about this later"). Students' first reactions may not represent the way they will react after having time to think about what you have said. The following suggestions offered by Williams and Long (1983, p. 330) can make feedback more palatable to students:

1. Offer feedback in a tentative rather than an absolute manner. For example, you might say, "Is this a possibility?" "Have you noticed . . .?" or "I wonder if you have thought about . . .?"

2. If the student becomes defensive, refrain from being defensive yourself. Stop talking and listen. You might comment, "You're surprised I'm saying this," or "You're upset that I'm giving you this information." This approach may help the student understand that you sense his or her frustration, and, consequently, he or she may permit you to provide more feedback at a later time.

3. Give precise feedback. Rather than attacking the student, indicate how often you have observed the behavior. For example, you might say, "I've noticed you had three arguments today," rather than, "You're always arguing with somebody."

4. If you pinpoint an inappropriate behavior, suggest how the student might improve the behavior. Tell the student about any improvement you have noticed.

LOOKING FOR THE REASONS

According to Dreikurs, Grunwald, and Pepper (1982), one of children's basic aims is to belong and find their place within different groups. But children may develop short-term goals that do not support their basic aim. Indeed, they may develop what these authors refer to as mistaken goals (i.e., goals to gain attention, power, or revenge, or goals to display inadequacy). Teachers can use a disclosure strategy to help students recognize their mistaken goals and gain a better understanding of the purposes behind their behaviors. The suggested strategy begins with the teacher's posing a question related to the goal ("Could it be that . . . ?"). For example, if the teacher suspects the child's goal is to gain attention, the teacher might ask, "Could it be you want to keep me busy with you?" (p. 29). If this "guess" proves inaccurate, the teacher would continue with other possibilities.

Dreikurs, Grunwald, and Pepper (1982) provide a specific sequence of questions for each mistaken goal. They caution against confronting the child with an accusation, such as "You are doing this to gain attention." The idea is not to confront, but to suggest possibilities. With young students, correct disclosure of the child's goal frequently is followed by a recognition reflex. A "recognition reflex" may be a smile, an "ah-ha" expression, or other behavior that indicates "You may have something there!" Older students' reactions may be less obvious than young children's reactions, but the students' body language can confirm a correct guess. Once the mistaken goal is identified, students are in a better position to choose more appropriate goals and behaviors.

Talk with students about appropriate behavior before problems arise.

5. Try giving positive feedback in addition to any negative feedback. Always start and end on a positive note.

6. Finally, feedback should be focused and limited. Don't overpower students by bringing up a succession of past mistakes. Stick to the present and remember that unsolicited feedback cataloging past misbehaviors is likely to produce more resentment than change.

Conversations with Students

Students can be invaluable partners in preventing and dealing with misbehavior. Mobilizing their help requires timely conversation with them. The best time to talk with students about appropriate conduct at school is before problems arise. A good starting place is to discuss school and class rules and procedures at the beginning of a school year (see chapter three). The teacher and students jointly can decide what is appropriate and inappropriate, as well as establish the consequences for each type of behavior. For example, you might decide that side conversations prevent both the offenders and their peers from getting their lessons done in a timely fashion. If offenders don't desist from such conversation after your first request, then these students will lose a specified amount of credit toward class privileges that day.

Teachers should take advantage of informal opportunities (e.g., over lunch, before or after school) to chat with students about what behaviors bother them and what they think can be done to reduce those behaviors. Franse (1998) suggests that teachers establish an informal, nonjudgmental tone in the conversation to encourage students to open up. Letting students express their concerns without interrupting them, acknowledging their feelings about school problems, and suspending judgments about the merit of their recommendations are among Franse's suggestions for creating a partnership with students in addressing misbehavior at school.

Despite your preventive efforts, there will be situations that require you to speak with an individual student, several students, or the entire class about problem incidents. If the situation involves only one or two students and doesn't require an immediate disciplinary action, you might ask the offending student(s) to remain after class or to meet with you privately. In some cases you will need to separate students who are arguing, pushing, or hitting one another, but a long-term solution often can best be found by having a private conversation "to get to the bottom" of the matter.

A STUDENTS' BILL OF RIGHTS

Five-year-olds who enter kindergarten have few academic skills and are socially immature. However, by the end of their formal school training, these same individuals are expected to have advanced academic skills and exhibit mature social conduct. In brief, society expects them to take their place in the adult world as responsible citizens. Such expectations can hardly be achieved if students do not have the opportunity to participate in decisions as they progress through the educational system.

One comprehensive and democratic model for managing classrooms at all academic levels is "judicious discipline," a framework developed by Foster Gathercoal (1997). This model is based on the Bill of Rights, which serves as the foundation for teaching students about their rights and responsibilities for life in the classroom and beyond. A major premise of the approach is that living effectively in a democratic society and meeting societal expectations of education involves giving students opportunities to participate in decisions affecting their lives. Although a discussion of the approach is beyond the scope of our text, the model has been widely tested and has considerable promise for enhancing personal ethics and good citizenship (Grandmont 2003; Landau and

Gathercoal 2000). See Gathercoal's text (1997) to learn details about implementing the approach in a single classroom or in a school-wide program. Student rights in classrooms devoted to student participation can include the following:

1. Every student has a right to be heard in discussions about classroom management and content issues.

2. No student should be subjected to ridicule from either the teacher or other students.

3. Every student has the responsibility to listen when others are expressing their views.

4. Every student has the responsibility to respond respectfully to others' ideas.

5. When votes are taken, each student's vote should count the same.

Although there is no single, best way for conducting private conversations to resolve problems, here are some guidelines that should contribute to constructive conversations:

1. Remain calm and avoid jumping to conclusions as to who did what to whom.

2. Be respectful of all involved and expect similar treatment from them.

3. Identify what you see as being the problem and ask if the participants see the problem as you do.

4. Once the problem has been clarified, ask what the offending student(s) think would be more appropriate behavior in the situation. If no suggestions are forthcoming, ask the student(s) to respond to your recommendations.

5. Ask what you can do to support the recommended changes in behavior and to make sure students avoid similar problems in the future.

Discussions with an entire class also may prove useful in dealing with disciplinary concerns. The teacher's role in such discussions is largely to facilitate listening and sharing of ideas. Student ideas should be invited, without ridicule from others, and all students should have an opportunity to express their views about behaviors that concern them and possible ways to reduce those behaviors. A suggestion box might first be used to elicit student ideas about topics that should be discussed. Although whole-class discussions may not resolve all problems, they can be a means of identifying problems and possible solutions. They also give students a sense of ownership about what occurs in the class and can foster cooperation for making the class better for everyone.

Logical Consequences

Earlier we mentioned how teachers might help students recognize mistaken goals and better understand the purpose for their behaviors. Another strategy proposed by Dreikurs, Grunwald, and Pepper (1982) is the use of logical consequences, an approach that serves as an alternative both to punitive measures and to the use of rewards. Logical consequences are outcomes that will likely follow a particular behavior under real-life circumstances. For example, if you greet others, they are more likely to greet you. Logical consequences may be applied by teachers or chosen by students. Dreikurs, Grunwald, and Pepper refer to the former as *applied logical consequences* and to the latter, those chosen by students, as *logical consequences.* An example of an applied logical consequence is the teacher's telling students who have made a mess to clean up after themselves. Ideally, applied logical consequences are one-time occurrences. Subsequently, teachers would permit students to select their own logical consequences as motivation for developing responsible behaviors.

One teacher in an alternative school had a standing rule in his class that students would clean up their messes before they could proceed to the next rewarding activity (applied logical consequences). Thus, when students made a mess, deliberately or otherwise, the teacher would say nothing to the students, but they would not be allowed to engage in the next fun activity until they cleaned up their mess. Thus, students could elect to forego a fun activity when their mess remained unattended or decide that in order to engage in the fun activity, it was worth cleaning up after themselves (logical consequences).

Personal responsibility is one of the features distinguishing logical consequences from traditional forms of punishment, where consequences often are imposed by others. Dreikurs, Grunwald, and Pepper (1982) claim that punishment often fails to underscore the natural consequences of misbehavior. Artificially imposed consequences emphasize external control, whereas logical consequences shift the emphasis to personal responsibility for one's own behavior. Thus, the use of logical consequences is more likely to promote self-discipline. These authors also contended that rewards teach the wrong values because students may behave appropriately only to earn rewards rather than to learn the value of self-responsibility. However, we must add that enjoyable privileges under real-world circumstances are often predicated on acting responsibly.

In addition to Dreikurs, Grunwald, and Pepper's (1982) analysis of logical consequences, Gilbert (1989) provides categories of logical consequences and examples of student misbehavior. Two of the categories are suspension of privileges and restitution. Suspended privileges might include favorite activities, opportunities to interact, use of valued objects, and access to places. A logical consequence involving suspension of an opportunity to interact might consist of the teacher's being silent, withholding proximity and conversation with a student who is being sassy. A logical consequence for stealing or damaging objects might be replacing the objects (restitution). Again, a key in identifying a logical consequence is to find a link between the behavior and the proposed outcome, one that will help the student correct the misbehavior and develop greater personal responsibility for behaving appropriately.

Taking personal responsibility.

Behavioral Contracts

Formal agreements are sometimes necessary to ensure that all relevant parties (student, teacher, parents) are committed to working toward a constructive behavior change. Such agreements (often referred to as *behavioral contracts*) can be applied either on a classwide basis or on an individual basis. When only one student is misbehaving, it is best to develop an individual contract that targets the inappropriate behavior pattern exhibited by that student. The contract identifies the problem behavior (either excessive or deficient), specifies alternatives to the behavior, articulates agreed-upon goals, tells what each party will do to move toward those goals, and underscores the benefits that will follow attainment of the goals. Parents, as well as teachers and students, may be parties to the agreement, offering support for desired behaviors at home (such as designating a time and place for study and providing privileges for completing assignments).

For contracts to be successful, the teacher must follow the terms of the contract to the letter. We have seen many contracts go awry because teachers occasionally failed to provide the rewards specified in the contract. If contracts are maintained over extensive periods, however, the specifics of the contract may need to be periodically updated. For example, a specified privilege that is initially reinforcing may lose much of its appeal over time. The initial standards of performance may prove unrealistic or may need to be upgraded as the student gains in skills.

To better understand how an individual contract might be developed and implemented, consider the case of Tim. Unlike many students' serious behavior problems, Tim's major problem was simply not getting his work done, especially his homework. Tim's teacher knew from his closely supervised work in class that he could do the work quite well. Thus, the major paradox was why Tim was not getting his assignments done when he was working on his own. Was he daydreaming or doing something that directly interfered with working on his assignment?

One thing that could be said to Tim's credit was that he was a very sociable child, perhaps too sociable. The teacher would often have to remind him to desist from conversation with his buddies and get to work on his in-class assignment. Plus, he would sometimes linger after class to chat with his teacher, running the risk of being late to his next class. When he was at home in the afternoon and on the weekend, his favorite activity was—you guessed it—talking on the phone.

When this pattern of social reinforcement became more evident to the teacher, she approached Tim with the possibility of developing a contract to ensure that he would get his work done more efficiently. Collaborating with both Tim and his parents, the teacher prepared a draft of a contract that specified social rewards that Tim could earn for completing his homework assignments. All parties agreed to the terms of the contract and signed the contract, indicating their commitment to abiding by those terms.

BEHAVIOR CONTRACT

Timothy Jones has been completing his homework an average of one day per week. It appears that instead of doing his homework in a timely fashion, he spends much of his time talking on the telephone. The goal is for him to complete his homework every evening. To do this, he will need to choose a location in his home away from a telephone and start on the homework within an hour of arriving home from school. Social privileges both at home and school will be contingent on his completing homework assignments. Timothy, his parents, and his teacher are participants in the contractual arrangement described here.

Timothy Jones agrees to complete his homework everyday to earn social privileges at home and conversational time with his teacher.

The parents of Timothy Jones agree to check Tim's homework assignment each day as soon as either of them arrive home. If the homework assignment has not been completed, Tim must complete the assignment to their satisfaction before having telephone privileges that evening. If Tim completes his homework everyday during a week, he may invite a friend to spend the night with him one evening on the weekend.

Tim's teacher agrees to check Tim's homework each day and spend five minutes of conversational time with him for each day the homework has been completed. Tim may accumulate conversational time across days of the week and take all of that that time with her on Friday at lunch, provided he has earned twenty-five minutes of conversational time that week.

Name	Signature	Date
Timothy Jones	_____	_____
Mr. Karl Jones	_____	_____
Ms. Rhonda Jones	_____	_____
Ms. Mary Lou Barker	_____	_____

Negative Interventions

Schools traditionally have used a number of punitive consequences for misbehavior, among which are verbal reprimands, time-out, response cost, and in-school suspension. All of these consequences can be used effectively, but some have far greater possibilities than others. As we discuss each option in the next few sections, we identify the circumstances under which it can best be used and offer guidelines for its use.

Verbal Reprimands

Reprimands take a variety of forms. They may be short or long, soft or loud, personal or impersonal. They may be represented in a statement as simple as "Stop that!" or in a critical remark aimed at embarrassing someone ("When will you ever learn?"). When used sparingly and directed toward behavior, not at the person, reprimands may suppress unwanted behaviors, at least temporarily. Although Williams's (1987) review of classroom management concludes that certain forms of verbal reprimands can weaken undesirable behavior, no researchers suggest using reprimands as a substitute for positive interventions. Teachers should ensure that any use of reprimands is coupled with positive strategies for teaching desired behaviors.

There are many reasons teachers should be cautious in using reprimands. If a teacher uses reprimands repeatedly, students can develop negative reactions toward him or her and the classroom setting. Criticism of children also can cause them to develop poor self-images. Saying a child is uncooperative or lazy, for example, casts personal aspersions on the child. It is far more useful to tell students what they should be doing instead of dwelling

MEMORIES FOR A LIFETIME

Many teachers take liberties in what they say to students that they wouldn't dare take in talking to an adult. The psychological pain resulting from these thoughtless comments can sometimes endure for a lifetime. A middle-aged teacher enrolled in an off-campus university course approached the instructor after class one evening to tell him how uncomfortable she was in the class. It turned out that her discomfort had nothing to do with the course content or even with the instructor, but rather with the location of the class. The teacher center where the class was being conducted was in a renovated old school building where this teacher had attended school as a youngster. In the very room where the university class was being taught, she had experienced humiliating treatment from her teacher decades ago. Just being in that same classroom again, thirty to forty years later, precipitated near panic attacks.

on what they are doing. "You should be working on your math assignment rather than looking at a comic book" redirects the student to what he or she should be doing without implying anything negative about the child. Harsh, personal reprimands should be avoided at all cost. Criticism, sarcasm, and ridicule of others can result in extreme emotional pain, sometimes greater than the physical pain from corporal punishment.

Although verbal reprimands are often overused and misused, there are ways to use reprimands constructively. In general, soft reprimands audible only to the misbehaving student are more effective than loud reprimands in reducing inappropriate classroom behavior (O'Leary and Becker 1968; O'Leary et al. 1970). O'Leary and colleagues (1970) note several advantages of soft reprimands. First, soft reprimands do not call the attention of the entire class to the misbehaving student. Second, because they may be different from what disruptive youngsters customarily receive at home and school, they should be less likely to trigger emotional reactions. In addition, Abramowitz, O'Leary, and Futtersak (1988) suggest that short reprimands result in less off-task behavior than long reprimands, which encourage "talking back."

Based on available research, the following suggestions may enhance the effectiveness of your reprimands:

1. Use reprimands sparingly.

2. Direct the reprimands at the behavior in question. Don't make derogatory remarks about the student.

3. Indicate what the student should be doing instead of what the student did wrong.

4. Be brief. Don't continue to chastise the student once you've made your point.

5. Deliver the reprimand quietly and in close proximity to the misbehaving student.

6. Pair any reprimand with positive intervention strategies aimed at teaching appropriate behavior for the situation.

Time-out
This procedure involves removing a child for brief periods (typically five to ten minutes) from the setting that provides reinforcement for the child's bad behavior. The use of time-out requires a quiet, relatively secluded area adjacent to the classroom. The offending child is put in this area until peer reactions to the offending behavior can be defused. Because many classrooms do not have an adjacent space removed from the sights and sounds of the regular classroom, attempts to use time-out often are compromised. The use of time-out

INSTRUCTIVE OR DESTRUCTIVE?

Marc surprised Mr. Turner when he retorted, "Go ahead and take me to the principal's office. See if I care!" Mr. Turner actually hadn't planned to take Marc to the office. He realized immediately that he had triggered Marc's stormy reaction by reprimanding him loudly in front of the classmates. He knew threatening Marc was unnecessary, but what could he do now? He didn't want to lose face.

Mr. Turner resolved to change how he reprimanded students in the future. He wanted his corrections to be more instructive than destructive, and he didn't want to treat students any differently than he expected to be treated by his supervisors. Mr. Turner also recognized that the public or private context for a critical remark can have a significant impact on how a student responds to the reprimand.

typically is limited to classes with young students.

Powell and Powell's (1982) review of the uses and abuses of time-out indicates that time-out is most effective in managing aggression, temper outbursts, and noncompliant behavior maintained by others' responses. If the peer reactions cannot immediately be stopped, the teacher can remove the offending child from that source of reinforcement. Powell and Powell suggest that time-out is generally ineffective with behavior that is self-stimulating. For example, time-out will likely be ineffective in stopping rocking and day-dreaming. Because time-out can be a controversial practice, you want to be sure you are operating within school guidelines regarding its use and that your students' parents are well informed regarding the nature and purpose of the time-out practices in your classroom.

A modified version of time-out that has general acceptability among parents and teachers involves excluding the child for a short period from an activity in which he or she is being disruptive. This type of exclusion is a natural consequence of disrupting an activity. In this case, the child doesn't have to go to a secluded area, but rather sits on the sidelines while the activity continues. The child is allowed to reenter the activity after a specified period, so long as he or she hasn't caused trouble during the time-out period. If the child has attempted to disrupt the activity from the sidelines, the exclusion from participation can be extended, or the child may then be placed in the regular time-out area for a specified period.

Response Cost

This strategy has far more generalized applicability than either verbal reprimands or time-out. Response cost is perhaps most commonly used in the context of a token economy, in which students earn and lose credit linked to backup privileges (Pazulinec, Meyerrose, and Sajwaj 1983; Walker 1983). In a typical token economy, students earn tokens (e.g., points, coupons, stickers) for appropriate behavior and forfeit tokens for inappropriate behavior. Whatever tokens remain after a work period can later be used to purchase backup privileges (e.g., listening to music, looking at magazines). A response cost procedure essentially conveys the message (via tokens earned and forfeited) that appropriate behavior pays, but inappropriate behavior costs something.

Response cost also can be used outside of a full-scale token economy. Students, for example, might forfeit privileges for engaging in a variety of inappropriate behaviors. The fine or cost should be appropriate to the transgression (i.e., small fines for minor offenses and large fines for major offenses), and it should not leave students in an all-is-lost position (with no avenue to improve their standing with respect to privileges or grades). For example, our university students lose a small amount of credit each day their work is turned in late. Under this arrangement, it is still worthwhile for students to turn in a late paper, but the sooner the better.

It is especially important that the unacceptable behaviors and the cost of those behaviors be specified in advance. However, it is possible to be too detailed in identifying inappropriate behavior. Your specification should not leave any question regarding the nature of a targeted inappropriate behavior ("coming to class late" is more specific than "showing a bad attitude"), but attempting to list every unacceptable behavior may challenge students to find ways of making trouble not on your list. A workable compromise includes identifying general categories of inappropriate behaviors, with specific examples provided for each category. Interfering with other students' learning is a general category, whereas nudging others, moving around the room without permission, and engaging in side conversation are specific examples of interfering with others' learning.

In-School Suspension

Although certainly not the strategy of first choice, in-school suspension is preferable to out-of-school suspension and expulsion. It is best used for aggressive acts and repeated disruptions in the regular classroom. Generally, with in-school suspension, the offending students remain in school but are removed from their regular classes and meet in a designated schoolroom to complete classroom assignments and follow prescribed rules (Sheets, 1996). The approach is different from time-out, in which students are temporarily removed from the source of reinforcement for their unacceptable behavior and do not take their schoolwork with them to the time-out area. In-school suspension might range from a single class period to several days, if not longer, depending on the offense. The strategy is apt to be used with middle school and high school students. In a survey of eight hundred school districts, 91 percent of the districts indicated they had used in-school suspension as a disciplinary measure (U.S. Department of Education 1992). Special rules, however, must be followed if suspensions and expulsions are used to discipline students with a disability (see chapter seven).

For this approach to be most successful, students must have opportunities to receive academic instruction while in suspension and to learn appropriate ways of behaving before returning to their regular classrooms. Although part of the impact of in-school suspension presumably results from the students' separation from their friends, being relegated to a sterile setting to do their work doesn't ensure better work habits and improved social demeanor. Thus, students experiencing in-school suspension typically will need mentoring to help them learn how to do their work rather than pester their fellow students. Teachers, of course, must ensure that instruction in their own classrooms meets these students' needs; otherwise, the offensive behaviors are likely to reemerge once the suspended students return to the regular classroom.

Even though a decision to use in-school suspension ultimately falls to an administrator, anyone making a referral should ensure that students' rights have not been violated. Different options should be tried before removing a student from the regular classroom even for brief periods. And, certainly, parents should be informed before in-school suspension is initiated. They may have helpful input regarding their child's problem behavior or may be able to add home support for the school's attempt to help their child. In-school suspension also can be combined with other strategies, such as behavioral contracts, to make the strategy more positive and move students toward responsible citizenship in the regular classroom.

Critical Choices

This chapter has described a variety of preventive and remedial strategies for dealing with misbehavior or even with the prospect of misbehavior. What considerations will help you determine what action to take in response to a particular incident of bad behavior? Perhaps the first consideration is the fairness of an option to the student who has committed the offense. What led to the incident? Was the student goaded or entrapped? Is there any strategy you would not want applied to your own child, given a similar misbehavior? Second, your concerns about misbehavior should not overshadow your primary interest—strengthening appropriate student behavior. What disciplinary actions have the best chance of illuminating the path to constructive behavior? Third, you should consider suggestions from others (e.g., teachers, parents, school counselors, school psychologists) regarding how to deal with a particular kind of misbehavior or how to relate to a particular child.

One way to boost your confidence in dealing with behavior problems is to become more skilled in encouraging positive behaviors (Martin, Linfoot, and Stephenson 1999).

Indeed, some studies (Elliott et al. 1984; Witt, Martens, and Elliott 1984) report that teachers rate positive strategies, such as reinforcing behavior that is incompatible with misconduct, more acceptable for managing problems than negative procedures such as time-out. If you find yourself in a power struggle with misbehaving students, first consider how you can highlight their good behavior rather than publicize their bad conduct. This may be your best avenue of achieving good rapport with students who cause trouble.

Teachers also will find that students can provide useful insights into how misbehaviors should be managed. In a study reporting high school students' views about misbehavior in physical education classes, the comments suggested they are less likely to misbehave in classes where rules and structure clearly distinguish

These students chose jazz dance over calisthenics.

between appropriate and inappropriate behavior (Supaporn 2000). The students indicated they want teachers to monitor student behavior and follow through on what they say they will do. They were particularly insistent that teachers stop harassment and teasing among students. Students also commented that teachers should ask them what they want to do and to plan interesting activities in which they are less likely to misbehave.

Other studies confirm the merits of considering students' opinions and preferences. Turco and Elliott's (1986) research with fifth, seventh, and ninth graders in two schools indicated that students had clear preferences among disciplinary methods. In rating solutions to disruptive behavior, the students showed a strong preference for being disciplined at home for school offenses rather than being reprimanded publicly at school. This preference may relate to the possibility of more lenient treatment at home or to embarrassment in the presence of their peers at school. Even for adults, public reprimands can be among the most humiliating experiences possible. We do not favor routinely asking parents to apply disciplinary actions for school offenses, but we do recommend caution in using disciplinary procedures that might humiliate students in front of their peers.

Additional factors are worth considering in deciding on corrective strategies. For example, getting to know your students will help you determine how to respond to their misbehavior. Some students are very sensitive and need only be reminded of what they should be doing. Using strong reprimands with such students would be hurtful, whereas strong messages may be necessary to get the attention of other misbehaving students. The nature of the offense and the student's age are also important considerations. Time-out, for example, is a more useful strategy for managing aggressive behavior in younger students. As students demonstrate the ability to manage their own actions, they should be given opportunities to suggest potential remedies for inappropriate behaviors and to identify more appropriate ways of behaving.

We suggest that in choosing alternatives for managing misbehavior you consider the following guidelines:

1. Use less-intrusive methods (e.g., having private discussions with students) before going public (e.g., sending the child to the principal, contacting the child's parents);

2. Exhaust positive alternatives before implementing punitive strategies, such as time-out;

3. Strengthen appropriate behaviors as alternatives to inappropriate behaviors;

4. Select strategies you feel comfortable in using (for example, those that would be acceptable if you or your child were the offender);

5. Consult with other school professionals (e.g., counselor, school psychologist) and parents about useful ways of managing different types of problems;

6. Determine students' preferences and give them choices in selecting disciplinary actions that will help them develop more constructive behaviors;

7. Use strategies appropriate for the child's age and disposition;

8. Match the strategy to the severity of the offensive—for example, cheating on an exam and engaging in side conversation during a class discussion require very different corrective strategies.

Specific Problems

Examining two important problem areas teachers encounter at school illustrates how some of our suggested strategies can be applied. Two problems that differ considerably in their effects on students and teachers are *bullying* and *tattling*. Although bullying affects students directly and teachers more indirectly, it is a problem behavior that teachers must decisively confront. Unequivocally confronting bullying will help teachers demonstrate their concern for students and establish a safer climate for everyone. Tattling, in contrast, is more of a direct concern to teachers, but it also has an effect on student relationships. Being "told on" by another student is unlikely to bolster good feelings between the culprit and the informant.

Bullying: Types and Victims

Bullying appears to be increasing in American schools. In a survey of U.S. public schools, reports of being bullied (i.e., picked on or made to do things they didn't want to do) among students ages twelve to eighteen increased from five percent in 1999 to eight percent in 2001 (Devoe et al. 2003). Reports of bullying were greater among males (nine percent) than females (seven percent). Furthermore, 29 percent of the schools reported daily or weekly incidents of bullying, with middle schools reporting more instances than elementary and high schools. Students also were more apt to fear attacks at school than in other settings.

Although often regarded as a physical act, bullying also can involve verbal and social actions. A student, for example, may be subjected to name calling and exclusion from a group. Dan Olweus, a noted authority on bullying, claimed that "a student is being bullied when he or she is exposed, repeatedly over time, to negative actions on the part of one or

Exclusion from a group is a form of bullying.

more other students" (1993, p. 9). Negative acts include intentionally harming or attempting to harm someone, but they can also involve excluding someone from a group. Olweus further restricts the use of the term *bullying* to instances where there is an imbalance of power, with one party less able than the other to make a defense.

Unfortunately, a consensus definition of bullying has yet to emerge among educators. The presence of physical contact alone can lead to a wrong conclusion and response. Hazler and colleagues (2001) have found that teachers and counselors are more likely to classify physical conflicts as bullying even when the incident does not fit the definition of bullying (i.e., involve repeated harm and an imbalance of power). Plus, teachers and counselors judge physical abuse as more severe than verbal or social abuse. The researchers stress the importance of recognizing and dealing with the long-term consequences of repeated low-level abuse. Such consequences may be far greater for the victim, as well as for the bully, than single instances of inappropriate behavior, such as a fight between schoolmates or one episode of harassment.

Other research (e.g., Yoon and Kerber 2003) suggests that teachers are more likely to intervene in verbal and physical bullying than in situations involving social exclusion. Teachers' responses to bullying scenarios in Yoon and Kerber's research indicate that teachers are most likely to be lenient in their response to social exclusion. These researchers emphasize that failure to take disciplinary action in bullying situations can send the wrong message to students. Even instances of social exclusion should not be ignored because such inaction suggests that socially ostracizing students is acceptable within the school culture. Leaving some students outside respected social circles in school will undoubtedly create morale problems for these students and may lead to violent consequences even for students regarded as popular and powerful in the school culture.

Knowing who is apt to be victimized may be vital in dealing with the problem. Olweus (1993) identified two types of victims: *passive-submissive victims* and *provocative victims*. In general, the first type tends to transmit behavioral signals that they will not defend themselves if attacked. They are often quiet and sensitive individuals who have few or no friends at school. Olweus notes they tend to be anxious and insecure and hold low opinions of themselves. Provocative victims, in contrast, may exhibit aggression as well as anxious behaviors. The latter students often have trouble concentrating on their work and may pester others instead.

Reduction of Bullying

Bullying cannot be managed by the teacher alone. Educators have long suggested a whole-school approach to the problem (Rigby and Bagshaw 2003). A whole-school approach typically involves all school employees, students, parents, and the community, working together to ensure procedures are in place to provide for students' physical and emotional

ABOUT BULLIES, VICTIMS, AND BULLY-VICTIMS

In a study of 1,985 fifth graders, the majority of whom were Hispanic and African American, seven percent were classified as bullies, nine percent as victims, and six percent as both (Juvonen, Graham, and Schuster 2003). The classifications were derived by having students nominate peers whom they perceived as bullies (e.g., pushed others around, made fun of others) and as victims (e.g., those who were pushed around). The bully-victims were students who were frequently identified as being a bully as well as a victim.

All three groups had difficulties in school and in their relationships with others (Juvonen, Graham, and Schuster 2003). Teachers, for example, indicated that bullies, victims, and bully-victims were more disengaged in school than were their classmates. Although bullies enjoyed the highest ratings for social status and popularity, they were avoided by classmates,

as were victims and bully-victims. Overall, victims suffered from low social status, ostracism by peers, high levels of self-reported emotional distress (e.g., depression, social anxiety, loneliness), and school disengagement. Bully-victims fared the worst of any group. They were the most likely to present conduct problems and to be avoided. They also displayed high levels of depression and loneliness.

Although the bullying group in this study had the lowest adjustment problems, all three groups presented problems for teachers. As the researchers note, when bullies are regarded as "cool" by peers and have high standing among them, teachers need to examine the social support afforded them and the lack of support given to victims. The failure to change the school culture for both bullies and victims leaves the door open for catastrophic acts of violence within the school.

safety. In working with others, teachers can do many things to minimize bullying in their classrooms and schools. Let's review how some of the previously discussed strategies can be used to create a school culture where each student has a place.

Respect for All Students. Respect can be demonstrated in many ways: listening to students' concerns, involving them in classroom decisions, assisting them with academic tasks, and praising their accomplishments. Respect shown by teachers sets the tone for the classroom and serves as a model for students to follow in their interactions with one another. Our professional experience has revealed that when teachers show respect for students who seem a bit odd, other students are more likely to stop their giggling and show respect also.

We recall two instances where student behavior in our university classes seemed somewhat askew. In one case, a young woman would get out of her seat and walk to where the instructor was standing to ask her question privately during class discussion. In another case, a student brought a large carrying case to class and put it directly in front of himself at the table where he sat. This large carrying case, which actually looked like a piece of luggage, completely shielded the student from the instructor's view. Although the student attempted to participate in class discussion, it was always when he was shielded from the instructor's view.

In both cases, both instructor and students were somewhat taken back by the unusual discussion episodes. However, the instructor maintained a serious demeanor and responded to these students as he would have to any other student's comment, which set the tone for other students to respond accordingly. The instructor did have some follow-up conversation with the students exhibiting the unusual behavior to help them learn to respond in ways less likely to invite ridicule from their peers.

Discussions with Students about Bullying. The comments on interpersonal communication in chapter two should provide a framework for discussing bullying with students. You should facilitate the open sharing of feelings about interpersonal behaviors, while at the same time restricting comments that might be highly offensive to others. Your discussion can help students become more aware of the nature of bullying and how it makes others feel (Harris and Isernhagen 2003). Otherwise, students may not recognize the cumulative gravity of repeated put-downs. One perspective you want to strengthen in these discussions

The classic "schoolyard bully"

is empathy, the ability to put oneself in the shoes of another who is the recipient of demeaning treatment.

Reinforcement of Behaviors Incompatible with Bullying. Although you must let students know that disrespect for others, whatever its form, will not be tolerated, you also must be ready to reinforce behaviors counter to bullying. Bullies need help in acting nonaggressively. Acts of cooperation and goodwill toward others can be encouraged. Similarly, victims need help in developing behaviors that will keep them from being a target of bullying. Feldman (2004) suggests children can lessen the likelihood of being bullied through such behaviors as looking others in the eye, speaking up, and standing up straight. A wide array of social skills should be described, modeled, and reinforced among all students.

Awareness of Bullying. In chapter three, we discussed the need to monitor students' academic and social behavior. Monitoring is especially important in dealing with bullying. You need to be aware of vulnerable areas in the school where teacher supervision can help reduce bullying. This behavior can occur in any area of a school, but restrooms, hallways, lunchrooms, and playgrounds are common trouble spots. A key to reducing bullying is to have more adults in these areas so that they can confront incipient signs of bullying. In fact, Olweus (1993) reports that bullying in school is lowered when the number of teachers supervising break areas increases.

Furthermore, you need strategies to ensure that students will let you know when bullying is occurring (see the section on tattling for important distinctions, though). Acting upon their input will demonstrate that their input matters. Timid students, however, may only be willing to report problems anonymously. A complaint box might be used ("Keep a Lid on Bullying" 2003), or you can tell students to provide input via a general classroom suggestion box.

As noted earlier, in reference to a whole-school approach, you should cooperate with other school personnel and parents in monitoring and reporting inappropriate student behaviors. Input from school bus drivers and cafeteria workers can be especially important in efforts to reduce bullying (Chamberlain 2003). You should take special note of parental complaints about peer mistreatment of their children. In a word, all reports of bullying should be taken seriously and thoroughly investigated.

Student Interest in Learning. An instructional approach that keeps all students actively involved in activities suited to their needs can be pivotal to preventing bullying. Among other things, students' interests need to be considered as you plan instructional activities (see chapter three). Students who demonstrate interest in school are less likely to bully or to be bullied. In fact, one large study of seventh to twelfth graders showed that students who liked school the most were least likely to be mistreated and that those who disliked school were more apt to be treated disrespectfully by peers (Eisenberg, Neumark-

Sztainer, and Perry 2003). Academically poor students were more likely to be the targets of harassment than academically successful students.

Consequences for Bullying. If you have conclusive evidence that a particular student is bullying other students, you must take decisive action whether or not the bullying involves students for whom you are directly responsible. If you happen to encounter an episode of bullying, you must intervene immediately to stop the unfolding scenario. To stand back will cause you to lose credibility with both the bully and the victim. However, you should alert the principal's office right away as to what is taking place because the incident may be too much for you to handle by yourself. Whatever the severity of the incident, the principal should be fully informed as to what has happened. Your school will undoubtedly have established procedures for dealing with alleged or actual episodes of bullying, such as contacting the parents of both the bully and the victim.

If you are serving in an administrative role in your school, you may be directly responsible for meting out consequences for bullying. If there is an obvious injury, police personnel must be contacted to investigate the incident. They may bring charges against the bully and remove him or her from the school. Otherwise, if the attack has resulted in no apparent injury, some type of suspension for the bully may be in order (in-school suspension for more minor incidents and out-of-school suspension for more major incidents). If in-school suspension is ordered, the school should prescribe human-relations training and school-service activity in addition to the suspension experience. Students can be required to participate in school projects that involve helping others, such as tutoring younger students or assisting disabled students in some way. The strategy is to reshape the way the bully derives social reinforcement, shifting the emphasis from hurting to helping.

Exploration of Other Resources. An Internet search will yield many materials you can use in developing approaches for dealing with bullying. Comprehensive reviews of the subject are available from Drake, Price, and Telljohann (2003) and from Espelage and Swearer (2003). Articles by Migliore (2003) and by Harris and Isernhagen (2003) offer a number of specific strategies for managing bullying. Olweus's text (1993) provides an extensive discussion of procedures that have been used successfully in reducing bullying. Useful material can also be found at the website of the Center for the Study and Prevention of Violence.

Tattling

Tattling may appear to be far removed from the more serious problem of bullying, but in an odd way the two problems are linked. On the one hand, teachers expect students to tell them about bullying. On the other, teachers often show frustration when students, usually younger students, tell them about trivial incidents. A critical question, then, is how teachers can encourage students to report some behaviors but discourage them from reporting other behaviors. Efforts to resolve this dilemma in dealing with tattling can include the following strategies.

Distinctions Between "Tattling" and "Telling." If you are to get students to report some incidents but not others, making a distinction between *tattling* and *telling* is a must. Violence-prevention experts believe parents can begin teaching their children the difference between tattling and telling when they are around age five, with the difference being that tattling is done to get someone in trouble and telling is done to get someone help (Dickinson 2001). You can use this distinction in clarifying what behaviors you want students to report and what behaviors you don't need to know about. The overall purpose of such clarification is to help students feel comfortable in coming to you with problems rather than to limit their contacts with you.

There is often a fine line between tattling and reporting information of a serious nature. Although you want to minimize tattling, you don't want to inhibit vital input from students. Students can learn what is appropriate and inappropriate input, but time is usually needed to teach the difference. Don't allow your frustration with a single episode of tattling to block further input from a student. A simple head nod combined with the instruction to get back to work may be sufficient for dealing with an incident of tattling. In contrast, a reprimand such as "Please don't interrupt me again with this kind of stuff" may block all future input from that student.

Reinforcement of "Tootling." Even after discussions about tattling and telling, one or two students still may feel a need to report "anything and everything" happening in class (e.g., "Mary's not doing her work," "Jimmy is whispering to Billy"). Such students may be more desirous of your attention than of actually tattling on others. They think you will applaud their reporting misbehavior. Ensuring that these students receive reinforcement for their academic work should help reduce their need to visit your desk in order to gain attention. Also, researchers (e.g., Skinner, Cashwell, and Skinner 2000) have demonstrated that students can be reinforced for "tootling" rather than tattling. Tootling involves students' reporting on their classmates' appropriate behaviors. This strategy might be particularly useful, given that students are telling about good things that a teacher might otherwise miss.

Awareness of Classroom Behaviors. Locating your desk so you can easily observe students, walking about the classroom to assist students, and in general being aware of what is happening ("withitness") were discussed in chapter three as ways for promoting appropriate behaviors. These procedures also can minimize tattling. If you already know what is going on and are acting to correct problems, students will be aware of your efforts and should be less likely to inundate you with reports of alleged misbehavior.

We also caution you against leaving students under the supervision of other students. This practice places too much responsibility on students, especially if they are asked to report on others' misbehavior upon your return. If you must leave for an emergency, send for another school professional to be in your room before you leave. Remember, you are responsible for the supervision and safety of students under your care. If bad things happen when you have left your room unsupervised by a school professional, you are putting yourself in a position of legal vulnerability.

Other Options. Instead of totally ignoring a student who is reporting on someone else's behavior, you can listen attentively and then decide on an appropriate response. For trivial matters, you can acknowledge the student's report and simply reply by saying something like "I understand" or "I'm aware of that." For situations where you should take preventive or remedial actions, you can thank the student and then address the problem at hand. If students continue to present trivial information, you might suggest they monitor their own behavior by listing the number of times they report on others. They can be positively reinforced for limiting themselves to serious matters, such as when someone is sick or needs help or when the reported behaviors fit the definition of bullying.

Concluding Comments

This chapter has virtually ignored one procedure still used in some school systems to cope with student misconduct: corporal punishment. In good faith, we cannot recommend corporal punishment as a viable option for dealing with any form of student misbehavior. The side effects of corporal punishment far outweigh the benefits. Among the most prominent side effects are modeled aggression, counteraggression, displaced aggression, passive aggression, social withdrawal, and negative associations with school life. Nonetheless, you may be in a school where corporal punishment is still used for certain types of misbehavior. If you would like to broaden your perspective of the legal status of corporal punishment and the extent of its use, you may want to examine the appendix.

The recommended strategies in this chapter, especially the negative interventions, are based on the premise that these strategies will not have to be frequently used. You should be aware that frequent occurrences of misconduct may be an indication of necessary changes in your overall management system. Perhaps the instructional program needs revision, or students are not receiving sufficient support for desired behaviors. Working to develop students' academic and social skills remains the most proven method of reducing classroom-management problems. It should remain your goal even when you are dealing with specific inappropriate acts. The underlying theme of your classroom management should always be the strengthening of academically and socially constructive classroom behaviors.

References

Abramowitz, A. J., S. G. O'Leary, and M. W. Futtersak. (1988). The relative impact of long and short reprimands on children's off-task behavior in the classroom. *Behavior Therapy* 18: 243–47.

Ayllon, T., and M. D. Roberts. (1974). Eliminating discipline problems by strengthening academic performances. *Journal of Applied Behavior Analysis* 7: 71–76.

Chamberlain, S. P. (2003). S. Limber and S. Cedillo: Responding to bullying. *Intervention in School and Clinic* 38(4): 236–43.

Devoe, J. F., K. Peter, P. Kaufman, S. A. Ruddy, A. K. Miller, M. Planty, T. D. Snyder, and M. R. Rand. (2003). Indicators of School Crime and Safety. *National Center for Education Statistics (NCES)* no.2004-004/NC J 201257. Washington, D.C.: U.S. Departments of Education and Justice.

Dickinson, A. (2001). To tattle vs. to tell. *Time* 157: 11, 82.

Drake, J. A., J. H. Price, and S. K. Telljohann. (2003). The nature and extent of bullying at school. *Journal of School Health* 73(5): 173–81.

Dreikurs, R., B. B. Grunwald, and F. C. Pepper. (1982). *Maintaining Sanity in the Classroom: Illustrated Teaching Techniques.* 2d ed. New York: Harper and Row.

Eisenberg, M. E., D. Neumark-Sztainer, and C. L. Perry. (2003). Peer harassment, school connectedness, and academic achievement. *Journal of School Health* 73(8): 311–17.

Elliott, S. N., J. C. Witt, G. A. Galvin, and R. Peterson. (1984). Acceptability of positive and reductive behavioral interventions: Factors that influence teachers' decisions. *Journal of School Psychology* 22: 353–60.

Espelage, D. L., and S. M. Swearer. (2003). Research on school bullying and victimization: What have we learned and where do we go from here? *School Psychology Review* 32(3): 365–84.

Feldman, S. (2004). Bullying prevention. *Teaching PreK–8* 34(6): 6–7.

Franse, S. R. (1998). Conversations with children. *Kappa Delta Pi Record* 35(1): 24–26.

Gathercoal, F. (1997). *Judicious Discipline.* 4th ed. San Francisco: Caddo Gap.

Gilbert, J. I. (1989). Logical consequences: A new classification for the classroom. *Individual Psychology* 45(4): 425–32.

Grandmont, R. P. (2003). Judicious discipline: A constitutional approach for public high schools. *American Secondary Education* 31(3): 97–117.

Harris, S., and J. Isernhagen. (2003). Keeping bullies at bay. *American School Board Journal* (November): 43–45.

Hazler, R. J., D. L. Miller, J. V. Carney, and S. Green. (2001). Adult recognition of school bullying situations. *Educational Research* 43(2): 133–46.

Juvonen, J., S. Graham, and M. A. Schuster. (2003). Bullying among young adolescents:

The strong, the weak, and the troubled. *Pediatrics* 112(6): 1231–237.

Kazdin, A. E. (2001). *Behavior Modification in Applied Settings.* 6th ed. Belmont, Calif.: Wadsworth/Thomson Learning.

Keep a lid on bullying with a complaint box. (2003). *Curriculum Review* 43(4): 11.

Kindall, L. M., E. A. Workman, and R. L. Williams. (1980). The consultative merits of praise-ignore versus praise-reprimand instruction. *Journal of School Psychology* 18 (4): 373–80.

Landau, B. M., and P. Gathercoal. (2000). Creating peaceful classrooms. *Phi Delta Kappan* 81(6): 450–54.

Martin, A. J., K. Linfoot, and J. Stephenson. (1999). How teachers respond to concerns about misbehavior in their classroom. *Psychology in the Schools* 36(4): 347–58.

Migliore, E. T. (2003). Eliminate bullying in your classroom. *Intervention in School and Clinic* 38(3): 172–77.

O'Leary, K. D., and W. C. Becker. (1968). The effects of the intensity of a teacher's reprimands on children's behavior. *Journal of School Psychology* 7: 8–11.

O'Leary, K. D., K. F. Kaufman, R. Kass, and R. Drabman. (1970). The effects of loud and soft reprimands on the behavior of disruptive students. *Exceptional Children* 37: 145–55.

Olweus, D. (1993). *Bullying at School: What We Know and What We Can Do.* Oxford, United Kingdom: Blackwell.

Pazulinec, R., M. Meyerrose, and T. Sajwaj. (1983). Punishment via response cost. In *The Effects of Punishment on Human Behavior,* edited by S. Axelrod and J. Apsche, pp. 71-86. New York: Academic Press.

Powell, T. H., and I. Q. Powell. (1982). The use and abuse of using timeout procedure for disruptive pupils. *Pointer* 26(2): 18–22.

Rigby, K., and D. Bagshaw. (2003). Prospects of adolescent students collaborating with teachers in addressing issues of bullying and conflict in schools. *Educational Psychology* 23(5): 535–46.

Sheets, J. (1966). Designing an effective in-school suspension program to change student behavior. NASSP Bulletin 80 (579): 86–90.

Skinner, C. H., T. H. Cashwell, and A. L. Skinner. (2000). Increasing tootling: The effects of a peer-monitored group contingency program on students' reports of peers' prosocial behaviors. *Psychology in the Schools* 37(3): 263–70.

Supaporn, S. (2000). High school students' perspectives about misbehavior. *The Physical Educator* 57(3): 124–35.

Turco, T. L., and S. N. Elliott. (1986). Assessment of students' acceptability ratings of teacher-initiated interventions for classroom misbehavior. *Journal of School Psychology* 24: 277–83.

U.S. Department of Education. National Center for Education Statistics. (1992). *Office for*

Civil Rights Survey Redesign: A Feasibility Survey. Washington, D.C.: U.S. Department of Education.

Walker, H. M. (1983). Applications of response cost in school settings: Outcomes, issues, and recommendations. *Exceptional Education Quarterly* 3(4): 47–55.

Williams, R. L. (1987). Classroom management. In *Historical Foundations of Educational Psychology*, edited by J. A. Glover and R. R. Ronning, pp. 297–325. New York: Plenum.

Williams, R. L., and J. D. Long. (1983). *Toward a Self-managed Life Style.* 3rd ed. Boston: Houghton Mifflin.

Witt, J. C., B. K. Martens, and S. N. Elliott. (1984). Factors affecting teachers' judgments of the acceptability of behavioral interventions: Time involvement, behavior problem severity, and type of intervention. *Behavior Therapy* 15: 204–9.

Yoon, J. S., and K. Kerber. (2003). Bullying: Elementary teachers' attitudes and intervention strategies. *Research in Education* 69: 27–35.

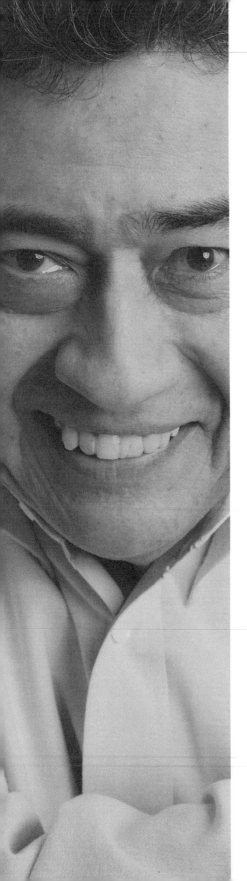

"Rafael, what do you really think about this movement to get parents more involved with their children's schoolwork? I've had more grief than I want from parents. My experience is they usually take their children's side, and they seldom come to school without some complaint."

"Well, I've had problems with parents too. But in the long run, I think we can't lose by working more closely with them. You'll have to admit that parents who are willing to complain and stand up for their children are at least interested in what's going on at school."

"You've got me there. But I still think it's just one more thing for us to do."

"It will take time, but it may save time in the end, too. I've found that the more good things I can tell parents about their children, the more willing they are to help and to listen to me when problems arise."

"Yes, but you have an advantage. You understand parents from minority backgrounds."

"I'm not so sure being Hispanic gives me an advantage. I just believe all people, regardless of their heritage, want the best for their children. We need to let them know we share their dream and are working hard to help their children."

6

◄○►

The Home Connection

Working with Parents

Research dealing with parents' involvement in schools clearly indicates that their involvement is an important contributor to their children's school success (Chen and Chandler 2001; U.S. Department of Education 1994). The benefits may come from parental involvement either at home or at school. Unfortunately, parental involvement is often limited or nonexistent. In fact, students with the greatest need for support may experience the least parental participation in school matters.

A number of factors impact the extent to which parents initially get involved with their children's schoolwork, including the children's grade level, the parents' education, and the parents' income (U.S. Department of Education 1998). Parents of children in elementary school are more apt to be involved than parents of children in middle or high school, even though involvement is helpful at all levels. Involvement also increases as household income and parental educational levels increase. Moreover, data from the National Center for Education Statistics (U.S. Department of Education 1998) show that parents who are highly involved in their children's schools are apt to have higher "social capital"—that is, they are more apt to share activities with their children, such as reading together or visiting a library together.

Family structure also plays a major role in the degree to which parents are involved in their child's school. Nord and West (2001) reported that students who belong to traditional families, with two biological parents present, are more likely to have their parents involved in school than are children who belong to non-traditional family arrangements. A high level of involvement means that the parents (or parent) participate in three or more school activities (e.g., school meeting, parent-teacher conference, school event, and volunteer work). For example, in the two biological parent living arrangement, 62 percent of the students had high parental involvement in school activities, whereas only 48 percent of the students in mother-only family living arrangements had high parental involvement, and only 37 percent of students living with non-parent guardians had high parental involvement. (As used here and throughout the chapter, the term *parent* is used to refer to anyone who acts in the *role of a parent*—that is, anyone who serves as the principal caregiver for the student.)

The percentage of school children living in non-traditional family structures has increased substantially over the past several decades. In 1970, 11 percent of children under eighteen in the United States lived in single-parent families, whereas 25 percent did in 1994 (U.S. Department of Education 1996). In 1996, 43 percent of the students in grades 1 through 12 lived in non-traditional family arrangements (Nord and West 2001).The percentage of children living with grandparents is also increasing. The number of grandparent maintained households rose by 19 percent from 1990 to 1997, with 3.9 million children living in grandparent-maintained households in 1997 (Casper and Bryson 1998). Many of these families are living below the poverty line, and parental involvement in the schools is often low.

We mention the different levels of parental involvement not in an accusatory spirit, but rather to emphasize the need for schools to become more assertive in enlisting assistance from parents. Overall programs to involve parents usually begin at the administrative level and then get communicated to teachers in the system. Moreover, the *No Child Left Behind Act* of 2001 requires schools to develop strategies that promote parental and community involvement in schools (Jacobson 2002). Therefore, all schools probably have a philosophy of how to develop better relationships with parents. The key to a strong relationship between the home and school resides with teachers; they have the most contact with students, and most parents have a vested interest in assisting those who have daily contact with their children.

Getting Started: Working with Administrators

To be effective in building strong relationships with parents, teachers need to work with administrators and follow administrative guidelines with respect to school-parent communication. Otherwise, competing messages may be sent to parents. Getting involved early in planning for communication with parents can give teachers some control over what might be undertaken in a particular school system. Interested teachers can volunteer to serve on committees charged with developing and maintaining programs for working with parents. Even if not on parent-participation committees, any individual teacher can still advocate for school initiatives such as providing transportation for elderly parents and parents with disabilities, hiring interpreters for parents with low English proficiency, and providing in-school child care so parents can attend school events. In other words, teachers need to be involved in formulating plans for building good home-school relationships, and they need to be advocates for programs aimed at enhancing parent participation.

Teachers should communicate closely with the school principal in developing collaborative linkages between the school and parents. The principal should be kept informed of unusual projects, interesting units of study, and special events the teacher is planning that might be particularly interesting to parents. Principals need to know what is going on in each classroom so as not to be surprised by parents' inquiries. Furthermore, their being able to tell parents about notable progress in your classroom will likely further parental interest and involvement. If principals are well informed about your classroom activities, they also can be more supportive should problems arise over alleged events in your classroom. The viewpoint of the principal may be especially helpful when you and a parent are seeing an event differently.

Principals may be able to arrange workshops on working with parents or provide necessary funds for projects to involve parents in your class. Principals also can make life easier for teachers in scheduling conferences with parents. In many cases, they expect teachers to schedule conferences with parents after school hours. By providing early input to the principal on scheduling, you may be able to influence him or her to permit parent-teacher meetings on teacher workdays (i.e., when students are not present and you have time allotted for academic planning, completing term grade reports, and conducting other school business), thus reducing your time away from home. The remainder of the meetings, for parents who work during school hours, can then be reserved for before and after school hours. Together, teachers and administrators can forge a strong bond with parents. Alone, neither is apt to be effective.

Having a Willing Attitude

The fact that school systems develop programs to involve parents does not mean every teacher will endorse the total program. Some teachers may simply be reluctant to invite more participation from parents. They may see parental involvement as encroaching on their responsibilities, or they may not want to invest the time needed to increase parental

involvement in school activities. Tacit agreement with a concept is always easier than fully-fledged implementation. Lazar and Slostad (1999), however, note that teachers gain professional status and authority, rather than lose control of the classroom, by relating well with parents. These authors also note that avoiding contact with parents for fear of conflict actually increases the potential for conflict. In the end, more time, not less, is apt to be involved in dealing with parents.

In addition to feeling parents might usurp the teacher's authority; some teachers believe that enlisting parental involvement is the responsibility of other school personnel. For example, Schweiker-Marra (2000) found that middle school teachers initially regarded other school personnel, such as the principal and guidance counselor, as having the responsibility for developing better communications with parents. These teachers believed their primary role was to inform parents about students' grades and inappropriate behaviors.

According to Schweiker-Marra (2000), two strategies that reduced teacher reluctance to becoming more extensively involved with parents were a monthly school newspaper, prepared by students in an eighth-grade technology class, and "good news" postcards. All teachers contributed information about activities in their classrooms to the newspaper, and the paper contained other sections informing parents about important meetings, ways to help with homework, and other school-related events. The school office provided the postcards (with pictures of various sites around school), which the teachers sent home to highlight positive things about students. These strategies produced many positive responses from parents, and the teachers perceived them as improving communication with parents.

The extent to which teachers pursue home-school relationships is affected by how they view parents' potential contributions. Recognizing the value of parent involvement is an important motivational factor for teachers. It is easy to look for someone to blame when things go wrong, and parents often become the targets, especially when they have been minimally involved in school activities. In reality, parents can be a teacher's chief ally in strengthening students' academic and social skills. Research (U.S. Department of Education 1994) even suggests that the school performance of all children improves when parents get involved in school activities. A willing attitude on the teachers' part can get things started. And from there, the list of things teachers and parents can do together to help children will continue to grow.

Writing Home

One of the things you can do early on, perhaps even before the beginning of the school year, is to write a letter introducing yourself to your students' parents. If you are an elementary teacher, you might obtain a roster of your students before the school year begins. One teacher used a notebook system to facilitate regular two-way communications with parents; for example, a letter was sent to parents prior to the school year to stress the importance of education for their children, to specify expectations for the students, to solicit parental input, and to describe the notebook system (Williams 1997). Indeed, an early letter to parents can signal your interest in all of your students and your desire to establish a partnership with parents, as well as describe any special projects in which you wish to involve parents.

A notebook system can also be a means of maintaining relationships with parents throughout the year and better meeting your students' needs. As described by Williams (1997), the notebook system typically involves having a spiral notebook for each child in which the teacher makes daily entries about information related to the child's work or school matters that might be of interest to the child's parents. The child takes the notebook home each day, and the parents respond to the teacher's comments and provide comments that can be useful to the teacher in working with their child.

Although Williams's letter to parents included a description of her notebook system, specification of her expectations for students, and encouragement of parental participation in promoting their child's learning, you can develop your welcoming letter around any special arrangement for students to make the school year more productive. You might describe, for example, how you will be integrating writing into the various subjects you teach or how students will be using computers to develop research skills. You certainly should specify what materials students will need each day, and you should welcome their suggestions for working with their child. If you are a high school teacher or teach multiple class sections, you will undoubtedly want to wait until the school year begins before sending a welcome letter to all your parents.

All communications with parents ought to be "user friendly" (Robinson and Fine 1994). You should avoid educational jargon—either talking over parents' heads or talking down to parents. A precise, straightforward, and respectful tone is best. Let others read your letter and offer suggestions about the content and tone. Also, be sure to proof carefully all written communication with parents. Administrative approval should be sought before launching a program to solicit parental support. You want your efforts to be in harmony with the broader program at your school.

An Introductory Letter Home

Although each teacher's letter home needs to be adapted to the grade level or subject he or she is teaching, the following letter illustrates what a welcome letter might include:

Dear Mr. and Mrs. *(Parents' Names):*

I want to take this opportunity to introduce myself and tell you how pleased I am to be working with your child, *(name of child),* this year. I recently graduated from State University with a major in elementary education and a concentration in English. I will be working as the language arts and social studies teacher for two groups of fifth-grade students who will rotate between their math-science class and my class. The math-science teacher and I will be working very closely together to ensure your child has an interesting and challenging fifth-grade experience.

One of the principal things we will be doing this year is integrating writing assignments across the curriculum. Many of your child's writing assignments will be related to current topics in science and math. For example, students will learn how to write up a science experiment, and they will often have choices about writing on science topics of greatest interest to them. Students also will be taught how to use math facts and develop graphs and figures that can be used in their writing projects. In addition, they will be using computers with special writing programs to help further their writing and research skills.

Your child also will be asked to maintain a daily writing journal. In the journal, students will describe school events they found to be interesting that day or discuss problems they have encountered. Journals will be turned in each day. I will read and make comments on the journal entries and return them the next day. Although the journal entries are not formal writing assignments, I believe in expanding opportunities for students to express themselves in writing. It also will help me get to know them better and plan activities around their interests and needs.

Although what I have spelled out may sound like a lot of work for your child, be assured most of the work will be done in school. Your child should have no more than thirty minutes of language arts and social studies reading and/or writing to do each school night. I will work with the math-science teacher to coordinate assignments so your child is not overburdened with out-of-class assignments. It would be helpful to your child, however, if you would read your child's work and my comments once the work has been returned. I hope you will also encourage your child to read and write at home.

On the opening day of school, your child will need a loose-leaf notebook, paper, and pencils for use on in-class assignments. Also, please arrange for your child to bring a spiral-bound notebook that can be used as a writing journal. Your child should have these materials each day of class.

Once again, let me express my delight in having your child in my class. If you have any suggestions for working with your child, please share them with me. Or, should a problem arise at any time, feel free to contact me by phone *(phone number)* or by e-mail *(e-mail address)*. I look forward to meeting you soon. I know that together we can make this a happy and rewarding year for your child.

Sincerely,
Mrs. Anne Dawson

The Monthly Trumpet

MRS. WADOSKI'S THIRD GRADE

September • Volume 1

Greetings from Our Class!

As a class project we will be preparing a monthly newsletter to keep you informed of upcoming events and of exciting things we are doing. We held a class meeting to select our newsletter name and to decide what to include in our first newsletter. The students and I hope you will you will be better informed about our class activities as a result of news items being trumpeted your way.

NEWS FLASH

With the help of our school technology assistant, we have developed a class web site that you can view on the World Wide web. Our web site address is _____. Group pictures of students engaged in various class activities are available at our web site. We will also be posting student poems and artwork in the near future. A creative product from each student will be included. You can also e-mail from our web site to offer your suggestions, comments, and direct questions to the class. If you don't have a computer in your home, please visit the library or the Community Center on Trade Street, where you will have access and assistance in retrieving our class web site.

UPCOMING EVENT

A school open house will be held on September 23. Please make plans to attend. Students will be providing a tour of our classroom and will share products of learning. Student art will be on display, and you will have a chance to look at your child's most recent writing project. Child care is available at the school, and buses will be running from several locations if you need transportation. Please call the school office at _____ for more details. REFRESHMENTS will be served in our class for all who attend.

VOLUNTEERS NEEDED

We are looking for classroom volunteers. Many options are available, including tutoring, supervising at lunchtime, teaching arts and crafts, chaperoning for class trips, translating from English to Spanish for our newsletter and for other documents for parents, sharing your expertise or talent(s), and many more. If you have time to assist us with any of these activities, please contact either the principal's office or your child's classroom teacher.

Spreading the News

Some teachers also find periodic (e.g., monthly) newsletters a good means of establishing regular communications with parents. Such newsletters can include a calendar of upcoming events, news about what students will be studying in the future, tips to parents on providing help with special assignments, overall progress being made by the class, requests for parent volunteers, and any other item of importance. The newsletter also may contain a special section prepared by students or one that includes contributions from the students (e.g., poems, drawings, comments).

A good time for a first newsletter is soon after your initial meeting with your class. Such a newsletter will give you an opportunity to introduce yourself to parents and to outline what you hope to accomplish in your class. An early newsletter can be used to identify ways parents can help their children at home. Community resources for parents and their children might be identified as well. Another advantage of an early newsletter is that it can be sent home with the school handbook, which outlines school policies and procedures.

If you should have a large enrollment of students whose parents have limited proficiency in English, you may need assistance in translating your newsletter into the parents' native language. For example, if you have Hispanic students, you may also need to send home an English or Spanish version of your class newsletter. Your goal, of course, is to communicate with all parents in a friendly and inviting manner, whether you are doing so in a welcoming letter, a regular newsletter, or other format.

Telephoning and E-mailing Home

Parents don't typically get a phone call from a teacher unless something is wrong. This need not be the case. Lazar and colleagues (1999) reported on a teacher who taught 120 biology students and used telephone contacts to praise students' achievements and to discuss ways of helping the students be successful. The teacher also made initial telephone calls to all parents to introduce himself and to learn more about his students. Of course, you may need to make an occasional call to discuss a problem or arrange a conference, but this task should be much easier if you have already established a supportive relationship and are not using your communications primarily to convey bad news.

In addition to making positive calls home, you may want to lobby your school administration to establish a telephone hotline. Parents can access hotlines at any time to receive relevant school information. Hotlines are most often established to inform parents about homework assignments. Each teacher spends a few minutes each day recording the students'

MEETING A PARENT'S NEED

Mrs. Peterson was a very eager mother who constantly called her son's teacher, Miss Pannell, at home to talk about her son's progress. At first Miss Pannell welcomed the calls as sincere expressions of interest. However, Mrs. Peterson also liked to chat about unrelated things, and Miss Pannell found that the calls began to take an inordinate amount of her time. Rather than appreciating the calls, Miss Pannell began to feel resentful when the phone rang. A discussion with her colleagues about the problem helped her to better understand Mrs. Peterson's motivations. The Peterson family had moved to town within the past year, and it seemed likely the phone calls represented a way for Mrs. Peterson to meet some of her social needs, which were probably inadequately met through other channels.

To help Mrs. Peterson develop other social contacts, Miss Pannell suggested volunteer activities for her that were social in nature, such as calling other parents about the annual parent's night, chairing the refreshments committee for the special event, and arranging for cleanup following the parents' night. Mrs. Peterson's calls to Miss Pannell became less frequent and less extended as Mrs. Peterson became more involved with other parents and made new friends. The occasional calls she subsequently made related more to her son's school progress and less to tangential events.

assignments. Parents can then call to hear a recording from their child's teacher. Other brief messages can also be added to a homework hotline, such as what to do if questions arise or tutoring is needed.

E-mail is increasingly used to make initial contact with parents and to communicate with them on a regular basis. Obviously, not all parents have access to a computer or the needed expertise to communicate via e-mail, but you can still provide your e-mail address for parents with access to a computer. Your school also might be willing to sponsor a workshop that will focus on the common teacher uses of a computer and alert parents to their being able to use computers in libraries and at other community resource centers.

Making Homework Useful and Palatable

In early communication with parents, you need to address the issue of homework. Although well intended, homework can become a contentious area for teachers, students, and parents (Paulu 1998). Some parents may come home too exhausted to check their children's homework, or they may not have the expertise to provide assistance with difficult assignments. The students may perceive the assignments as busywork or as too difficult or too long and consequently they may not do the homework or do it haphazardly. And some students may have a troublesome home life, making attention to their homework problematic both for themselves and for their parents.

Benefits of Homework

Despite the problems and anxieties associated with homework, there is still much to be gained by appropriate out-of-school assignments. Students can practice and strengthen skills learned in class, learn responsible time management, and increase their overall knowledge. All homework, however, is not created equal. Parents' support will be needed to ensure that students attend to their assignments, and teachers will need to give assignments manageable in length and difficulty to produce maximum benefits from homework.

There are numerous procedures you can use to gain student commitment to homework and to maximize the likelihood of their doing the tasks you assign. Foremost, you want to ensure that homework assignments are *practical* as well as academic. As discussed in chapter three, practicality has to do with focusing on what will help students cope better in the world outside of the classroom. For example, will the assignment help the child develop better interpersonal skills, develop better health practices, be a more informed citizen, or learn basic skills useful in getting a job? You will need to help students be aware of how an assignment is linked to important life goals that will benefit them both now (e.g., help them to improve their grades, to learn to write better, to know how to use a computer, and to get along well with others) and later as adults (e.g., help them to get a good job, to be a good parent, and to have a more enjoyable life). In other words, each assignment should have a definite purpose that fits into an overall plan leading to outcomes beneficial to the student.

Demands of Homework

Students should have a clear understanding of the homework they are to do each day. Again, as noted in chapter three, you may write assignments on the board or use a hand-out. Older students may wish to record their assignments in a daily planner. You want to let students know early on how frequently you will be giving homework assignments (e.g., twice each week or daily). In addition, students need to have an idea of how much time you expect them to be spending on homework each night.

The actual time students spend on homework will vary from student to student and from grade level to grade level. National organizations for parents and teachers suggest between ten and twenty minutes per night for students in kindergarten through second grade and from thirty to sixty minutes for children in grades three through six (U.S. Department of Education 2003). The amount of homework usually increases as students get older, but even students in higher grades should not be overburdened with homework.

Spending between one and two hours on homework each night should be sufficient for most students to practice skills learned in class. But the amount of homework given depends on the students' abilities and their need for additional practice. We say more in chapter eight about how students spend their time after school and what might be done to help them develop good work habits, such as those related to completing school tasks.

If you are not the students' only teacher, you will want to coordinate your homework assignments with their other teachers (Patton, Jayanthi, and Polloway 2001). Patton, Jayanthi, and Polloway note that this task can be difficult, but that attention to what other teachers are requiring can reduce the likelihood that students will have inordinate amounts of homework. Teachers in different subject areas can agree, for example, to give homework on different days or agree to limit the homework given each day. Teachers might also work out a testing plan, so tests in different subjects fall on different days.

Help with Homework

Before sending students home with an assignment, you want to be certain they can do the work. It's usually a good idea to let them begin the assignment in class. This practice serves two purposes. First, getting started is often the most difficult part of any task. By providing encouragement and supervision at the start of an assignment, you are bolstering motivation to continue the task until it is finished. Second, if problems arise, you are available to offer the required assistance and to make suggestions regarding what remains to be done. Moreover, if the homework assignment involves something new to the students, be certain to provide step-by-step instruction as to how they are to proceed.

Homework ordinarily should be related more to practicing what students are learning at school than to developing new skills on their own. Nonetheless, inform student where they can get help if problems arise later. Perhaps they can telephone you before a certain time or call a classmate. Some schools have homework centers located in apartment complexes, community centers, libraries, churches, or other locales, where tutors and other paid personnel are available for a limited time each afternoon and evening.

As has been suggested, you might clarify your expectations and seek parental support through a class newsletter, telephone conversations, or e-mails. (Meeting with parents, discussed later in this chapter, is another option for discussions about homework.) You might also have additional written materials describing how parents can help their children be successful in school. One very useful government publication you can make available to parents in English or Spanish is *Questions Parents Ask about School* (U.S. Department of Education 2003). The handbook, which is only sixteen pages, offers many tips on how parents can help their child succeed in school. For example, there is a unit on how parents can monitor their child's schoolwork. The tips for parents include the following recommendations:

- Create a home environment that encourages learning (e.g., have a set daily time for doing chores and homework);

- Model behaviors that show the importance of learning (e.g., let the child see you read);

- Make sure the home has books, magazines, and newspapers;

- Limit television-viewing time;

- Show interest in the child's schoolwork (e.g., by attending school events);

- Offer praise and encouragement for school achievements.

Other units in the booklet provide answers to such questions as: How much homework should my child have? How should I help my child with homework? How can I be more involved with my child's school? The booklet is in the public domain, so you can download it to your computer and make the booklet or some part of it available to parents. You can also order the booklet. For more details, we suggest you go to www. ed.gov/offices/OIIA/pfie/questions/. Plus, you can go to the U.S. Department of Education website on the Internet and do a search on helping students with homework. *Questions Parents Ask about School* and many other useful resources will surface in your search.

Your communication with parents should clarify their role in helping with homework. You may want them to look over their child's work and offer occasional guidance, but you are not expecting them to teach academic skills. Be sure you are clear on this point; you don't want to convey the message that parents should go beyond a supportive role and perhaps end up doing the homework for the child. Parents need to know that the homework is not for them.

You can provide parents with a list of questions they can ask their child regarding homework. Paulu (1998) has suggested including the following queries in your list of questions:

- What is the day's assignment?
- When is the assignment due?
- Are special resources required (e.g., access to a computer)?
- What supplies will you need (e.g., graph paper)?
- Have you already started? Finished?
- Would a practice test be helpful?

Homework in Perspective

Finally, in making homework assignments, you need to be respectful of students, parents, and yourself. You don't want students to be overburdened with homework. Sometimes you will need to consider other things that are happening in your students' lives. Special events and celebrations in which students are involved, for example, might be a reason to postpone an assignment. Similarly, you don't want to put the parents in the position of trying to teach material to students in order for the assignment to be completed. Instructions about homework should occur at school, although you can give your telephone number and e-mail address so students and parents can contact you if problems arise. You also want to avoid giving more homework than you and your assistant(s) can assess. In short, be kind to all involved. This strategy will reap more rewards than turning homework into a Herculean task for everyone.

Meeting with Parents

Face-to-face meetings are generally the best way to communicate with parents and to form relationships that will enhance cooperation between teachers and parents. Research indicates that parents are most likely to attend school events involving contact with their child's teacher (Carey and Farris 1996). In their study, Carey and Farris noted that 57 percent of public elementary schools reported most or all parents attended regularly scheduled schoolwide parent-teacher conferences and that 49 percent reported most or all parents attended open-house or back-to-school nights. In contrast, only 12 percent of the elementary schools said most or all of the parents attended sporting events, such as field days or other athletic events. Inasmuch as open houses and parent-teacher conferences are widely attended and are crucial components of good parent-teacher relationships, let's look at each in more detail.

Open House at School

An open house near the opening of school allows the school to put its best foot forward and tell about what students will be doing over the course of the school year. Open houses are generally not the time for conferences about individual children. However, if a parent indicates a need for an individual conference during the open house, you can schedule a meeting for later. You can also indicate when regularly scheduled parent-teacher conferences will be held.

In one survey, 97 percent of all public elementary schools reported holding an open house or back-to-school night (Carey and Farris 1996). If your school happens to be one of the few not holding such events, you may want to offer your assistance in organizing one. Getting parents involved in planning an open house is also a good way to ensure the event's success (Moles 1996). Your school principal probably has ideas about how to involve parents in planning an open-house agenda, but you may wish to have parents involved in planning what will take place in your own classroom. In addition, teachers may make the program more interesting to parents by giving them an option to try an activity students have been doing or by having students conduct a few learning activities to do with parents (Moles 1996).

Attendance at school open houses may be improved by providing baby-sitting services and offering transportation for parents. These options can be advertised in any advance publications conducted in an open-house campaign (Moles 1996). Moles also notes that having students design invitations, mailing an invitation to every parent, placing posters in local businesses, telephoning parents, and making school announcements on the day of the event may be helpful ways of increasing participation in open houses. (Many other strategies for involving parents can be found in the booklet edited by Moles, which includes strategies adapted from *Parent Involvement Fact Sheets* and *Parent-School Collaboration: A Compendium for Parent Involvement*, both of which were published by the Massachusetts Department of Education.)

Parent-Teacher Conferences

Parent-teacher conferences are among the most frequently used means for communicating with parents. An initial parent-teacher conference is often held at the end of a grading period. Other conferences may be scheduled when a student is having difficulty related to conduct or to academic standards. The focus in a regularly scheduled conference is to describe the teacher's expectations and to identify ways in which the teacher and parents can work together to improve the child's chances for success. The focus of the problem-centered conference, in contrast, is finding a solution to a specific problem a student is having in school.

A friendly conversation between a father and a teacher.

APPRECIATING CULTURAL DIFFERENCES

Ms. Wilson, a sixth-grade teacher, recently relocated to a new city. Her first introduction to her new classroom yielded an array of names unfamiliar to her and foretold a great deal of cultural diversity in her classroom. Ms. Wilson decided to take advantage of the differences by devising teaching units that would allow students to share unique aspects of their cultural background with others. She reasoned such an approach would increase students' knowledge and foster an appreciation of cultural differences.

In preparation for parent-teacher conferences, Ms. Wilson spent time researching cultural differences and strategies for working with families and children from different backgrounds. Her goal was to understand the values, beliefs, and concerns of her students' families. She reviewed her expectations for each student in light of her knowledge about the student's background. During the conferences, she encouraged parents to provide their expectations both of her and of their child. Some beliefs were very similar to hers, but others were different from her personal cultural heritage. By considering each parent an ally and a resource, she attained a better understanding of each student and an appreciation for the motivations underlying her students' behavior.

Unlike an open house, which is group oriented, parent-teacher conferences are one-on-one encounters and consequently can be more intimidating for both parents and teachers. Parents entering a classroom to meet with a teacher may face a flood of memories, both positive and negative. They may have failed in school, faced ridicule at school, or never completed school. They may view their educational level as quite limited. The teacher may represent an authority figure with whom they may not agree, but with whom they feel powerless to disagree. As a result, their ultimate reaction may be a passive one. That is, they may simply be hesitant to interact openly with the teacher or to follow through on suggestions made by the teacher.

Teachers may be overwhelmed and frightened by the prospect of meeting so many parents for individual conferences, especially parents whose background is different from their own. The teacher also may fear that questions will be raised about what they are teaching or how they are meeting students' needs. Thus, it is important to both teachers and parents to reduce anxieties and make the conference as pleasant as possible for all parties. The teacher needs to take the initiative in this case.

Demonstrating Respect. An essential facet of reducing anxieties about parent-teacher conferences is building respect. Any number of seemingly small gestures can prove beneficial. Potter and Bulach (2001), for example, suggest that scheduling conferences at a convenient time and location for parents, being punctual, smiling and shaking hands when greeting parents, providing comfortable adult seating, and removing physical barriers between you and parents are ways to build trust and respect. You also want to ensure privacy and meet in a setting free of noise, with no interruptions. Moreover, you want to regard parents as equals. Jordan and colleagues (1998) proposed that parents be viewed as partners and treated with the same respect as a colleague. They recommended that educators acknowledge parents as the primary advocate for their children. Such a view can help you understand and appreciate parental perspectives should disagreements arise.

Beginning a conference on an affirmative note can set a comfortable tone for the conference. Showing the parents examples of their child's better work, especially work demonstrating progress, provides a good starting point. Recounting a positive behavioral incident involving their child can also increase positive parent responses and thus help reduce teacher tensions. Behavior and academic areas needing improvement should be discussed. Having a clear-cut agenda is a way of showing others you respect their time. Allowing enough time for them to ask questions and not feel rushed is also important. Finally, we suggest the conference end on a positive note. As you summarize the meeting and discuss any follow-up that might be required, you can express your appreciation for the parents meeting with you.

Listening. Talking and listening are mutually exclusive, so be prepared to share talking time during the conference. Parents can tell you a great deal about their children's likes and dislikes and effective ways of relating to them. They can tell you what they see as important educational goals for their children and how they might work with you to promote attainment of those goals. As you listen to parents, be sure to communicate nonverbally your interest in what is being said. For example, you should make eye contact with the speaker and avoid tapping your feet, fidgeting in your chair, or shuffling papers. Do not interrupt. Although at times you may anticipate what the parent is going to say, give him or her the opportunity to say it. Don't be in a hurry. Try to put yourself in the parent's place. Ask questions and reiterate your understanding of what he or she has said. You may be surprised at the improvement in your communication with parents if you master the principles of good listening.

Seeking Feedback. In addition to listening to parents, you must be able to convey information to them about their children. You may sometimes feel they are not listening or understanding what you are saying. At such times, you might ask them to reflect their understanding of what you have said. For example, you might ask, "How are you interpreting what I am saying?" or "What is your understanding of the point I'm trying to make?" This technique should allow you to clear up misunderstandings that might otherwise impair further communication. If you find parents are misinterpreting what you say or if you detect hostility, anger, or strong defensiveness, communication has probably broken down. In that case, you will need to search for common points of agreement and renew the communication process.

PARENT-TEACHER MISCOMMUNICATION

Mrs. Jarvis came to school one afternoon to talk about her son Bob's recent dislike for school. She said he had always liked school previously, but now complained about school every morning during breakfast. Before Mrs. Jarvis could finish the story, the boy's teacher, Ms. Jordan, began to tell about how much she liked Bob and what a pleasure it was to have him in class. She said she didn't know what she might have done to cause the problem. She continued to direct the conversation and was feeling hurt she was being unfairly criticized for something she didn't feel was her fault.

In reality, Mrs. Jarvis was not there to criticize the teacher. Her son, a first grader, was actually intimidated by having to eat lunch with older second- and third-grade students. When Mrs. Jarvis finally got a chance to relate all the details of her son's problem, Ms. Jordan was relieved she hadn't done anything to upset the child, but she was also embarrassed at having jumped to conclusions. She indicated she would have her students eat together with their peers rather than mixing them in with older students. In a few days, Mrs. Jarvis reported Bob was fine and once again felt comfortable at school. Better communication between the parent and teacher, however, could have resulted simply from the teacher's taking time to listen.

If you have parents with limited proficiency in English, you may need to seek the help of an interpreter to ensure that you and the parents have a clear understanding of what the other is saying. Sometimes other family members may have English proficiency greater than the parents. In such cases, you might encourage parents to invite a family member to join the conference to serve as the interpreter.

Managing Problems. Sometimes you may be faced with parents who are dissatisfied either with a past incident in your class or with a school procedure. Parents occasionally become irate and may come calling unexpectedly. How do you deal with an angry parent, especially if a meeting has not been scheduled? Your agenda should be twofold: defuse some of the parent's anger and keep control of your own emotions. Keep in mind that both of you are committed to helping the child. The following suggestions may be helpful in coping with such a crisis:

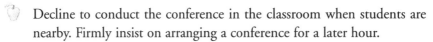

- Decline to conduct the conference in the classroom when students are nearby. Firmly insist on arranging a conference for a later hour.

- Speak calmly during the conference, and the parent may eventually do likewise. Measure your words carefully and refrain from going on a counterattack.

Respond to the feelings that lie behind parental statements rather than to the content (e.g., "You are really concerned about . . ." or "You're very angry about what happened in class yesterday"). This response communicates that you understand parents' feelings and reduces the likelihood of an incident being turned into something personal against you.

Help the parents explore the ramifications of different solutions, with the mutual goal being to help their child. Attempt to work out at least a beginning solution to the problem. If possible, arrange for both of you to implement some aspect of that solution.

Arrange for follow-up communication. Ask the parents to call and report, positively or negatively, on what has happened with their child since the conference. Do not be afraid to say, "I don't know," "I may be wrong," or "Call me if things don't go well." Hearing teachers admit they are not always right may be reassuring to an irate parent.

Utilizing Resource Specialists. Resource specialists often have more contact with some parents than do regular classroom teachers because they are involved with students who have problems requiring specialized services. School social workers, for example, often

---

A SECOND OPINION

Mrs. Ruth, a ninth-grade teacher, was surprised at Mr. Pritney's angry reaction to her assessment of his son's academic problems. Her intention had been to make him aware of the problems as she saw them, but Mr. Pritney strongly disagreed with her and tried to prove his point with examples. She felt compelled to defend her position, given that she saw the boy in a different context than did Mr. Pritney. After much discussion and no agreement, Mrs. Ruth asked that the conference be terminated and suggested they meet again after they had time to think more about the problem areas.

During the week, Mrs. Ruth made an appointment with the school counselor to discuss what had happened and to consider how to handle the conference next week. The counselor arranged a role-play session to explore the implications of reacting in different ways. Through the session, Mrs. Ruth became aware that her desire to have Mr. Pritney agree with her had resulted in a failure to hear or accept what he had to say. The result was an impasse. With the insight Mrs. Ruth gained from working with the counselor, she and Mr. Pritney were subsequently able to begin understanding each other in addressing the problems related to his son.

It is important that teachers and resource personnel are committed to helping the child.

work with parents to identify community programs that can help address families' personal and financial needs and ensure proper care of the child. Similarly, a speech pathologist may be working with parents in promoting speech development of their child, or a technology specialist may be helping parents develop computer skills needed for working with a child at home or for communicating with the school via e-mail. It is important for classroom teachers to work with all resource specialists, including the special educator, school psychologist, guidance counselor, school nurse, or other resource personnel to facilitate good relationships with parents.

Team-planning conferences constitute a way for resource personnel and the regular classroom teacher to combine their collaboration with parents of a student who is having problems. Planning prior to the conference should be done jointly. The contribution each professional can make toward the child's development should be delineated, and the ways the services complement each other should be outlined for the parents. All school professionals involved in the conference should make an effort to help parents feel at ease during the planning conferences. Having someone to greet them, introduce them to others in the meeting, and talk with them casually about nonthreatening topics before the formal beginning of the conference helps create a comfortable climate. Resource personnel and teachers can respond to parents' expressed concerns during the conference.

Both resource personnel and regular classroom teachers can help maintain close contact between the school and the home by sending frequent progress reports home and calling occasionally to check on a child. Inviting parents of children with exceptional abilities to visit the classroom and resource room can do much to allay parents' fears about whether a certain placement is right for their child.

Finally, although the principal is available to provide administrative guidance and support, you may occasionally wish to consult other support personnel such as the school counselor or school psychologist for specific suggestions as to how to relate to a particular parent (e.g., "What should I do if Jody's mother totally disagrees with what I have to say about Jody?"). Or you may wish to discuss a recent conference with a parent and receive feedback concerning the appropriateness of your own comments in the conference. Did your behavior help to reassure the parent that the two of you are working together to help the child?

A Final Note of Caution. When you are communicating with parents, you should realize that they will often attempt to cooperate with you or school authorities even though they have misgivings about what they are asked to do. Parents take seriously and may rigorously implement any casual suggestions made by teachers. Teachers should take care to ensure that the ideas they present to parents are both workable and likely to succeed for their child. A method of evaluating success and failure should be given to the parents. Failure can create self-blame for not doing things correctly, although the technique itself may have proven inappropriate. Parents should be told, "This may be helpful, but if it doesn't work, we will try something else." The teacher should follow up on any suggestions he or she offers to parents.

And More Can Be Done

Teachers and other school personnel can do a number of other things to strengthen communication with parents. Potentially useful approaches include workshops for parents (on topics such as how to handle discipline in the home setting), lunches for parents hosted by the principal, breakfasts with the teacher, and neighborhood coffees (Moles 1996). Besides gatherings between school personnel and parents, greater parental involvement can be achieved by using parents in a variety of volunteer roles, ranging from serving on curriculum committees to tutoring in classrooms. Much depends on the school's willingness to reach out to parents. Brainstorming sessions between teachers and parents may yield many creative ways of developing partnerships between the school and home. What additional ideas can you suggest for building bridges between you and your students' parents?

Final Thoughts: Benefits and Cautions

Involving parents is not always easy. If such involvement occurred naturally, the government would not need to mandate that schools develop policies to involve parents. Mandated policies, however, do not ensure the development of good relationships between parents and teachers. There has to be a willingness from both parties to work in the children's best interest. Teachers often have to take the initiative to help parents feel welcome in the schools. They may need to communicate, however, that parental involvement does not mean taking the role of the teacher in instructing their children. Alleviating fears in this area might be accomplished by clear delineation of the roles parents can play, such as listening to their children read, limiting television-viewing time, and making daily inquiries about homework. Teachers occasionally may need to refer parents to community agencies that can assist them with personal problems that are keeping them from being more involved in their children's education.

The benefits to the school in involving parents are numerous. Increased cooperation between the home and school can result in fewer disciplinary problems. Parents who understand and agree with a teacher's goals for their child can be expected to value the educational process and to communicate these values to their children. Community pride, enthusiasm, and commitment to the school can be increased. Conversely, when parents are left out of the educational process, lack of commitment to the school and misunderstanding of school goals are likely outcomes. Contacting parents only when problems arise with a child may impede the development of a cooperative relationship between the home and school. When parents have negative feelings about their child's school or teacher, these feelings are often communicated to the child, who may then act out those feelings by creating disturbances in the classroom. Parents also talk to other parents. When a parent is happy with the school program, this satisfaction will likely be communicated to others. Better to have parents as allies working to resolve discipline problems and build good relationships than to have them uninvolved or unhappy.

Cooperation between the home and school also may reduce absenteeism. When the parents become involved and see the opportunities available to their children, they will be more willing to ensure that their children are in school. Much of students' underachievement is simply a result of being absent too frequently. Students must be in school if you are to be optimally effective in promoting their academic development. Parents represent your best partners in ensuring that their children are in school on a regular basis.

SURFING THE WEB

As with other topics, you can find invaluable information about working with parents by perusing the World Wide Web. For example, if you go to the US Department of Education website and enter the phrase "parental involvement," you will find 500 resources related to working with parents. You will find topics such as "perceived barriers to parent involvement in school programs," "ways schools encourage parent involvement in children's learning, "school-sponsored activities to promote parent involvement," "Florida Center for Parent Involvement," and much more. At the Florida Center for Parent Involvement, for instance, you will find a series of resources organized by themes (such as family empowerment, parenting support) that includes fact sheets for parents and professionals. You will also find translations in Spanish. You can also go to your own state's website and find useful information for working with diverse cultural groups.

If you don't find what you are looking for under "parental involvement," try looking under "parents and families." At the U.S. Department of Education website, you will find a number of editor's picks on this topic, including "parental involvement resources." In your web search, you will also discover clearinghouses that provide information related to working with parents. One such clearinghouse is the Clearinghouse on Early Education and Parenting, part of the Early Childhood and Parenting Collaborative within the College of Education at the University of Illinois at Urbana-Champaign. Their site provides numerous resources about parenting and early childhood education. Your favorite university may also have a website within their college of education that relates to parenting issues.

In case you want to do some translating in your work with parents, you can also look for translation services on the web. Enter English to Spanish, for example, in your search engine and you will find several free translation services. (There are also services that charge a fee, but we have found the free services to be very useful.) You merely type your message in English and select a language for the translation (Spanish is only one of many languages you may obtain). Once again, the resources are out there, but it will take a little time and effort to locate what you need.

In addition, teachers' job satisfaction may be increased as a result of positive relationships with parents. Nothing boosts their morale more than having a parent say, "I never really knew until now how much the school is trying to do for my child," or "I really feel good about Juan's school experience." There may be little difference in the academic programs of two adjacent school systems, but parent attitudes toward the systems can be significantly different. When parents are enthusiastic about a school program, teachers usually feel their efforts are being recognized, and, consequently, their enthusiasm also increases.

References

Carey, N., and E. Farris. (1996). *Parents and Schools: Partners in Student Learning.* Washington, D.C.: U.S. Department of Education, Office of Educational Research and Improvement.

Casper, L. M., and K. R. Bryson. (1998). *Co-resident Grandparents and Their Grandchildren: Grandparent Maintained Families.* Washington, D.C.: U.S. Census Bureau.

Chen, X., and K. Chandler. (2001). *Efforts by Public K–8 Schools to Involve Parents in Children's Education: Do School and Parent Reports Agree?* National Center for Education Statistics (NCES) no. 2001-076. Washington, D.C.: U.S. Department of Education, NCES.

Jacobson, L. (2002). Summit connects parents and teacher ed. *Education Week* 22(12): 3.

Jordan, L., M. E. Reyes-Blanes, B. B. Peel, H. A. Peel, and H. B. Lane. (1998). Developing teacher-parent partnerships across cultures: Effective parent conferences. *Intervention in School and Clinic* 33(3): 141–47.

Lazar, A., P. Broderick, T. Mastrilli, and F. Slostad. (1999). Educating teachers for parent involvement. *Contemporary Education* 70(3): 5–10.

Lazar, A., and F. Slostad. (1999). How to overcome obstacles to parent-teacher partnerships. *Clearing House* 72(4): 206–11.

Moles, O. C., ed. (1996). *Reaching All Families: Creating Family-Friendly Schools.* Washington, D.C.: U.S. Department of Education.

Nord, C. W., and J. West. (2001). *Fathers' and Mothers' Involvement in Their Children's Schools by Family Type and Resident Status.* National Center for Education Statistics (NCES) no. 2001-032. Washington, D.C.: U.S. Department of Education, NCES.

Patton, J. R., M. Jayanthi, and E. A. Polloway. (2001). Home-school collaboration about homework: What do we know and what should we do? *Reading and Writing Quarterly* 17: 227–42.

Paulu, N. (1998). *Helping Your Students with Homework: A Guide for Teachers*, edited by L. B. Darby. Washington, D.C.: U.S. Department of Education, Office of Educational Research and Improvement.

Potter, L., and C. Bulach. (2001). Do's and don'ts of parent-teacher conferences. *Education Digest* 66(9): 37–40.

Robinson, E. L., and M. J. Fine. (1994). Developing collaborative home-school relationships. *Preventing School Failure* 39(1): 9–15.

Schweiker-Marra, K. E. (2000). Changing teacher attitudes and actions to promote better parent-teacher communications. *ERS Spectrum* (summer): 12–18.

U.S. Department of Education. (1994). *Strong Families, Strong Schools.* Washington, D.C.:

U.S. Department of Education.

———. (1996). *Youth Indicators 1996/Children of Single Parents.* Washington, D.C.: U.S. Department of Education, National Center for Education Statistics.

———. (1998). *Factors Associated with Fathers' and Mothers' Involvement in Their Children's Schools.* National Center for Education Statistics (NCES) no. 98-122. Washington, D.C.: U.S. Department of Education, NCES.

———. (2003). *Questions Parents Ask about School.* Washington, D.C.: U.S. Department of Education, Office of Intergovernmental and Interagency Affairs, Educational Partnerships and Family Involvement Unit.

Williams, V. I. (1997). Passing notes to parents. *Teaching Exceptional Children* (September–October): 30–34.

Our very accomplished friend, Pat

7

◄○►

Including Everyone
Teaching Students with Special Needs

Pat, a long-time friend of ours, was born with cerebral palsy. Her illness slowed her speech, and she sometimes had difficulty getting her words out. She was also unable to walk until she was almost six years old.

After much physical therapy, Pat was eventually fitted with leg braces and corrective shoes. Her parents taught her at home until she was ready for third grade. Then her parents tried to enroll her in public school, but school officials suggested she be placed in a special-education class primarily for students with mental retardation. Her parents objected because they realized Pat was a bright child with physical disabilities requiring accommodations. Her uncle, a physician, also tried to convince school officials to permit Pat to be placed in a regular classroom. When his efforts failed, her parents enrolled Pat in a private school for girls, where she remained until she was ready for the seventh grade.

They again made efforts, without success, to enroll her in a regular public school classroom. Once more Pat was taught at home, but she later entered a private church school where she graduated from high school at age sixteen.

Pat went on to earn a bachelor's degree in mathematics from a major university, taught school for several years, and eventually earned a master's degree and a Ph.D. in statistics. She taught statistics at the university level until retirement, winning awards for teaching and coauthoring several statistics books. She also coauthored a number of articles with the authors of this text, developing and conducting statistical analyses.

Pat is well known for her pleasant disposition and helpfulness, especially to those needing assistance with statistics. If Pat were entering school today, she would have the right to be taught in a regular classroom thanks to the *Education for All Handicapped Children Act* of 1975. But parents' dreams to have their children's special needs properly identified and properly met have been fulfilled very slowly, or are yet unrealized.

To some degree, all students have special needs. What works with one student may not work well for another. Thus, effective teaching necessitates adapting one's academic program so that each child is appropriately challenged and engaged in learning activities, even though some students may have disabilities that make learning difficult. Some students also have negative life experiences that can adversely affect their ability to learn, and others may have special talents that need to be nurtured.

This chapter addresses the possibilities of teaching students with disabilities, students who experience home abuse or neglect, and students who are academically gifted. It is not intended to deal extensively with all special-education needs, but rather highlights the principal exceptions likely to be represented in your classes.

A Brief Background on the Development of the *Individuals with Disabilities Education Act* (IDEA)

Like Pat, many students in the 1950s did not have access to an appropriate education in the public schools. Even up to 1975, most regular classroom teachers had little contact with students who were known to have a disability; students with disabilities were often taught in special classes separated from their nondisabled peers. Students with undiagnosed problems, of course, were in regular classrooms, but the degree to which their needs were being met is questionable. Opportunities for students with disabilities improved when Congress enacted the *Education for All Handicapped Children Act* of 1975 (EHA) (Public Law [PL] 94–142). The law sought to improve the identification and education of children with disabilities and to ensure their rights to equal educational opportunities. Furthermore, the law was a congressional response to the fact that one million children with disabilities were being excluded entirely from the public schools and that more than half of the students with disabilities had only limited access to the educational system (Office of Special Education and Rehabilitative Services n.d.).

EHA guaranteed a *free appropriate public education* to *all* children, including those with any disability. The law also mandated that a written *individualized education plan* (IEP) be developed to meet the specific needs of each child receiving special-education services. Children with disabilities were also to receive their free appropriate public education in the *least restrictive environment* (LRE), which meant that students with disabilities were to be educated in regular classrooms when that would be for the mutual benefit of children with and without disabilities. EHA also extended legal protections to children with disabilities by giving parents access to their child's records (with the right to amend) and the right to participate in evaluation and decision-making procedures regarding their child's education. The law also mandated fair, nondiscriminatory, and appropriate evaluation by trained professionals of students with potential disability conditions.

> ## FOR MORE INFORMATION ON PARTICULAR DISABILITIES:
>
> Fortunately, you can quickly access many resources when you need more details. The world wide web, for example, can help you obtain information on virtually any disability and special need. The U.S. Department of Education is a primary source on every aspect of education and is easily accessed on the web. Moreover, your local education agency can provide guidance in meeting all students' needs.

Since the implementation of the EHA, which covered individuals between the ages of three and twenty-one, a number of amendments have been added to broaden coverage for children with disabilities. For example, legislation in 1986 expanded services under the EHA to children ages three to five through a mandated preschool program and established the Early Intervention State Grant Program for infants and toddlers (to age two). Amendments in 1990 changed the name of the law from EHA to *Individuals with Disabilities Education Act* (IDEA), placing "the child" ahead of "the disability." The 1990 amendments further expanded the original list of categories of students eligible to receive special-education and related services. Other amendments were made in 1992, primarily affecting services to infants and toddlers (Goodman 2003).

Substantial changes were made to IDEA in 1997 (discussed later in this chapter), which were still the law when this book was written. IDEA 1997 has maintained many of the components from earlier amendments, but has placed a new emphasis on educating students with disabilities in regular classrooms and having them follow the regular curriculum. Children from birth to age two currently receive services through early-intervention programs, and those from age three through twenty-one receive special education and related services through the public schools (Goodman 2003). If you are interested in more details in the law affecting students with disabilities, see Goodman's report entitled *What's Reauthorization All About* (2003) and the Office of Special Education and Rehabilitative

Services report entitled *History of the IDEA* (n.d.). You can also find updates and any amendments to the law at the web site of the National Dissemination Center for Children with Disabilities (NICHCY).

Important Provisions in IDEA 1997 Affecting Regular-Education Teachers

Provisions added to IDEA 1997 affected the regular-education teacher's role in working with students having disabilities. These changes are summarized in a publication entitled *IDEA–Part B Final Regulations: Provisions of Special Interest to Teachers* (1999b) prepared by the Office of Special Education Programs. Several of the changes impacting the teacher and increasing students' chances for success in regular classes are described in the next section.

IEP and the Regular-Education Teacher

One of the important regulations of IDEA 1997 is a requirement that at least one regular-education teacher be included as a member of the IEP team if the child is or may be participating in the regular classroom environment (Office of Special Education Programs 1999b). To the extent appropriate, the teacher must be involved in developing, reviewing, and revising the child's IEP (Office of Special Education and Rehabilitative Services 1999). Among other things, the teacher's role includes helping to determine appropriate positive interventions and supplementary aids for the child, as well as supports to be provided the child by other school personnel. Moreover, all regular-education teachers and special-education teachers who have responsibilities in implementing the child's IEP must have full access to the IEP. Parents must also have access to the IEP and be informed of their specific responsibilities and any accommodations that must be made to meet the child's needs.

Although regular-education teachers do not have to attend every IEP meeting, such as discussions unrelated to the teacher's role, failure to meet their obligations can result in serious consequences. Weishaar (2001), for example, notes four possible consequences for not following a student's IEP: a request by parents for a due process hearing, possible legal actions against the teacher, administrative evaluation of the teacher (with potential employment implications), and an inappropriate education for the child. Teachers should want to be involved in the IEP to the greatest extent possible—not because they must, but because they have direct contact with the child and can make recommendations concerning teaching approaches they have found useful in working with the child. Their involvement in discussions is also a means of obtaining helpful suggestions from other team members (e.g., parents, special educators, and educational specialists who can interpret test results) about how best to meet the child's needs.

Components and Development of the IEP

The IEP under IDEA 97 must include specific statements ensuring that a special-education student receives an educational program and related services that are appropriate for his or her needs. At the very least, the IEP must include the following information:

- Present levels of student performance, including a statement of how the disability affects the student's involvement and progress in the general education curriculum;

- Measurable annual goals, including benchmarks or short-term objectives;

- A statement of educational needs resulting from the child's disability;

- A statement of all needed services and supports, including special education, related services, and program modifications and supports for school personnel;

- Extent of nonparticipation with nondisabled students;

- Progress reporting;

Modifications needed for participation in statewide or districtwide assessments, or, if it is determined that the child cannot participate, why the assessment is inappropriate for the child and how the child will be assessed;

Transition needs for students age fourteen and older (Warger 1991, p. 1).

In developing the IEP, team members are responsible for considering the child's strengths and weaknesses, parents' concerns regarding the child's educational needs, and the results of the initial or most recent evaluation of the child. In addition, the team must consider a number of special factors:

Language needs for children with limited English proficiency;

Need for instruction in Braille if the child is blind or visually impaired;

Communication needs, including opportunities for a child who is deaf or hard of hearing to interact (in his or her language mode) with peers and professional personnel;

Need for positive behavior intervention or other supports if the child's behavior interferes with his or her own learning or that of others;

Need for assistive technology devices and services.

A summary of these requirements can be found in Warger's (1991) article in the NICHCY publication *IDEA Amendments of 1997* (National Dissemination Center for Children with Disabilities 1998).

Disciplinary Issues

The current IDEA has put certain disciplinary safeguards in place to balance concerns about school safety, while protecting the rights to a free appropriate public education for students with disabilities (Office of Special Education Programs 1999a). For example, the law permits schools to place a student in an alternate education setting for up to forty-five days for weapon and drug offenses. This zero-tolerance provision for serious acts of misconduct applies equally to students with or without disabilities. However, "95% of students in special education who are suspended or expelled do not exhibit the violent or aggressive behaviors that are the intended targets of 'zero tolerance' policies" (National Association of School Psychologists 2002, p. 2).

IDEA also guarantees no cessation of services when a change in placement occurs for a student with disabilities. (A change in placement results when a student is removed from his or her current placement for more than ten days or when a pattern of removals accumulates to more than ten days in a school year.) Further, the law requires that the IEP team develop positive behavior-intervention plans for a student with a disability whose behavior interferes with his or her learning or with that of others and when there is a change of placement.

The regular teacher who is a member of the IEP team will be involved in deciding whether a behavior is actually a manifestation of a disability and will then participate in developing plans to address the troubling behavior. If the student's behavior is found not to be a manifestation of the disability, discipline can be the same as that for other students, but services must continue so the student can progress in the general curriculum and move toward meeting goals set forth in the IEP.

As we have mentioned many times, the teacher's primary approach to discipline should be on teaching behaviors that will help all students be successful inside and outside the classroom. The current IDEA promotes a proactive approach by requiring the IEP team to consider the need for positive behavior supports. Positive behavior interventions, strategies, and supports "emphasize the importance of making positive changes in the child's environment in order to improve the child's behavior" (National Association of School Psychologists 2002, p. 3).

Departments of education in each state generally offer information on appropriate disciplinary strategies for all students and on procedures that IEP teams should use in

FUNCTIONAL BEHAVIOR ASSESSMENT

"'Functional Behavior Assessment (FBA)' is a process for analyzing the reason why students engage in certain behaviors. The FBA examines the context (antecedents and consequences) in which behaviors occur. The process provides educators an opportunity to develop effective intervention plans as part of the IEP for the students with disabilities" (Tennessee State Board of Education n.d., p. 6).

In conducting the FBA, the assessor, typically the school psychologist, makes classroom observations to determine what is happening prior to a troubling behavior (the antecedents) and what the payoffs for the behavior are (the consequences) that sustain the behavior. The observer, for example, might look at academic activities taking place prior to the behavior, who was present with the student, time of day, physical context, and a range of other setting events that might be setting the stage for troubling behavior. The observer also assesses whether the student is getting peer attention, teacher attention, a desired item, or other payoffs. The student is possibly avoiding a frustrating task by exhibiting the problematic behavior. Once the assessment is made, plans can be implemented to develop appropriate, alternative behaviors. Ideas suggested in chapter three can be used to prompt desirable behaviors, and strategies suggested in chapter four can be used to strengthen and maintain those behaviors.

developing positive support systems, including the development of behavioral intervention plans based on *functional behavior assessments*. Finally, you should not be concerned that following a child's IEP and focusing on positive strategies will make your job more difficult. Instead, appropriately meeting each student's needs will prevent many student problems, making your classroom experience much more pleasant.

Technology Devices and Services

As noted earlier, the IEP team must determine if the child needs technology devices and services and then specify in the IEP the type of assistance needed. In addition, if it is determined that the student needs assistive technology devices in the home or in other settings, school-purchased devices must be provided (Office of Special Education Programs 1999b). Indeed, all services provided through special-education programs are to be provided at no cost to parents. The term *special education* "means specially designed instruction, at no cost to the parents, to meet the unique needs of a child with a disability, including—(i) instruction conducted in the classroom, in the home, in hospitals and institutions, and in other settings; and (ii) instruction in physical education" (Code of Final Regulations [CFR].

TECHNOLOGY DEVICES AND SERVICES

An *assistive technology device* is defined under IDEA as being "any item, piece of equipment, or product system, whether acquired commercially off the shelf, modified, or customized, that is used to increase, maintain, or improve functional capabilities of a child with a disability."

Assistive technology service is defined as "any service that directly assists a child with a disability in the selection, acquisition, or use of an assistive technology device. It includes:

a. The evaluation of the needs of such a child, including a functional evaluation of the child in the child's customary environment;

b. Purchasing, leasing, or otherwise providing for the acquisition of assistive technology devices by children with disabilities;

c. Selecting, designing, fitting, customizing, adapting, applying, maintaining, repairing, or replacing assistive technology devices;

d. Coordinating and using other therapies, interventions, or services with assistive technology devices, such as those associated with existing education and rehabilitation plans and programs;

e. Training or technical assistance for a child with a disability or, if appropriate, that child's family;

f. Training or technical assistance for professionals (including individuals providing education or rehabilitation services), employers, or other individuals who provide services to, employ, or are otherwise substantially involved in the major life functions of that child." *(IDEA 1997, 34 CFR § 300.5 and § 300.6.)*

§300.26). Furthermore, a student does may not have to be eligible for special-education services in order to receive services. Section 504 of the *Disabilities Act* of 1973, a law prohibiting discrimination against persons with disabilities, requires that all students with disabilities be provided a free, appropriate public education (ERIC Clearinghouse 2003). Any student with a disability who is not eligible for services under IDEA should be referred

SPECIAL-EDUCATION TEACHERS AND THEIR ROLE

All special-education teachers must be licensed as such, which requires special training in working with individuals with disabilities. Licensure requirements, however, vary by state. A minimum of a bachelor's degree, with special-education coursework, is required in all states, and some states also require a master's degree in special education. Because of the additional coursework requirements for special education, training to be a special educator is typically longer than that required to be a regular classroom teacher.

Special-education teachers work with students in a variety of settings. Some special educators, for example, team teach with a regular-education teacher, offering special instruction to students with disabilities. Others serve as a resource teacher in several classrooms, providing individualized instruction for a few hours each day in each classroom. Still others work in a resource room where students receive special instruction for a portion of each day. Some have their own classrooms in which they teach only students with disabilities. Special educators also work in homebound programs and in residential and hospital settings. Some also work primarily with infants and toddlers.

Like regular-education teachers, special-education teachers perform many work functions, including:

• Providing special teaching strategies, such as individualized instruction, problem-solving assignments, and small group work;

• Ensuring that students with disabilities who need special accommodations, such as having tests read orally, receive the accommodation;

• Working as a member of the IEP team to help others on the team develop IEPs suited to the needs of each student with a disability;

• Interacting cooperatively with parents to see that they are aware of their child's progress and to offer helpful suggestions for promoting learning at home;

• Designing and implementing appropriate curricula for students with special needs;

• Helping students develop appropriate social behaviors;

• Preparing students with life skills needed after graduation;

• Working with other school personnel to see that the curriculum is adapted to meet the needs of each child with a disability;

• Coordinating activities to meet requirements of inclusive education programs. (U.S. Department of Labor 2004–2005)

to the local school system's Section 504 Committee to determine what service can be provided (see the section "Related Services" below).

Of course, you do not have to rely solely on your technical skills to identify the technology devices and services needed by a student. The IEP team or the Section 504 team or both will provide guidance regarding what is required. Your school system should also provide training in using assistive technology, and there should be someone employed in the system whose role is to provide technology assistance to teachers and others (including parents and students). Those offering related services to students (e.g., audiologists, physical therapists, speech therapists, occupational therapists) will have expertise in technologies related to their specialties and will be a source of much useful information and assistance in using those technologies. On the Internet, you can also find articles related to the use of assistive technology and an extensive array of assistive technology devices, including many discussing computer programs and computer adaptations for students with and without disabilities. Your primary role will be to ensure that you use the resources available and that students use the accommodations available to them.

Expansion of Disability Categories

IDEA 1997 identifies twelve categories of disabilities (Office of Special Education and Rehabilitative Services 1998): specific learning disabilities, speech or language impairments, mental retardation, emotional disturbance, multiple disabilities, hearing impairments,

RELATED SERVICES

Students eligible for special-education services under IDEA are also eligible to receive related services. Students with disabilities who do not fall within the categories designated for special-education services, however, may be eligible for related services under Section 504 of the Disabilities Act. The regulations for IDEA define *related services* as including transportation and such developmental, corrective, and other supportive services as are required to assist a child with a disability to benefit from special education, and includes speech-language pathology and audiology services, psychological services, physical and occupational therapy, recreation, including therapeutic recreation, early identification and assessment of disabilities in children, counseling services, including rehabilitation counseling, orientation and mobility services, and medical services for diagnostic or evaluation purposes. The term also includes school health services, social work services in schools, and parent counseling and training. As with special-education services, related services are to be provided without cost to the parents. (IDEA 1997, 34 CFR § 300.24 [a]).

orthopedic impairments, other health impairments, visual impairments, autism, deaf-blindness, and traumatic brain injury. Students must be evaluated and found to be eligible under specific provisions of IDEA in order to participate in special-education programs and receive services provided under the law. IDEA 1997 also has added provisions permitting students with attention deficit disorder (ADD) and attention deficit hyperactivity disorder (ADHD) to be served under the category of other health impairment (Office of Special Education Programs n.d.).

The law also gives individual states the discretion to extend services to children ages three through nine who are experiencing developmental delays. This latitude includes a child (1) "who is experiencing developmental delays, as defined by the State and as measured by appropriate diagnostic instruments and procedures, in one or more of the following areas: physical development, cognitive development, communication development, social or emotional development, or adaptive development; (2) and who, by reason thereof, needs special education and related services..." (IDEA 1997, 20 U.S.C. 1400 § 300.7).

Assessment of Your Approach to Teaching Students with Disabilities

Students with disabilities may require special accommodations to help them make the most of their educational opportunities. For example, a student who has a disability that makes spelling difficult might need a hand-held electronic speller as well as appropriate computer programs to aid in the development of spelling skills. Others might need to use computer programs, such as text-to-speech software, to assist in the development of reading skills. Students who have a disability affecting the learning of mathematics would probably benefit by having instruction with math manipulatives and by using a calculator. Accommodations are not adjustments teachers make only for students with disabilities, however. Desiring the best educational results possible and making appropriate accommodations are basic to teaching all students.

Teachers will also need to pay special attention to the information contained in a student's IEP and to the guidance offered by others who provide related services to students with disabilities. For example, each IEP will include long-term goals and benchmark objectives that can be incorporated into the regular curriculum for special students and help to ensure that the student is making progress. The IEP will also include details regarding technology services and devices required for addressing the student's needs. As emphasized earlier, you should be familiar with each student's IEP and carefully follow all recommendations. If you have any doubts about your role on the team, you should schedule a meeting with the special-education teacher or the IEP team. An IEP team can make other recom-

ADDITIONAL GUIDELINES FOR WORKING WITH MOST STUDENTS

The following guidelines should be useful in working not only with students with disabilities, but with all students in your classroom.

• Break down assignments into small, manageable units that will provide the student with more immediate feedback and frequent success experiences.

• Make directions simple and present them one at a time unless the student has demonstrated the ability to handle multiple directions.

• Modeling how to follow directions, in addition to giving verbal direction, can be extremely beneficial for some children.

• Review and regularly practice previously learned skills.

• Keep distractions to a minimum. Some students may benefit from the use of study carrels when working on difficult assignments.

• Reward students for successful completion of a task or task segment.

mendations when a student is not progressing as expected, and guidance can be sought in implementing the recommendations that might have proven problematic.

You should keep in mind several questions as you attempt to address the needs of students with and without disabilities:

Do you have high expectations for all students?

Are all students treated with respect?

Do you know the present performance level of all your students, as well as their strengths and weaknesses?

Have you developed goals and objectives to move students to higher levels of performance? (And are you familiar with the IEP goals and objectives for each student?)

Have you made necessary accommodations so that all students are involved in class activities and are progressing in the general curriculum?

Do your instructional activities allow each child to be properly challenged and to experience success?

Are students being reinforced for their efforts and achievements?

Have you provided opportunities for success through use of techniques such as behavior shaping?

Are students being helped to appreciate their own efforts and achievements rather than relying solely on you for reinforcement?

Have you involved parents in their children's education, and do you keep them informed of their children's progress?

Are you working closely with others (e.g., special educator, technology service providers, related services personnel) in addressing students' needs?

Do you have strategies in place so that students learn skills needed for working in cooperative group activities and for working independently?

Initiative in Making Referrals

Although IDEA mandates that school systems develop "child find" programs to identify children in need of special-education services, including children in private schools, the identification of children with disabilities is not automatic. For example, children of immigrants, homeless parents, itinerant workers and others who move frequently, as well as children whose problems don't emerge early in life, may not be readily identified as needing special-education services. In fact, teachers may be the first to recognize a student who needs special services.

As a general rule, you should seek assistance in dealing with student problems you cannot correct and that are interfering with students' academic achievement and personal development. Never assume someone else has already sought or will seek proper assistance. When in doubt about making a referral, you should consult a resource specialist in your school system (e.g., school nurse, school social worker, counselor, school psychologist, special-education teacher). Your school, however, has referral forms you will need to complete when making a referral. An intervention assessment team typically determines whether the child requires evaluation to establish the presence of a disability. If the child needs only a different instructional approach or a change in management strategies, you will have at least a better understanding of how to proceed with the child. With such assessments, you can better meet a child's immediate needs irrespective of whether he or she has been formally identified as having a disability.

As a teacher of regular-education classes, you won't always be able to tell whether the problems a child is exhibiting fit within the parameters of a specific disability. It is the job of other professionals, who evaluate the child to determine whether the child is eligible for special services under IDEA or Section 504 of the Disabilities Act. Once you make a referral, other professionals can determine what specific disability, if any, the child has and what services are needed.

Home-Related Problems

Many legislative and public-school initiatives are aimed at ensuring that children have equal educational opportunities. Obviously, not all children come to school from equal home environments. Chapter six highlighted ways you can work with parents to enhance the educational opportunities of their children. However, there are times when outside intervention is needed. According to the U.S. Department of Health and Human Services (2004), 896,000 children were the victims of abuse or neglect in 2002. More than sixty percent of these children were being neglected by parents or other caregivers. Other children were subjected to maltreatment in the form of physical, sexual, or emotional abuse. For example, twenty percent of the child maltreatment cases in 2002 were related to physical abuse, ten percent to sexual abuse, and seven percent to emotional abuse. Indeed, child abuse is widespread and not restricted to any socioeconomic level.

All states now have laws requiring that neglect and abuse be reported. Absolute proof of neglect or abuse is not necessary for you to file a report; suspected abuse also should be reported. You should be aware that your report needs to be treated as confidential information. School policies will dictate to whom reports should be made, which typically includes the school principal. However, you should follow up to see whether the problem is being addressed. You can also make direct reports to your local Department of Social Services and other child protection agencies.

As pointed out in Crosson-Tower's manual (2003), physical signs of maltreatment are among the most readily observable. A child, for example, may have extensive bruises in different stages of healing, adult bite marks, burns, signs of

RECOGNIZING CHILD ABUSE AND NEGLECT IN THE CLASSROOM

The National Clearinghouse on Child Abuse and Neglect Information has an excellent document, Recognizing Child Abuse and Neglect in the Classroom (2004), which you can obtain on-line at its website. The article emphasizes that educators can pick up on signs of abuse and neglect through observations of students' classroom behaviors and physical appearance, as well as during routine interviews with their parents. The article notes that educators should attend to a cluster of signs rather than relying on any single indicator of abuse or neglect.

malnourishmnet, have poor, or have inappropriate clothing for the time of year. Wearing too much clothing might be a way of covering up bruises or other injuries. Too little clothing might be an indication of neglect. However, your report should specify only what you observe rather than propose a diagnosis of child abuse.

Behavioral clues of abuse may exist alone or can accompany physical signs of maltreatment (Crosson-Tower 2003). For instance, children may have sexual knowledge beyond that of their age group or act in a sexually aggressive manner toward younger children. Abrupt changes in children's behavior, such as a drop in academic performance or loss of interest in activities that the child previously enjoyed, can be symptomatic of maltreatment. Being fearful of adults or exhibiting low self-esteem and withdrawing from others can also be indicative of maltreatment.

Educators may also recognize signs of maltreatment though contacts with parents or other caregivers. Child abuse or neglect, for example, can be indicated when a parent frequently does any of the following:

- Blames or belittles the child;

- Treats the child as very different (in a negative way) from his or her siblings;

- Describes the child as "bad," "evil," or a "monster;"

- Shows minimal concern about the child;

- Fails to keep appointments or refuses to discuss problems the child may be having in school;

- Misuses alcohol or other drugs;

- Behaves in a bizarre or irrational way (Crosson-Tower 2003).

Conversations with children can also provide indicators of abuse and neglect. In talking with children, however, teachers should avoid pressuring students for information or making promises of confidentiality they cannot keep. When children reveal information that suggests abuse or report maltreatment, teachers should let the child know they will be supportive but will also have to report the information. The National Clearinghouse pamphlet suggests that interviews with the child should be by the person in the school who is most competent in interviewing. That person should be caring and supportive and someone the child trusts. The school counselor or other member of the school staff (e.g., social worker) who is familiar with problems of abuse and interviewing processes is the logical choice for conducting preliminary interviews. Referrals to appropriate personnel not only are required, but also provide the avenue for getting help for the child and for others involved in the neglect or abuse.

Intellectually Gifted Students

Giftedness is not covered under IDEA. However, funding for gifted student programs is available through grants provided under the *Jacob K. Javits Gifted and Talented Education Act*, which was reauthorized in 2001 (U.S. Department of Education 2003). State and local school systems also provide funding for gifted student programs. To receive special services, students have to meet specified definitions for being gifted or talented, which vary by state. In Tennessee, for example, *giftedness* "means a child whose intellectual abilities and potential for achievement are so outstanding that special provisions are required to meet the child's educational needs" (Tennessee State Board of Education n.d., p. 4).

Children who are academically gifted are typically identified by the high scores they achieve on standardized intelligence tests. Such tests rely heavily on verbal and mathematical measures, however, and may not identify all children who are intellectually gifted in other areas. For example, many students who have specific talents or who are highly creative may not obtain high scores on general measures of intelligence. Moreover, students from

A child with a special talent

diverse cultural backgrounds may not perform well on standard measures of intelligence. Students of color and students with limited English proficiency, perhaps for this reason, are under-represented in special programs for the gifted (Schwartz 1997). Teachers should also be alert to evidence of giftedness in children in magnet schools as well as in regular schools, irrespective of the students' background. Also, students who are not eligible to participate in programs for the intellectually gifted may be eligible to participate in other programs your school system offers to students with other special talents.

Just as children with disabilities are best served in regular-education classroom, students who are gifted also receive much of their education in regular classes. Parke (1992) indicates that the challenge for educators in meeting these students' needs is twofold: gifted and talented students must have a full-service education and must experience a challenging education suited to their needs and achievement levels.

Winebrenner and Berger (1994) suggest that gifted students benefit from alternative activities that expand basic concepts and allow them to pursue personal interests. This is not to be confused with extra-credit work, however. Instead, Winebrenner and Berger recommend *compacting* and *contracting*. In *compacting*, students who demonstrate previous mastery spend less time with the regular curriculum and more on enrichment opportunities. *Contracting* involves written agreements between the student and the teacher that permit students to work on alternative projects once they have learned the concepts the whole class will learn. The alternative projects agreed upon are selected sometimes by both teacher and student and sometimes by the student alone. Supervised independent activities and work at learning centers may also prove beneficial in working with students who are gifted.

Although educating students who are gifted in the regular classroom is most in keeping with the concept of inclusion, programs for the gifted are varied. Programs may include enrichment activities in the regular classroom or acceleration to a higher-level class. Acceleration may happen at any age of a student's academic career from kindergarten to college. Some students who are gifted receive instruction in selected subjects in a separate classroom, while maintaining contact with nongifted peers in a regular classroom for other activities. For example, they may take minicourses, advanced-placement courses, and honors classes, or they may attend special classes during vacation periods.

Gifted children frequently come to teachers' attention through a history of outstanding grades in the academic areas. Teachers may also be alerted to the presence of a gifted child by the child's superior score on a group-ability test or on standardized achievement tests. Students who complete especially creative projects in writing, science, or other subject areas and whose expressed ideas and questions are above expectation based on age and grade are also candidates for assessing their eligibility for gifted services. General signs of giftedness may be evidenced in one or more of the following characteristics (adapted from ERIC Clearinghouse on Handicapped and Gifted Children 1990, p. 4):

- Superior reasoning powers, such as being able to generalize from specific facts and ability to see subtle relationships;

- Intellectual curiosity—asking insightful questions;

- Broad range and depth of interest, particularly of an intellectual nature;

- Superior quality and quantity of written or spoken vocabulary or both;

- Avid reading;

- Quick learning, with good retention of what is learned;

- Insight into arithmetic problems and ready grasp of concepts;

- Creative ability or imaginative expression (e.g., in music, art, drama, and dance);

- Ability to concentrate for long periods and high level of personal responsibility in independent work;

- High standards, with the capability to evaluate and correct own work critically;

- Initiative and originality in intellectual tasks and flexibility in approaching problems;

- Keen observation skills, high responsiveness to new ideas;

- Skill in communicating with adults;

- Enjoyment of intellectual challenges and a subtle sense of humor.

The student who is gifted may not necessarily be the top academic student in the class. Owing to boredom and lack of motivation, some gifted students achieve well below their potential. Some students may also be poor spellers, have poor handwriting, or display other academic problems that keep them from being recognized as gifted and getting the services they need. Many also disdain routine and drill. Some are skeptical of what they are told. Bored with having completed tasks and not having work to do, students can also create disturbances or be viewed as being noncooperative. Indeed, teachers must look to the positive qualities of all students and be alert to any sign of superior cognitive skills and refer these students for participation in programs for the gifted and talented. It is better for teachers to over-refer than to miss students who may need special instruction to develop their superior talents.

Concluding Comments

Passage of the EHA opened new opportunities for a full and equal education for many students. Subsequent revisions of that act have further expanded services and the categories of disabilities being served. The current law, IDEA 1997, places a new emphasis on inclusion, the process of educating students with disabilities in regular classrooms and of having them follow the regular curriculum, as well as on the production of verifiable evidence of student progress.

With the new legislation, regular-education teachers have expanded roles that provide new and exciting professional opportunities. We think nothing is more exciting than helping students learn, especially students whose dreams for equal educational opportunities are finally becoming a reality. Furthermore, the dreams of students who come from environments where they have been maltreated may be fulfilled only by a loving and caring teacher who sees the potential for changing hurt lives. Other great opportunities exist in working with students who are gifted. The teacher who focuses on the development of each child's potential, whatever the level and nature of that potential, is the one most likely to find the greatest joy in teaching.

References

Crosson Tower, C. (2003). *The Role of Educators in Preventing and Responding to Child Abuse and Neglect.* Washington, D.C.: National Clearinghouse on Child Abuse and Neglect Information. Retrieved March 24, 2005 from http://research.acf.hhs.gov/pubs/usermanuals/educator/educators.cfm.

Education for All Handicapped Children Act of 1975. (1986). Public Law No. 94–142. 20 U.S.C. 1145. §§ 1401 et seq.

ERIC Clearinghouse on Disabilities and Gifted Education. (2003). *Section 504 of the Rehabilitation Act—Frequently Asked Questions.* Arlington, Va: ERIC. Retrieved August 18, 2004, from http://ericec.org/faq/sectn504.html.

ERIC Clearinghouse on Handicapped and Gifted Children. (1990). *Giftedness and the Gifted: What's It All About?* ERIC Digests no. E476. Reston, Va.: ERIC. Retrieved September 13, 2004, from http:www.ericfacility.net/ericdisgests/ed321481.html.

Goodman, S. (2003). *What's Reauthorization All About?* Washington, D.C.: National Information Center for Children and Youth with Disabilities (NICHCY). Retrieved July 16, 2004, from http://www.nichcy.org/reauth/Goodman.htm.

Individuals with Disabilities Education Act Amendments of 1997. (1997). 20 U. S. C. §1400 et seq.

National Association of School Psychologists (NASP). 2002. IDEA *Reauthorization: Challenging Behavior and Students with Disabilities.* Bethesda, Md.: NASP. Retrieved July 7, 2004, from http://www.naspcenter.org/factsheets/idea_fs.thm.

National Dissemination Center for Children with Disabilities. (1998). *The IDEA Amendments of 1997.* News Digest no. 26. Washington, D.C..: National Dissemination Center for Children with Disabilities. Retrieved July 23, 2004, from http://www.nichcy.org/pubs/newsdig/nd26txt.htm.

Office of Special Education and Rehabilitative Services. Office of Special Education Programs, U.S. Department of Education. (1998). *Twentieth Annual Report to Congress on the Implementation of the Individuals with Disabilities Education Act.* Washington, D.C.: Office of Special Education and Rehabilitative Services, Office of Special Education Programs.

———. (1999). *Regular Education Teachers as IEP Team Members.* Washington, D.C.: Office of Special Education and Rehabilitative Services. Retrieved August 8, 2004, from http://lobby.la.psu.edu/063_IDEA/Agency_Activities/Education/ED_Regular_Ed.

———. (n.d.). *History of the IDEA.* Washington, D.C.: Office of Special Education and Rehabilitative Services. Retrieved August 4, 2004, from http://www.ed.gov/policy/speced/leg/idea/history.html.

Office of Special Education Programs. (1999a). *Discipline for Children with Disabilities: Q*

& A Document from OSEP. Washington, D.C.: Office of Special Education Programs. Retrieved August 4, 2004, from http:www.ideapractices.org/law/addl_material/discipline.php.

———. (1999b). *IDEA—Part B Final Regulations: Provisions of Special Interest to Teachers*. Washington, D.C.: Office of Special Education Programs. Retrieved July 21, 2004, from http:www.ideapractices.org/law/briefs/teachers.php.

———. (n.d.). IDEA 97 *Final Regulations: Major Issues*. Washington, D.C.: Office of Special Education Programs. Retrieved August 4, 2004, from http://www.ideapractices.org /law/addl_material/majorissues.php.

Parke, B. N. (1992). *Challenging Gifted Students in the Regular Classroom*. ERIC Digest no. E513. Reston, Va.: ERIC Clearinghouse on Handicapped and Gifted Children.

Schwartz, W. (1997). *Strategies for Identifying the Talents of Diverse Students*. ERIC/CUE Digest no. 122. New York: ERIC Clearinghouse on Urban Education. Retrieved September 6, 2004, from http://www.ericfacility.net/ericdigests/ed410323.html.

Tennessee State Board of Education. (n.d.). *Rulemaking Hearing Rules of the State Board of Education*. Nashville, Tenn.: Tennessee State Board of Education.

U.S. Department of Education. (2003). *Jacob K. Javits Gifted and Talented Students Education Program*. Washington, D.C.: U.S. Department of Education. Retrieved September 7, 2004, from http://www.ed.gov/programs/javits/legislation.html.

U.S. Department of Health and Human Services. Administration for Children and Families, Children's Bureau. (2004). *Child Maltreatment 2002*. Washington, D.C.: U.S. Department of Health and Human Services. Retrieved September 5, 2004, from http://www.acf.hhs.gov/programs/cb/publications/cm02/summary.htm.

U.S. Department of Labor. Bureau of Labor Statistics. (2004–2005). Teachers—Special education. In *Occupational Outlook Handbook*. Retrieved October 18, 2004, from http://stats.bls.gov/oco/ocos070.htm.

Warger, C. (1999). *New IDEA '97 Requirements: Factors to Consider in Developing an IEP*. ERIC Digest no. E578. Reston, Va.: ERIC Clearinghouse on Disabilities and Gifted Education. Retrieved August 8, 2004, from http://lobby.la.psu.edu/063_IDEA/ Agency_Activities/Education/ED_IDEA_andIEP_0899.

Weishaar, M. K. (2001). The regular educator's role in the individual education plan process. *The Clearing House* 75(2): 96–98.

Winebrenner, S., and S. Berger. (1994). *Providing Curriculum Alternatives to Motivate Gifted Students*. ERIC Digest no. E524. Reston, Va.: ERIC Clearinghouse on Disabilities and Gifted Education. Retrieved September 6, 2004, from http://www.ericfacility. net/ericdigests/ed372553.html.

"Well, John, how are your students this year?"

"My students are OK . . . except that they don't work together very well and have trouble working independently."

"Hey, how can you say your students are OK if they can't work together or work independently? What else is there in schoolwork?"

"Actually there's a lot. As long as I am providing detailed instructions and close supervision, especially on a one-to-one basis, my students do OK. It's just when they have extended time on their own or when they're put in groups that things don't go well."

"What happens under those circumstances?"

"Well, when they're working independently, they may quickly get sidetracked to something else, usually trivial stuff, and then don't get their work done in a timely fashion. And if they encounter the slightest problem, instead of trying to work their way through it, they head for me to tell them what to do. In fact, they often have difficulty even getting started with independent work.

They can't find their pencils, the handouts I gave them, or paper to write on—there's always something missing. And when I put them in groups to review for an exam or to work on a project, they'll soon start talking about anything but the assignment unless I hover right over them. Even when they appear to be on-task in their groups, a few students will be doing all the work, and the other students will be sitting on the sidelines. Hey, I'm sorry. I'm telling you more than you wanted to know."

8

The Complete Package

Helping Students Develop Effective and Efficient Work Habits

Are John's students that different from students in most American classrooms? Although schools and even classes within schools vary widely with respect to independent work and group activity, a great deal of closely supervised individual work occurs in most classrooms. Certainly, this practice is not inherently bad. Students must understand how to do their work, and much of that understanding must come from the teacher. A significant amount of instruction can be given to the class as a whole, but some students will still have difficulty proceeding on their own. And as complete as the teacher's instructions might have been, some students won't be paying attention and will have trouble getting started or will soon get stuck.

One is likely to find more independent seat work than group activity in a cross-section of American classrooms. This pattern may be attributable to classroom-management problems that often emerge in group activities. Although students often need considerable teacher assistance even with independent work, there is less likelihood of off-task and disruptive behavior than when they're put in groups. Plus, the noise level in a classroom with much group activity, even when groups are on task, will be much higher than when students are working individually at their desks. Many teachers find this increased noise disquieting, and they fear giving the wrong impression about their class when the principal happens to drop by. There is still the notion among many practitioners that a good classroom is a quiet classroom.

Reasons for Promoting Good Work Habits

Even if self-directed work and group collaboration would be a welcomed change from dependence on teacher instruction, are they worth the necessary time and energy to mobilize and sustain them? Neither can occur without substantial teacher instruction. If there is more relevant content to teach than can be taught within the school day, why add the task of teaching independent and collaborative work habits? Why not teach just your subject matter, giving whatever degree of individual assistance is necessary, and call it a day?

Content versus Work Habits

There must be a greater outcome of schooling than just teaching content that students may or may not find useful in their adult lives. Admittedly, students need literacy and basic mathematical skills to function well as adults. A better understanding of the natural and social world also would be beneficial, especially if students are to make informed judgments

Working together could not occur without substantial teacher instruction.

about the use of natural resources and about the improvement of international relations. However, despite the long-term significance of some content taught in school, students will forget by adulthood much of the specific content they learned in school.

If our long-term aim as educators is to prepare students to function well as adults, then we must be concerned about how well students can manage their own work and how well they can work with others. Most students will eventually find themselves in work situations where both working independently and working together are at a premium. Individuals who must be supervised every step of the way, or who work well only on their own, are not the workers most companies and agencies want.

Independent versus Collaborative Skills

If we assume that both independent and collaborative work habits are important, which of them should be targeted first in helping students improve their work habits? It is unlikely that a student will be an important contributor to collaborative work without also having independent work skills. The student who lacks independent work skills will have to be told what to do in group work and will be inclined to let others take the initiative and assume the responsibility for accomplishing group tasks. Taking the initiative in organizing and doing one's own work is a practice that also can be valuable in group settings. Although some skills are somewhat specific to group work, they must be built on a foundation of independent work skills.

Independent work skills will benefit students not only when they become adult workers, but also while they are in school, for at least three reasons. First, students who develop the skills to acquire new knowledge and to monitor their own learning should be able to function more effectively in a variety of subject areas (Bransford et al.1986). Second, students may perform better both socially and academically when given increasing opportunities to manage their learning experiences. Research relating to opportunities for self-directed learning has suggested that students are more likely to accept responsibility for academic successes and failures if they can play a part in managing their own instruction (Arlin and Whitley 1978). Third, even though students cannot always make good judgments regarding what they should learn and how they should learn it, they sometimes can provide valuable input to the teacher as to what they can learn, what they want to learn, and how they can best learn it. Teachers would be wise to solicit and consider such student input in planning instructional activities.

The benefits of group-learning experiences can be as significant as learning to work independently. First, research indicates that, given the right conditions, group learning leads to better academic achievement than either individualistic or competitive learning (Slavin 1984, 1991). But the social and personal benefits of students' working together can be even greater than the academic benefits. The opportunity to bond within a group can provide some of the greatest incentives for coming to school. Plus, the social benefits of group work often reach beyond one's immediate work group. One learns to work more comfortably with those from different backgrounds and to develop friendships across a broader spectrum of peers.

Although effective work skills have numerous benefits, they can never completely free a student from some dependence on teachers. Students will always need instruction, encouragement, and feedback from teachers. In most cases, they must explicitly be taught how to manage their own academic work and how to relate well within groups. This chapter focuses on providing support for students as they attempt to acquire effective and efficient work habits. By *effective*, we mean working on important tasks rather than engaging in trivial activities, and by *efficient* we mean focusing on those tasks in a way that makes the best use of their time and resources. But before addressing the challenge of promoting effective and efficient work habits, we first examine American students' current work practices.

Problematic Work Tendencies

First, we must acknowledge that some students epitomize the best of both independent and group skills. Their family heritage undoubtedly contributes immensely to their exemplary work habits at school. At the other end of the spectrum, some students are repeatedly disruptive and off-task. Both of these groups represent the exception rather than the norm among American students. A majority of American students can be characterized as passively compliant (Spaulding 1992). They do enough to get by, while showing little initiative and enthusiasm about learning.

The percentage of passively compliant students varies from school to school. A private school that serves students from affluent homes with high academic expectations most likely has few passively compliant students. In contrast, a public school that has many students whose parents provide little support for education may have many passively compliant students, who see little purpose in attending school but still try to stay out of trouble at school. In addition, public schools often see a greater incidence of disruptive behavior than is evident in an elite private school.

Student habits that adversely affect academic performance are reflected both in school activities and in experiences beyond the school day. Because the teacher can have more influence on student work habits in the context of school, we first deal with habits related to school attendance and work patterns in the classroom. Then we examine how students' management of their time and activities outside of school can also affect their performance in the classroom. Obviously, some habits (such as attendance) are affected by what happens both in the classroom and out of school.

Work Patterns Related to School

Problems with student work habits are both dispositional and behavioral. On the one hand, some students appear to have either an indifference or an antipathy to working hard at school. They appreciate neither the satisfaction nor the importance of hard work. These students prefer to be doing almost anything besides schoolwork. On the other hand, some students attempt to do their schoolwork, but their approach is either misdirected or inefficient. Either they work hard on tasks that lead to trivial outcomes (ineffective), or they work toward important outcomes, but in such a halting and convoluted fashion that they seldom reach those outcomes (inefficient).

Absenteeism. No one can take full advantage of school opportunities without being present on a regular basis. Absenteeism is especially damaging in academic programs requiring sequential learning, where advanced skills cannot be developed in the absence of basic skills (Ediger 1987). School attendance can best be characterized as a necessary but insufficient condition for academic success (Haberman 1997). Missing school establishes a vicious cycle likely to become worse with time. As students miss school, they get further behind in their work, and the quality of their work suffers. Poor performance is likely to make school more frustrating and less reinforcing, leading to increased absenteeism (Georgiady and Romano 1994). Consequently, student attendance, or lack of, consistently predicts performance on both grades and standardized achievement tests (Lamdin 1996).

This cycle linking absenteeism and poor performance is especially pronounced for special students (such as those with learning disabilities, mild retardation, and emotional disturbance), resulting in higher rates of absenteeism than for regular students (Weitzman 1985). Nonetheless, the relationship between attendance and school achievement holds true for both youngsters with learning disabilities and those without (Heberling and Shaffer 1995). Research at the high school level also shows that absenteeism is substantially higher in inner-city schools than in other high schools (National Center for Education Statistics 1996). Nonetheless, African-American students who regularly attend classes at their urban high schools have higher grade point averages than those who attend less frequently (Steward, Steward, and Blair 2002).

Work Inhibition. One of the most mysterious work tendencies among students is what Bruns calls *work inhibition*, defined as "a history of not completing school assignments in all subjects for at least two years" (1992, p. 40). These students have the ability to do their schoolwork, but minimal motivation to do it. As many as 20 percent of public-school children may fall in this category, with three out of four work-inhibited students being boys. The pattern seems unrelated to socioeconomic level and typically does not include a high level of disruptive behavior. The paradox of work inhibition is that virtually everyone in the child's support network tries to promote the child's achievement. Parents of work-inhibited students may make extraordinary efforts to get their children academically mobilized, but to little avail.

Work-inhibited students are able to avoid schoolwork either by daydreaming or becoming preoccupied with almost any type of activity besides schoolwork. Although not well understood, work inhibition likely evolves from the failure to find satisfaction in the work experience. Work-inhibited students find little joy in the process of work and are indifferent to the widely perceived benefits of hard work. Thus, they are living in the moment, doing what is most comfortable in the present without regard to the future consequences of their choices.

Procrastination. Some students habitually run late in completing their work. They can always find something to do now instead of working on the target task. By putting things off, they make tasks increasingly difficult and reduce the payoffs for eventual task completion. Procrastinators usually have good intentions, worry about what they have not done, ignore negative feedback, and resent being reminded of work yet to be done (Broadus 1983). They appear to inflate the difficulty of tasks or perhaps underestimate their ability to meet task demands. Such phrases as "this is too hard" and "I can't do this" are common. Some regard their skills as so limited that they will look stupid by attempting the task. Thus, they would rather be judged as lacking effort than as lacking ability (Fiore 1989).

Although procrastination is often prompted by students' apprehension about their ability to do a task, it can also be fueled by mistaken notions about the choice of times to work on a task. This can be the case with either easy or difficult tasks. Some tasks are regarded as so easy that they can readily be done at any time, whenever the students might be in the mood. Other tasks appear so difficult that students wait for major blocks of time to begin work on those tasks. Because major time blocks (e.g., full days or full weeks) can be difficult to find, these students have difficulty getting started with larger tasks. Small blocks of time are seen as so inconsequential that students are disinclined to capitalize on them to begin major tasks.

A common mythical belief about the best time to work on a task is that many tasks can best be accomplished under time pressure (Szalavitz 2003). By delaying a task until the last minute, one still has not only the task to complete, but a very restricted time frame for completing it. No matter what one's mental or physical state at that time, the work must get done as the deadline nears. Yet many procrastinators claim that this time pressure energizes them to do their best work. Not true. Last-minute work is often done poorly, certainly at a lower level of quality than could have been accomplished by starting earlier and working steadily on the task.

Another impediment to initiating work on a task appears to be the lack of an organized strategy for attacking tasks. Even if a student understands that a particular task cannot be done at the last minute, his or her initiative in working on the task may be stalled by lack of clarity as to where to begin with the task, what subtasks will be involved in the larger task, and the optimal order for doing the subtasks. Indecision about any of these issues can keep the student in the starting block. For instance, the student understands that a term paper must be written and turned in by a specified date, but he or she has only a vague notion of how to proceed in identifying a topic and constructing different parts of the paper. Obviously, procrastination under these circumstances can heighten anxiety about what needs to be done to accomplish the task.

Weak and Erratic Effort. Muted and spasmodic effort is probably the number one contributor to underachievement in school. Many students are inclined to give up at the first sign of difficulty with a task. Unfortunately, children who give up easily in one situation are likely to do so in other situations (Hamilton and Gordon 1978; Stipek, Roberts, and Sanborn 1980). When students encounter difficult facets of assignments, their tendency may be simply to stop working or to wait for teacher assistance. The tendency to give up can have a pervasive effect on a child's learning. Children who persist at tasks learn more than those who give up when tasks become arduous (Stipek 1983).

Many students have problems in staying on task even when the tasks are within their skill range. On-task behavior is a strong correlation of academic performance (Cobb 1972; Prater, Hogan, and Miller 1992; Soli and Devine 1976; Wheldall and Panago-poulou-Stamatelatou 1991). Such behavior includes looking at the teacher as he or she gives instructions, taking notes as the teacher is talking, asking questions of the teacher, responding to the teacher's questions, and remaining actively engaged in independent and small-group learning activities.

Unfortunately, many urban students stay on-task no more than approximately twenty percent of the time, and their patterns of work tend to be disjointed (Haberman 1997).

Both teachers and students may overestimate or underestimate students' on-task behavior. Not surprisingly, students have a tendency to overestimate and overrate their level of on-task behavior (Mammolenti, Vollmer, and Smith 2002). And, in consulting with teachers, we have found that the teachers themselves often estimate the level of students' on-task behavior in keeping with their overall impression of the students. The same behavior (e.g., looking out the window, engaging in side conversations) may be judged as off-task for some students, but as neutral or positive behavior for other students. In fact, teachers can develop such a negative impression of some students that they claim these students are never on-task. Yet in our research projects that have assessed the on-task behavior of various types of students, we have yet to find a student who is never on-task. In fact, the minimum level of on-task behavior we have observed is approximately twenty-five percent.

Similar to giving up easily and getting off-task is submitting work prematurely when it is neither completely nor correctly done. Even when students are given feedback about changes needing to be made in their work, their revised work often reflects only the most superficial attention to that feedback. Students who submit their work prematurely seem to find relief in turning in their test papers or written assignments as quickly as possible. This tendency appears to be guided by the philosophy of doing the least possible to fulfill task requirements. The student may feel compelled to do the assigned work but have little incentive to do high-quality work.

"NOWNESS"

Martin Haberman (1997) has written about the concept of "nowness" that exists in many urban schools. The turnover in student enrollment from the beginning to the end of the school year may approach 100 percent in some urban classes. Plus, students are not inclined to take their textbooks home or complete homework assignments. In many urban classes, there is a virtual disconnect between what occurs in class today and what occurred yesterday or will occur tomorrow. Thus, each day's activities must stand alone, with no preparation required and no follow-up expected from the student. If students can be prodded or cajoled to participate in a class activity, even when the activity has no connection to activities on past and future days, urban teachers may regard the day's activity as a success.

A revered philosophical orientation to getting the most out of life is to live in the present. Certainly, one can become preoccupied with the past or the future at the expense of the present, but students must realize that what happens today can be closely linked to what happened yesterday and what will occur tomorrow. They cannot participate in a learning activity today for which they are unprepared, and the failure to benefit from today's learning activity can undermine their opportunities for future learning. There is probably no sphere in life more important than the classroom where each day's activity should build more directly on past activities and lay the foundation for future activities.

Disorganization of Work Materials. Student performance is often undermined by poor organization of work materials. The sheer amount of clutter at one's work station may impede finding what is needed for a particular task. Plus, the disarray can greatly undermine concentration on the task at hand. Organizational problems are legion within the classroom. Students forget, misplace, or lose even materials as basic as paper and pencil, textbooks, and instructional handouts. The jumble of materials in the student's desk or locker does not bode well for efficient retrieval of necessary materials. Research (Kops and Belmont 1985) has shown that low-achieving students typically have

Organizational problems are legion in lockers.

difficulty in organizing their work on school tasks and in selecting the right materials for the task at hand. Thus, these students need to be taught how to select task-related materials and how to arrange their materials to permit efficient retrieval of what is needed (Georgiady and Romano 1994).

Out-of-School Activities

Just as each day at school should be connected to past and future school days, what happens in the classroom is also connected to what occurs in the student's life outside of school. Students' choices about their use of out-of-school time can enhance or undermine their effectiveness in the classroom. If students spend seven hours a day at school, they have seventeen additional hours before the next school day that will significantly affect their performance that upcoming day. In those seventeen hours, students must find enough time for such activities as sleep, television viewing, and work responsibilities.

Sleep. Most students need more sleep than they get: they need nine to ten hours but are inclined to get seven to eight hours (Kantrowitz and Springen 2003). In fact, a recent survey by the National Sleep Foundation found that only fifteen percent of adolescents reported getting at least eight and one-half hours of sleep (the bare minimum according to health experts) on school nights. A web of lifestyle factors, some of which students have little control over, affect how much sleep they get. A troubled home marked by parental conflict can greatly erode time for sleep, and a financially poor home can require students to work long hours to help pay the family bills.

Obviously, time spent on such activities as TV viewing, Internet surfing, or working part-time affects time available for sleep. Rather than sleeping for whatever time remains after engaging in other high-priority activities, students first need to protect adequate time for sleep and then parcel out time for other activities. The failure to do so typically results in one of two outcomes: students come to school in a drowsy state, or they oversleep (thus missing school or coming to school late). Either outcome limits how much benefit these students derive from school, and affects the teacher's morale during the school day. Seeing glazed eyes and heavy eyelids surely does not boost the teacher's spirits, and missed class time greatly increases the challenge of providing a coherent learning experience for absent or tardy students.

Television Viewing. Some research and informal observation reveal that watching television is the most prevalent activity in which most students engage outside of school during their awake time (Wells and Blendinger 1997). Thus, one of the most critical choice areas for students is how much television they view and what programs they view. Children

Too much television, not enough sleep.

who watch television the most are regrettably also the most likely to watch programs that have little educational value (Fetler and Carlson 1982). Students from a lower socioeconomic background are most inclined to follow this viewing pattern, spending most of their after-school hours before bedtime watching programs replete with violence and frivolity.

Ironically, heavy television viewing may have a greater adverse effect on the academic achievement of students from professional families than on the achievement of students from less-educated families (Fetler 1984). Perhaps there is a greater contrast between television viewing and other options (e.g., books, newspapers) readily available to children in professional families than for children with less-educated parents. Whatever the family's educational level, it is heavy television viewing rather than moderate viewing that is counter to academic performance. In fact, viewing up to ten hours per week has been linked to school achievement in a positive way. Some television viewing likely helps the child stay in touch with events and options beyond his or her own community.

Part-time Work. As students progress to the high school years, increasing numbers are working part time, with work being a higher priority than school for many of these students (Kablaoui and Pautler 1991). High school students are twice as likely to have part-time jobs than was the case fifty years ago (Singh 1998). Unfortunately, research on the advantages and disadvantages of part-time work is relatively meager. Findings thus far on the relationship between part-time work and school experiences are mixed, with part-time work apparently contributing to academic performance under some circumstances, but detracting from school performance under other conditions. For instance, a part-time work experience is more beneficial if students have an opportunity to develop skills useful both in school and in future employment (Stern et al. 1995).

Another key issue in determining the effects of part-time work on school performance is how much time students are working. Cheng (1995) found that working up to fifteen hours a week was associated with greater time invested in homework and extracurricular activities as well as with a lower dropout rate. In some cases, these students are saving money for future educational opportunities (Wirtz et al.1988). However, the choice to work twenty or more hours a week is often prompted by disinterest in school and is followed by increased disengagement from school (Steinberg, Fegley, and Dornbusch 1993).

In general, students who work more than fifteen to twenty hours per week make lower grades, are more likely to drop out of high school, and are less likely to complete postsecondary programs (Stern et al. 1995). Some work experience may be beneficial, but long work hours are likely to undermine school success (Singh 1998). Overall, part-time work appears to have a slightly negative effect on academic performance in high school. The three major issues that will affect the potential academic benefits of work are the amount of work time, the nature of the work, and the use to be made of the earnings from the work.

School Strategies for Promoting Effective Work Habits

An overall approach for addressing most of the work patterns just described involves the following sequence of steps: (1) the teacher models good work habits, (2) the teacher creates a physical and academic environment conducive to focused task performance, (3) the teacher selectively rewards good work habits, (4) the teacher instructs students in how to talk themselves through difficult tasks, and (5) the teacher and students systematically assess work-related behaviors. The challenge is to make the classroom a place where effective work habits are expected and rewarded.

Modeling Good Work Habits

A culture of high, medium, or low work expectations characterizes most classrooms. That culture is defined in part by the behavior modeled by the teacher and by influential peers. It is unlikely that your insistence on good work habits for your students will be viewed as credible if your own work habits are suspect. What you model for your students may be the most powerful contributor to the development of their work habits.

The teacher's attendance, punctuality, organization of the classroom, and persistence at tasks are abundantly clear to students. For example, a teacher who begins a class or a school day without a clearly articulated plan can expect no better from students. Confused, misdirected, and off-task behavior are certain to ensue, potentially creating a multitude of discipline problems. Likewise, a teacher who announces planned activities and consequences, but who gets sidetracked from those plans hardly fosters student delivery on their commitments. A teacher whose handouts are replete with typos and grammatical mistakes cannot expect students to give close attention to the technical quality of their work. A teacher who fails to return student work in a timely fashion and even loses student work cannot expect students to be on top of their work.

Creating a Constructive Classroom Environment

Numerous facets of the classroom environment can affect the likelihood of productive student behavior, including the physical order, difficulty of learning tasks, oral and written explanations, and individual versus group tasks. Although these factors do not ensure that students will generally be on-task, they can at least create a climate conducive to on-task behavior.

Physical Order. A moderate amount of physical order in the classroom likely contributes to good work habits. The teacher must identify specific places to store materials used by both teacher and students, locate commonly used materials and equipment in readily accessible areas, have a scheme for putting things away when they are not in use, develop a system for minimizing clutter in the classroom, establish a routine for periodically cleaning furniture and work space, and add items that will increase the aesthetic appeal of the classroom (e.g., area rugs, easy chairs, lamps, and paintings).

The major objectives in helping students organize their work spaces are to promote easy retrieval of needed materials and to maximize concentration on assigned tasks. Developing a format that students can use in storing materials in their desks and lockers would be advisable. Because these spaces are small, it is all the more important to arrange one's materials in an orderly fashion and to keep those spaces generally free of clutter. Otherwise, too much time is spent trying to locate needed materials. To optimize focus on the current task, students also should keep their desk tops free of materials not currently in use. Having extraneous materials piled on one's desk not only takes up space, but serves as a distraction from the immediate task. Finally, student help should be enlisted in keeping the whole classroom orderly. Putting class materials away after use, picking up trash around one's desk, and putting furniture back in its place after activities are good starters.

Task Difficulty. Another facet of the classroom environment that affects the efficiency and persistence of students' on-task behavior is the difficulty of the tasks assigned. In working with preadolescents with behavior disorders, DePaepe, Shores, and Jack (1996) found that difficult tasks produced lower amounts of on-task behavior and higher incidence of disruptive behavior than did easier tasks. Although high-achieving students undoubtedly can tolerate greater task difficulty than can low-achieving students, even high-achieving students need to experience more success than failure. Dickinson and Butt (1989) found that on-task behavior for both high-achieving and low-achieving students can be optimized if task difficulty is manipulated to ensure at least 70 percent success.

The difficulty level of a task is directly affected by the clarity of instructions for doing the task. Most of us have had the experience of assembling a mechanical device from the written instructions that came with the device. Although putting the device together should be relatively easy (at least that's the story we got at the place of purchase), technical terminology and omission of steps in the instructions may make the task confusing and frustrating. In classroom instruction, task difficulty can be greatly reduced if the teacher divides tasks into smaller steps and then presents those steps in a logical sequence. Perhaps one of the most compelling marks of a good teacher is the ability to execute task analysis (divide large tasks into smaller subtasks) until subtasks (steps) are defined at a level the students can manage. Obviously, some students will need smaller steps than others. The challenge is to keep subdividing a larger task until a struggling student can proceed with the subtasks.

Written Explanations. As students develop literacy skills, it is valuable to provide a written explanation of the steps involved in performing a task. Students may initially understand an oral explanation, but later forget critical facets of that explanation. A

"THE END OF THE NEVER-ENDING LINE"

Steven Levy, a fourth-grade teacher in Massachusetts, recounted the difficulty he was having with students turning in incomplete and poorly done work (Levy 1999). The picture included in his article showed students in line waiting for the teacher to check their work. At any one time, several students waited in line for Mr. Levy to pass judgment on their work. As some students standing in line finally reached the teacher, other students would join the end of the line. The work presented to the teacher was often incomplete or carelessly done, causing the teacher to send students back to their desk to try again. They would eventually rejoin the line leading to the teacher's desk, but with no assurance they would get it right this time. Thus, the line seemed to have a life of its own.

Starting with the simple task of how to draw a straight line and then a curved line, Mr. Levy eventually developed rubrics (standards) for how to perform tasks of varying levels of complexity. When students began to use these rubrics to evaluate their own work, they could determine where they had met the instructional standards and where their work was still lacking. They had a much clearer idea of what acceptable work looked like even before submitting their work to the teacher. In evaluating student work, you have something in mind as to what represents complete and acceptable work. Why not put your standards in writing and give them to the students when they start on an assignment? As an added step, students can use these standards in formally evaluating their own work and then submit their self-evaluation with the assignment.

written explanation can provide the reminders necessary for them to progress efficiently through the steps of the task without having to come to you for directions. Time spent in writing explicit instructions will be redeemed manyfold by the time saved in re-explaining the task to students.

Group Tasks. The social climate in the classroom is the facet of the classroom environment that most directly affects teamwork skills. Although some students readily work well with others, most do not naturally develop group skills during conventional schoolwork. As a rule, team skills must be directly taught, practiced, and rewarded to become firmly embedded in the student's behavioral repertoire. Teachers who attempt to use a cooperative learning format can expect to devote at least as much time to developing social skills as to developing academic skills. Although putting students in groups does not assure that they will develop social skills, they most certainly will not develop social skills without some opportunity to work together. Academic and demographic diversity among group members appears to extend the benefits of group experiences. Students are most likely to develop an appreciation for diversity when they have an opportunity to help and be helped by students different from themselves.

Reinforcing Good Work Habits

The controlling factor of student work habits is ultimately the reinforcement of those habits. Students may be less likely than their parents to value hard work inherently or to see sustained and diligent effort as the road to success. A teacher practice that enables students to continue devaluing work is accepting late work, mediocre work, and weak excuses for work not done (Landfried 1989). Teachers do many things for students that students should do for themselves. This pattern of enabling students to be negligent and careless in their work habits is often prompted by teachers' desire to please students, their parents, and school administrators.

Before we can expect students to improve their work habits, we must stop reinforcing their poor work habits. For example, Haberman (1997) contends that urban schools allow many students simply to show up and do no work as long as they do not disrupt class. A student who is allowed to be idle in the classroom is unlikely to become a productive adult worker. A productive classroom has high standards respected by both teachers and students, with teacher reinforcement available only for meeting those standards.

Teacher-Managed Rewards. When students do not value work for its own sake or for the natural benefits it brings, how can we make good work habits important to them? Although not very palatable to those who appreciate hard work, one direct approach is to find ways to reward students immediately for demonstration of good work habits. Of course, our real agenda is to promote student engagement in productive work habits until those habits generate their own natural reinforcement. It is not beyond reason, however, that some work tasks (e.g., cleaning the board, picking up clutter) may always have to be maintained through artificial rewards.

Rewarding students for attending school regularly can be a starting point in making good work habits more positively reinforcing. Suppose students do not like schoolwork, see no inherent value in schoolwork, and do not believe that school will be instrumental to achieving desired outcomes in their lives. How can we possibly make school attendance rewarding to these students? One study (Licht, Gard, and Guardino 1991) with special-education high school students used a combination of rewards for good attendance and notes to parents about student absences. Students who did not experience this intervention showed substantial declines in attendance as the semester progressed, but students who received the combination of rewards and parent notices maintained attendance at a high level. Regular attendance puts the student in a position to be academically successful—eventually making attendance naturally valuable to the student (Heberling and Shaffer 1995; Romer 1993).

An extrinsic-reward approach has also been used to increase punctuality (Johnson 1995). Middle school students signed in on a daily time card and received points exchangeable for rewards when they arrived on time for class. Rewards included video game time, items from the school store, and longer lunch periods. In addition to the reward contingencies, a time-management workshop was offered to help students alter events contributing to their tardiness. The workshop targeted such strategies as preparing their clothes the night before school, going to bed earlier, using an alarm clock to wake up, and going to their lockers less frequently. All twenty students in the program earned rewards for timely arrival, and they reduced their class tardiness from an average of fifteen to zero times a week during the final weeks of the program.

Teacher-managed rewards also have been used to promote assignment completion among sixth graders who had rarely completed assignments (Poston 1991). Participating parties developed and signed a behavior contract specifying the contingencies between rewards and weekly assignment completion, with the criteria for assignment completion being increased weekly. Rewards included computer play time and bonus points for purchasing items from the school store. Under the reward contingencies, students increased their assignment completion rate by at least 50 to 80 percent.

Teacher-managed rewards need not be tangible items, such as trinkets and edibles. In one high school program, students with outstanding attendance records were rewarded with certificates, congratulatory letters, and positive phone calls to parents (VanSciver 1986). Rewards can also consist of activities readily available in the classroom. For example, access to a computer during free time decreased the tardiness and improved one middle school boy's achievement levels (Inkster and McLaughlin 1993). Similarly, for one underachieving seven-year-old, Johnston and McLaughlin (1982) used contingent free time to increase assignment completion, while maintaining accuracy of work.

Even though contingent privileges can be used to improve a variety of work habits, tangible rewards may remain the most powerful incentives for many students. For example, VanSciver (1986) found that awarding school T-shirts to the homeroom with the best attendance record had a more pro-nounced effect on student attendance than did less tangible rewards (e.g., congratulatory letters, positive phone calls to parents). The group nature of the reward contingency undoubtedly enhanced its effectiveness.

In promoting teamwork, reinforcement must be provided for both individual and group accomplishments to maximize the performance of group members (Slavin 1984, 1991). Having students work together on a project or on a test review will not be most effective if students are then evaluated only on an individual basis. Similarly, if rewards are available only

Productive teamwork.

for group results, some students may contribute little to the group's performance. In fact, the brightest and most energetic members of the group may do most of the work unless each member's contribution to the group outcome is determined and rewarded accordingly. Thus, for teamwork to be most productive, team members must be evaluated and rewarded on both an individual and group basis.

Student-Managed Rewards. Several studies have found student-managed rewards superior to teacher-managed rewards. Lovitt and Curtiss (1969), for example, found that the academic response rate of a twelve-year-old student was higher when the student specified the requirements for rewards than when only the teacher specified the requirements. Similarly, Bolstad and Johnson (1972) revealed that self-regulation of rewards (self-recording and self-dispensing of rewards) was more effective in reducing inappropriate behavior among the most disruptive students in ten first- and second-grade classrooms than was teacher regulation of rewards. By acquiring the logistics of self-rewarding, students may be able to function more independently in situations where teachers are not immediately available to reward productive behavior.

Student management of rewards is not practiced extensively in most classrooms. A full application of this concept would mean that students choose the consequences to be applied as rewards, set the standards for applying those rewards, and then actually apply those rewards when the self-chosen standards are met. Students sometimes have control over one of these dimensions (usually applying the rewards based on self-selected or teacher-selected standards), but seldom have control over all three of the dimensions. Even if students have some role in selecting consequences, their choices must be compatible with school rules. Also, teachers should exercise veto power over student-selected standards that are too liberal. Even when students determine when the reward standards have been met, teachers should keep a watchful eye on the integrity of that process.

Developing Constructive Self-verbalizations

All the prompts and reinforcers for appropriate work habits need not be external. Most people instruct themselves vocally or subvocally on what they should and should not do in various situations. Guevremont, Osnes, and Stokes (1986) found that preschool children who were taught to verbalize the behavior in which they were to engage showed improved behavior not only in the experimental setting, but also in times and places different from the experimental setting. There are occasions in the classroom when self-verbalization can help students achieve better control over their emotional and social reactions. Students can develop a personal script to counter outbursts of anger (such as counting to ten before making an aggressive response), to reduce anxiety associated with giving a speech, and to be more positive in the comments they make to others. The strategy is for students to plan ahead in determining what they need to say to themselves to behave constructively in potentially problematic situations.

A study by Meichenbaum and Goodman (1971) demonstrated that second graders exhibiting hyperactive and impulsive behavior could be trained to instruct themselves in performing tasks with multiple steps. They were trained on a variety of tasks, such as copying line patterns and coloring figures within boundaries. During the training sessions, students individually observed the experimenter performing the task while giving himself or herself instructions aloud:

> Okay, what is it I have to do? You want me to copy the picture with the different lines. I have to go slowly and be careful. Okay, draw the lines down, down, good; then to the right, that's it; now down some more and to the left. Good, I'm doing fine so far. Remember go slowly. Now back up again. No, I was supposed to go down. That's okay. Just erase the line carefully. . . . Good. Even if I make an error I can go on slowly and carefully. Okay, I have to go down now. Finished. I did it. (p. 117).

After observing the experimenter, each student performed the task while giving self-instructions aloud. Next, the student performed the task while whispering instructions. Finally, the student performed the task silently (without lip movements). The idea was to help students internalize self-instructions. The students who received training in self-verbalization subsequently performed significantly better on psychometric tests that measured cognitive impulsivity, performance IQ, and motor ability than did control students who were exposed to the training tasks but not trained to self-verbalize.

Self-Assessing Work Habits

To determine the impact of the previously discussed interventions on student work habits, educators must have systematic procedures for assessing the occurrence of the targeted habits. Many dimensions of work habits (e.g., attendance, punctuality, assignment completion, and quality of work) are reflected in the teacher's regular records. A more intricate analysis of work habits may require development of checklists to assess how well tasks are done. Although the teacher can make such an assessment, it is advisable to involve the students in this process. For example, a teacher trying to establish an orderly work environment should develop a checklist of organizational tasks (e.g., trash picked up around one's desk, materials put away when not in use, work space clear of unnecessary materials) that students can use in assessing order within their personal work space. At the very least, such assessments should be done before, during, and after any special intervention to determine its effects on students' work habits.

Benefits of Self-Assessment. Self-assessment not only provides useful evaluative information, but may also have a reactive impact on the behaviors being assessed (i.e., the process of assessing one's own behavior can affect the frequency of that behavior). For example, one of the best ways to help students maintain their focus on the assigned task is to teach them self-monitoring strategies, which typically involve both self-observation and self-recording of the target behavior (Nelson 1977). Students are compelled to pay attention to their behavior and to make a record of that behavior. The intent is to help students improve performance by becoming more aware of how they are progressing with their work (Mace, Brown, and West 1987). Poor achievers consistently fail to monitor and evaluate their work (Kops and Belmont 1985). Consequently, they may feel they are working well when systematic monitoring actually reveals the opposite.

Logistics of Self-Monitoring. Given that students must self-monitor their work habits to assess precisely the adequacy of those habits, research on student self-assessment has targeted primarily self-monitoring. The self-monitoring approach has been used by a wide array of students, ranging from average students to those with severe handicapping conditions (Ballard and Glynn 1975; Cole, Gardner, and Karan 1985; Hughes and Boyle 1991; Long and Williams 1976). Self-monitoring also has been applied to a variety of on-task, conduct, and performance indices. Various self-recording devices have been used, including wrist counters, pocket-size notebooks, note cards, sticker charts, and performance checklists (Dunlap et al. 1991).

Much of the research on self-monitoring has been done with students who have special needs (Mammolenti, Vollmer, and Smith 2002). In our own research (Long and Williams

1976), for example, we employed self-recording with a group of retarded adolescents. Each student had to maintain a point sheet on which points were recorded for appropriate responses. The students logged points for being ready to start lessons, having appropriate materials, completing assignments, working quietly for specified time periods, and performing similar actions. Recording of points increased levels of appropriate responding for the group by approximately 10 percent during spelling and by approximately 15 percent during reading.

An example of a written checklist for self-recording has been provided by Anderson-Inman, Paine, and Deutchman's 1984 study of neat-paper skills. Resource-room students used this checklist to improve the appearance of their written work. They simply checked off the different steps in the task as they completed them. The checklist included the following items:

> Leaving margins on both sides of the page
>
> Starting on the front side of each sheet
>
> Putting one's name in the proper place
>
> Writing a title for the assignment
>
> Staying on the lines with one's writing.

A basic requirement of self-monitoring a recurring behavior is learning how and when to record the target response. An unobtrusive cue, such as a beep on an audiotape or an alarm on one's wristwatch, is often used. This cuing procedure is typically used to guide students in self-monitoring on-task behavior. When the cue sounds, the student asks himself or herself, "Was I working?" and then marks his or her record sheet accordingly (Prater, Hogan, and Miller 1992).

Although some students are so distractible that they will need to continue self-monitoring indefinitely, the teacher's long-term goal is to teach them to pay attention to their behavior and accomplishments without the use of an artificial recording device. For example, after children's self-monitoring has been regulated by a systematic external cue, they can then be asked to self-record whenever they think about recording. Ultimately, the teacher wants the students to provide their own cues as to when to self-record.

The fading of external directions and cues is best done gradually. The recording device or checklist can be withdrawn in steps. The intervals between cues for self-recording can also be extended, starting with one minute and progressing step by step to much longer intervals. If a student is using a performance checklist in doing an academic task (for example, working math problems), he or she might first use the checklist after each problem is completed, but then later after every two problems are completed. Although students with handicapping conditions may require more extended transitions, most students can eventually be weaned from external prompts while maintaining improvement across time and settings (Koegel, Koegel, and Ingham 1986).

The impact of self-monitoring can be increased when combined with other techniques (Bolstad and Johnson 1972; Long and Williams 1976; Mahoney, Moura, and Wade 1973). For instance, self-monitoring can be used in combination with external reinforcement or self-reinforcement or both. Peer monitoring has also been successfully used in combination with self-monitoring (Fowler 1986). Having peers monitor one another's work habits increases the likelihood that the self-monitoring is being done accurately.

Selected Work Practices to Promote

Good work practices in school have both short-term and long-term dividends: they will help students do better in school and prepare them to be more successful in the adult workplace. These practices include attending school regularly, meeting commitments in a timely fashion, keeping their work space and work materials organized, sustaining concentration on work tasks, seeking and using supervisory feedback, and working effectively with other students. These work habits become especially important in the high school years as students near entry into the adult workforce, but their importance can be seen even as early as preschool (Stipek 1983). The previous section on procedures for promoting constructive work habits illustrated how many of these work habits can be promoted by various teacher-managed and student-managed strategies. In this final section, we highlight three target areas that are especially important to students' success in school and to their long-term success as adults.

Punctuality in Completing Work Tasks

Punctuality makes a difference in most school activities. The time when one arrives at school, completes assignments, and prepares for examinations can make a significant difference in a student's academic success. Surprisingly, little recent research has directly addressed this linkage, with most of this research focusing on tardiness in arriving at school (Din, Isack, and Rietveld 2003; Inkster and McLaughlin 1993; Johnson 1995; Ligon and Jackson 1988). Research done many decades ago (Dudycha 1936; Turney 1930) suggested that punctuality in general is related to measures of intelligence and grades earned.

Getting to class and completing assignments in a timely manner are affected by the ability to judge accurately the time needed to accomplish targeted tasks. Individuals who are consistently late in meeting their commitments often underestimate how much time will be required to do the specific tasks embedded in those commitments. If traveling to school typically requires thirty minutes, the consistently late student may estimate the travel time as twenty minutes. Thus, the challenge for the teacher is to teach these students to overestimate the time required to perform particular tasks. A good rule of thumb is to ask the student to estimate the time needed for a task and then to double that estimate. If this liberal estimation leads to arriving early at school or to completing assignments ahead of time, students can use the extra time to review for upcoming school activities.

Even if a time estimate is accurate for a particular task, there is no assurance that the student will accomplish the task in a timely fashion. Two factors can still undermine timely task completion: getting started late and getting sidetracked along the way. Of course, getting started late can result from a host of antecedent behaviors: going to bed late, failing to set the alarm clock, leaving late for school, and saving too many tasks for the last minute. But even if the student gets started in a timely way, his or her attention may be diverted by other potential tasks along the way. He or she can set out to do task A but wind up engaging in activities B through Z. This shifting of attention from task to task can produce a multitude of loose ends in tasks attempted or in the completion of minor tasks at the expense of major tasks.

The student who chronically runs behind schedule needs models and prompts to illuminate the path to timely completion of tasks. Teachers and selected peers can model the importance of starting early with tasks and saving ancillary tasks until one has completed the primary task. One tactic that prevents an individual from getting sidetracked from the primary task is having a small notepad nearby to jot down other activities or tasks that come to mind while the individual is working on the primary task. Once listed on the notepad, thoughts of these additional tasks can be put aside until completion of the primary task. This arrangement works far better than stopping the primary task to engage in the ancillary tasks, which may completely dilute the student's focus on the primary task.

Another way to make sure the larger task is completed in a timely fashion is to divide it into subtasks and then to proceed from one subtask to the next, rather than continually thinking in terms of the larger task (which can be a very intimidating prospect). Completing a task on time usually is directly related to when one starts on the task. Starting in a timely fashion lays the foundation for completing the task in a timely fashion. Just jotting down subtasks necessary to complete the larger task is a useful starting point. As soon as the student has a better sense of the smaller tasks to be done, doing at least one of those tasks will help to establish momentum in working on the larger task.

Openness to Supervision

Although being able to work well without continuing supervision is one of the hallmarks of student effectiveness, all students occasionally need supervisory input to proceed effectively and efficiently with a task or project. An effective student learns to accept supervision when given and to ask for supervision when needed. Students need to know when to request assistance, to make sure they understand instructions given, to question tactfully any directions that appear to be off target, and then to follow through with the recommended action.

First of all, students need to know when and how to ask for assistance. It is often better to ask for help early than to compound errors by proceeding with a flawed work strategy. To get the needed input, students must learn how to pinpoint precisely what they

HELP!

Getting stuck with a task is disconcerting for some students and challenging for other students. Students who feel overwhelmed may either disengage from the task or send an urgent SOS to the teacher. These students may plead that the task is either much too difficult or that they are totally baffled by the task. Either reaction is not very productive in getting clarification as to how to proceed with the task. In contrast, there are the students who refuse to ask for help and who may attempt to proceed with the task even when they are getting nowhere with their current strategy. These students can save themselves considerable time and likely will complete the task more efficiently and effectively if they ask for assistance at key points. Yet it is difficult to fault these students for persisting largely on their own.

Certainly, the student who insists that the task is too difficult or that he or she is totally stuck presents the greater difficulty to the teacher. The appeal for help may come in the form of "I can't do it." This capitulation usually prompts a line of questioning from the teacher designed to pinpoint where help is needed. The teacher may first ask the student to show what he or she has done thus far on the task. The student may have followed a line of reasoning that led to a dead end or to an erroneous conclusion. Thus, the teacher will ask the student to explain why these initial steps were taken, trying to help the student see the importance of thoughtfully considering each step rather than proceeding impulsively. The teacher will remind the student of what to do first, then second, and so on.

When the student appeals for help, he or she will eventually be able to articulate the steps taken to that point and to pinpoint the impasse to which those steps have led. The teacher's role at this point is to model questions the student will need to ask to figure out how to resolve that impasse. The major intent of this dialogue is to help the student go from global descriptions ("I don't know how to do this") to more precise descriptions ("I have done A and B, but they are not leading to C") and to related questions ("Should C actually follow from A and B? Is there a flaw in my application of A or B?"). Thus, when students get stuck or reach an erroneous conclusion, they will start retracing their steps with precisely focused questions to determine what steps they might have overlooked or misapplied.

do *not* know. A broad question—such as "How do I do this?"—may not yield the specific feedback needed to complete a task. A way for you, the teacher, to ensure that your feedback is explicit and relevant is first to identify exactly where the student's task performance broke down and the strategies used by the student in attempting to transcend the impasse. Otherwise, your feedback may be too general to benefit the student, or you may be targeting the wrong aspect of the student's task performance.

Collaboration with Peers

In recent years, industry has definitely moved in the direction of employees working together as teams (Erdman 1992). Solitary individual effort and individual competition among workers is viewed as less helpful than sharing ideas, building a collaborative approach to problem solving, and accomplishing team goals. Although some specific tasks are still done individually, larger tasks are usually done on a team basis. Nonetheless, schools have traditionally required students to work individually and often competitively (Slavin 1984).

A good team

In some instances, schools have deliberately separated students in performing work tasks, especially when students in a group are aggressively inclined toward one another (Haberman 1997). Although perhaps necessary over the short run, simply separating adversarial students does nothing to teach them how to work with individuals whose values and actions conflict with their own. The challenge is to help students see that more is to be gained by teamwork than by conflict. Although often underappreciated by educators and parents, teamwork skills are surely among the most important skills that students can learn at school.

Making teamwork activities successful requires the cultivation of three levels of student skills: behaving nondisruptively in group activity, learning to share ideas within groups, and reaching sound conclusions within groups. You may wish to use the following list of group skills in assessing how groups and individuals in your classroom are faring with respect to their group collaboration:

Working Together Nondisruptively
Getting into the group quickly and quietly
Staying with the group
Keeping hands to oneself
Talking in a quiet voice
Taking turns (as opposed to all group members talking at once)

Sharing within the Group
Avoiding put-downs
Encouraging others
Involving everyone
Restating others' ideas

Reaching Sound Conclusions within the Group
Checking for agreement
Asking for reasoning behind ideas
Criticizing ideas, not people
Reaching consensus
Making a plan

Practicing any and all of the actions listed here will help students be more successful in their cooperative learning. Yet another aspect of group work is equally vital in promoting group success—the reward contingencies for cooperative outcomes. Students often work together in preparing for an exam or developing a course project. If students are working together on a project in which they have an intrinsic interest (such as improving the appearance of the school playground or making the school schedule more student friendly), the completion and implementation of the project may be all the reward that is needed. However, if students are preparing for an exam in a subject area not particularly interesting to them, some extrinsic rewards may be necessary to maximize student effort on the task.

Reward contingencies that are most effective for group work take into account both group achievement and individual contribution to that achievement. Each group member's work must factor into the group accomplishment. For instance, if the group is being rewarded for its members' collective improvement in exam scores, each person's exam scores must be counted in the tabulation of group improvement. In this approach to cooperative

WHAT ABOUT THOSE HIGH PERFORMERS?

Research spanning the early grades through college shows that low and average performers appear to benefit substantially from cooperative group work. However, the evidence is not so clear-cut for high performers. One procedural difficulty related to high performers is that they have little room to improve their performance (such as from one test to the next), whereas low and average performers have a great deal of room for improvement. To adjust for this disparity in room for improvement, we give the high performers the same group credit for continuing to perform at a high level as we do to low and average performers for improving their performance (Williams, Carroll, and Hautau n.d.). Despite this accommodation, we have found that high performers may actually decrease their performance level somewhat under a cooperative-learning reward contingency, but the low and average performers are likely to improve considerably (Stockdale and Williams 2004).

When high, average, and low performers meet together to study for an exam, how do the high performers function in the group? They most often assume a leadership role and become a tutor for others in the group. They spend considerable time explaining difficult concepts to low and average performers. Because of this teaching role, the high performers presumably learn the subject matter at a deeper level than they would under an independent study or competitive arrangement. The assumption is that teaching subject matter produces a deeper level of understanding than simply learning it for one's self.

However, the down side of this scenario is that the time the high performers spend explaining concepts to low and average performers detracts from their time to master other concepts (Johnson and Johnson 1992). To counter this tendency for high performers to help their fellow group members at their own expense, we have used both group and individual contingencies in promoting group work (Williams, Carroll, and Hautau n.d.). If the composite test score for a group exceeds the composite score for their previous test by a specified amount, everyone in the group gets a certain number of bonus points. Plus, each individual in the group who improves his or her score or makes an A on the exam gets additional bonus credit. Thus, high performers must maintain a high level of performance and help other students improve their performance to maximize their own bonus credit. We have found that this added individual contingency helps high performers sustain their performance at a high level.

learning, rewards are usually based on improvement rather than on absolute performance level. Sometimes groups are competing against one another in improvement, and other times all groups are trying to reach the same criterion of improvement. In either case, all groups have a similar mix of high, average, and low performers, with the baseline composite level of performance very similar across groups.

Concluding Comments

This chapter has presented an analysis of several student work practices that may contribute both to success in school and to success in adult life: regular attendance, punctuality in meeting commitments, efficient organization of work materials, task persistence, openness to supervision, completion of high-quality work, teamwork skills, and constructive management of outside-of-class experiences. Teachers can aid the promotion of such practices by modeling exemplary work habits, developing a physical and academic environment conducive to effective work habits, and rewarding responsible rather than irresponsible work habits. The assessment and promotion of independent and collaborative work habits should be one of the highest priorities in contemporary education. Developing these work habits may provide more long-lasting benefits to students than keeping the focus of school primarily on the acquisition of subject matter.

References

Anderson-Inman, L., S. C. Paine, and L. Deutchman. (1984). Neatness counts: Effects of direct instruction and self-monitoring on the transfer of neat-paper skills to nontraining settings. *Analysis and Intervention in Developmental Disabilities* 4: 177–85.

Arlin, M., and W. Whitley. (1978). Perception of self-managed learning opportunities and academic locus of control: A causal interpretation. *Journal of Educational Psychology* 70: 988–92.

Ballard, K. D., T. Glynn. (1975). Behavioral self-management in story writing with elementary school children. *Journal of Applied Behavior Analysis* 8: 397–89.

Bolstad, O. D., and S. M. Johnson. (1972). Self-regulation in the modification of disruptive classroom behavior. *Journal of Applied Behavior Analysis* 4: 443–54.

Bransford, J., R. Sherwood, N. Vye, and J. Reiser. (1986). Teaching thinking and problem solving: Research foundations. *American Psychologist* 41: 1078–89.

Broadus, L. (1983). *How to Stop Procrastinating and Start Living.* Minneapolis: Augsburg.

Bruns, J. H. (1992). They can but they don't: Helping students overcome work inhibition. *American Educator* 16(4): 38–47.

Cheng, M. (1995). *Issues Related to Student Part-Time Work: What Did Research Find in the Toronto Situation and Other Context?* Research Department report no. 215. Toronto: Toronto Board of Education, Research Department.

Cobb, J. A. (1972). The relationship of discrete classroom behaviors to fourth-grade academic achievement. *Journal of Educational Psychology* 63: 74–80.

Cole, C. L., W. I Gardner, and O. C. Karan. (1985). Self-management training of mentally retarded adults presenting severe conduct difficulties. *Applied Research in Mental Retardation* 6: 337–47.

DePaepe, P. A., R. E. Shores, and S. L. Jack. (1996). Effects of task difficulty on the disruptive and on-task behaviors with severe behavior disorders. *Behavior Disorders* 21: 216–23.

Dickinson, D. J., and J. A. Butt. (1989). The effects of success and failure on the on-task behavior of high-achieving students. *Education and Treatment of Children* 12: 243–52.

Din, F. S., L. R. Isack, and J. Rietveld. (2003). Effects of contingency contracting on decreasing student tardiness. Paper presented at the Annual Conference of the Eastern Educational Research Association, February, Hilton Head Island, S.C.

Dudycha, G. J. (1936). An objective study of personality. *Archives of Psychology Columbia University* 204: 53.

Dunlap, L. K., G. Dunlap, L. K. Koegel, and R. L. Koegel. (1991). Using self-monitoring to increase independence. *Teaching Exceptional Children* (spring): 17–22.

Ediger, M. (1987). *School Dropouts, Absenteeism, and Tardiness.* Counseling and Student Services Clearinghouse. U.S., Ohio: ERIC, ED27991

Erdman, A. (1992). What's wrong with workers. *Fortune* (August 10): 18.

Fetler, M. (1984). Television viewing and school achievement. *Journal of Communication* (spring): 104–18.

Fetler, M., and D. Carlson. (1982). California assessment program surveys of television and achievement. Paper presented at the Annual Meeting of the American Educational Research Association, March, New York.

Fiore, N. (1989). *The Now Habit.* New York: Penguin Putnam.

Fowler, S. A. (1986). Peer monitoring and self-monitoring: Alternatives to traditional teacher management. *Exceptional Children* 52: 573–81.

Georgiady, N. P., and L. C. Romano. (1994). *Focus on Study Habits in School: A Guide for Teachers and Students to Increase Learning in Middle School.* Michigan Association of Middle School Educators. U.S., Michigan: ERIC, ED385347.

Guevremont, D. C., P. G. Osnes, and T. F. Stokes. (1986). Preparation for effective self-regulation: The development of generalized verbal control. *Journal of Applied Behavior Analysis* 19: 99–104.

Haberman, M. (1997). Unemployment training: The ideology of nonwork learned in urban schools. *Phi Delta Kappan* 78 (March): 499–503.

Hamilton, V., and D. Gordon. (1978). Teacher-child interactions in preschool and task persistence. *American Educational Research Journal* 15: 459–66.

Heberling, K., and D. V. Shaffer. (1995). *School Attendance and Grade Point Averages of Regular Education and Learning Disabled Students in Elementary Schools.* Elementary and Early Childhood Education Clearinghouse. U.S.,Ohio: ERIC, ED387264.

Hughes, C. A., and J. R. Boyle. (1991). Effects of self-monitoring for on-task behavior and task productivity on elementary students with moderate mental retardation. *Education and Treatment of Children* 14: 96–111.

Inkster, J. A., and T. F. McLaughlin. (1993). Token reinforcement effects for reducing tardiness with a socially disadvantaged adolescent student. *B.C. Journal of Special Education* 17: 284–88.

Johnson, B. (1995). A behavior modification program to reduce tardiness in middle school dropout prevention students. Disabilities and Gifted Education Clearinghouse. U.S., Florida: ERIC, ED387985.

Johnson, D. W., and R. T. Johnson. (1992). What to say to advocates for the gifted. *Educational Leadership* (October): 44–47.

Johnston, R. J., and T. F. McLaughlin. (1982). The effects of free time on assignment completion and accuracy in arithmetic. A case study. *Education and Treatment of Children* 5(1): 33–40.

Kablaoui, B. N., and A. J. Pautler. (1991). The effects of part-time work experience on high school students. *Journal of Career Development* 17: 195–211.

Kantrowitz, B., and K. Springen. (2003). Why sleep matters. *Newsweek* (September 22): 75–77.

Koegel, L. K., R. L. Koegel, and J. C. Ingham. (1986). Programming rapid generalization of correct articulation through self-monitoring procedures. *Journal of Speech and Hearing Disorders* 51: 24–32.

Kops, C., and I. Belmont. (1985). Planning and organizing skills of poor achievers. *Journal of Learning Disabilities* 18(1): 8–14.

Lamdin, D. J. (1996). Evidence of student attendance as an independent variable in education production functions. *Journal of Educational Research* 89(3): 155–62.

Landfried, S. E. (1999). "Enabling" undermines responsibility in students. *Educational Leadership* 47(3): 79–83.

Levy, S. (1999). The end of the never-ending line. *Educational Leadership* 56(6): 74–77.

Licht, B. G., T. Gard, and C. Guardino. (1991). Modifying school attendance of special education high school students. *Journal of Educational Research* 84: 368–73.

Ligon, G., E. E. Jackson. (1988). *Why Secondary Teachers Fail Students.* Assessment and Evaluation Clearinghouse. U.S., Texas: ERIC, ED311061.

Long, J. D., and R. L. Williams. (1976). The utility of self-management procedures in modifying the classroom behaviors of mentally retarded adolescents. *Adolescence* 41: 29–38.

Lovitt, T. C., and K. A. Curtiss. (1969). Academic response rate as a function of teacher and self-imposed contingencies. *Journal of Applied Behavior Analysis* 2: 49–53.

Mace, F. C., D. K. Brown, and B. J. West. (1987). Behavioral self-management in education.

In *Psychoeducational Interventions in the Schools*, edited by C. A. Maher and J. E. Zins, 160–76. New York: Pergamon.

Mahoney, M. J., N. G. Moura, and T. C. Wade. (1973). The relative efficacy of self-reward, self-punishment, and self-monitoring techniques for weight loss. *Journal of Consulting and Clinical Psychology* 40: 404–7.

Mammolenti, J., P. Vollmer, and D. Smith. (2002). *Self-monitoring: The Effects of Self-recording and Self-evaluation on Off-task Behaviors of Elementary Students with Mild Disabilities.* ERIC no. ED469850. Arlington, Va.: ERIC.

Meichenbaum, D. H., and J. Goodman. (1971). Training impulsive children to talk to themselves: A means of developing self-control. *Journal of Abnormal Psychology* 77: 115–26.

National Center for Education Statistics. (1996). *Student Absenteeism and Tardiness.* Indicator of the Month no. RIENOV96. Washington, D.C.: National Center for Education Statistics.

Nelson, R. O. (1977). Assessment and therapeutic functions of self-monitoring. In *Progress in Behavior Modification*, vol. 5, edited by M. Hersen, R. M. Eisler, and P. M. Miller, 263–308. New York: Academic Press.

Poston, R. (1991). Increasing assignment completion of sixth grade students through behavior modification. Elementary and Early Childhood Education Clearinghouse. U.S., Florida: ERIC, ED339455.

Prater, M. A., S. Hogan, and S. R. Miller. (1992). Using self-monitoring to improve on-task behavior and academic skills of an adolescent with mild handicaps across special and regular education settings. *Education and Treatment of Children* 15: 43–55.

Romer, D. (1993). Do students go to class? Should they? *Journal of Economic Perspectives* 7: 167–74.

Singh, K. (1998). Part-time employment in high school and its effect on academic achievement. *Journal of Educational Research* 91: 131–39.

Slavin, R. E. (1984). Students motivating students to excel: Cooperative incentives, cooperative tasks, and student achievement. *Elementary School Journal* 85: 53–63.

———. (1991). Synthesis of research on cooperative learning. *Educational Leadership* 48(5): 71–82.

Soli, S. D., and V. T. Devine. (1976). Behavioral correlates of achievement: A look at high and low achievers. *Journal of Educational Psychology* 68: 335–41.

Spaulding, C. L. (1992). *Motivation in the Classroom.* New York: McGraw-Hill.

Steinberg, L., S. Fegley, and S. M. Dornbusch. (1993). Negative impact of part-time work on adolescent adjustment: Evidence from a longitudinal study. *Developmental Psychology* 29: 171–80.

Stern, D., N. Finkelstein, J. R. Stone III, J. Latting, and C. Dornsife. (1995). *School to*

Work: Research on Programs in the United States. Washington, D.C.: Taylor and Francis.

Steward, R. J., A. D. Steward, and J. Blair. (2002). *School Attendance Revisited: A Study of Urban African American Students' GPA and Coping Strategies.* ERIC no. ED471343. Arlington, Va.: ERIC.

Stipek, D. J. (1983). Work habits in preschool. *Young Children* (May): 25–32.

Stipek, D. J., T. Roberts, and M. Sanborn. (1980). Mastery motivation in four-year-olds. Unpublished manuscript, University of California at Los Angeles.

Stockdale, S. L., and R. L. Williams. (2004). Cooperative learning at the college level: Differential effects on high, average, and low exam performers. *Journal of Behavioral Education* 13: 37–50.

Szalavitz, M. (2003). Stand and deliver. *Psychology Today* (July–August): 50–54.

Turney, A. H. (1930). *Factors Other Than Intelligence That Affect Success in High School.* Minneapolis: University of Minnesota Press.

VanSciver, J. (1986). Use rewards to boost student attendance (and public goodwill). *Executive Educator* 8(6): 22–23.

Weitzman, M. (1985). Demographic and educational characteristics of inner-city middle school problem absence students. *American Journal of Orthopsychiatry* 55: 378–83.

Wells, L., and J. Blendinger. (1997). Action research: How children in the fifth grade spend their time outside of school. Paper presented at the Annual Meeting of the Mid-South Educational Research Association, November, Memphis, Tenn.

Wheldall, K., and A. Panagopoulou-Stamatelatou. (1991). The effects of pupil self-recording of on-task behaviour on primary school children. *British Educational Research Journal* 17: 113–27.

Williams, R. L., E. Carroll, and B. Hautau. (n.d.). Individual accountability in cooperative learning at the college level: Differential effects on high, average, and low exam performers. Manuscript submitted for publication.

Wirtz, P. W., C. A. Rohrbeck, I. Charner, and B. S. Fraser. (1988). Situational and social influences on high school students' decisions to work part-time. New Orleans: Paper presented at the Annual Meeting of the American Educational Research Association, April.

Note: Selected portions of this chapter have been adapted from content included in (1) Student Work Habits: An Educational Imperative (2000), ERIC document (ED449446), by Robert L. Williams and Eun Jung Oh, and (2) the unpublished doctoral dissertation "The Psychometric Properties of the Student Work Habits Rating Form" (May 2000), written by Eun Jung Oh and edited by Robert L. Williams. This material has been adapted for this chapter with Eun Jung Oh's permission.

The reddish hue above the horizon signaled the day's last rays of sunlight. It was the time of day Sarah appreciated most of all. After spending several hours in a hot classroom, she loved the coolness of the evening on her back patio.

The hectic activity of the school day made her more than ready for the tranquility here. The lightning bugs and crickets were as much stimulation as she needed at that moment.

The cry of "Mom!" from inside the house abruptly brought Sarah back to the reality of all the things she had to do before she could retire for the evening. Dishes and clothes had to be washed, her children had to be helped with their homework, and her own preparation for the next school day had to be done.

9

In the Cool of the Evening

Your Life Beyond the Classroom

Contrary to what your students may think, a teacher's life does extend beyond the school day. In fact, it may not be an exaggeration to claim that the most important part of a teacher's life begins with the ending of the school day. If you treat the after-school hours as simply an extension of the school day (e.g., grading papers or preparing lesson plans), you will end up neglecting vital dimensions of your personal life. Eventually, you will have less to offer in the classroom because of this personal deprivation.

In afternoon in-service programs, we have seen that washed-out look on teachers' faces too many times! The impression we get is that by the completion of the teaching day many teachers are physically fatigued and emotionally drained. Some crucial things must happen in the next fourteen to sixteen hours to get them ready to function effectively again the next day. Our suspicion is that those "crucial" things often do not happen, and, thus, teachers return the next morning with negligible energy, which obviously makes the day exceedingly tough for them.

The purpose of this chapter is to address the possibility of your beginning the school day in a refreshed condition that will sustain you in meeting your students' myriad needs in the next six to eight hours. In this chapter, to help you make this possibility a reality, we focus exclusively on those fourteen to sixteen hours between the ending of one school day and the beginning of the next school day. We have divided your nonteaching time in the evenings and on weekends into seven areas: rest, physical activity, recreation, nutrition, social relations, domestic responsibilities, and academic preparation. We discuss how you can best handle each area in the nonteaching hours so that you can return to school with some sparkle in your eyes. We draw from a broad spectrum of literature because the educational literature has given little emphasis to the quality of the teacher's personal life.

Rest

Rest represents the major block of time in your nonteaching hours. However, as your teaching and nonteaching responsibilities accumulate, these responsibilities tend to encroach significantly on your resting time. After all, "burning the midnight oil" is a revered educational value. Unfortunately, if you burn too much of this oil, the cognitive illumination in your classroom may soon grow dim. What works better is to identify how much time you need for an adequate night's sleep and then to protect that time at all cost.

Importance of a Good Night's Sleep
Although lingering for a few minutes on your back patio qualifies as rest, the most essential rest comes in your nightly sleep. No amount of wakeful rest can compensate for a good night's sleep, which is essential for both physical and psychological rejuvenation. A classic study on longevity (Wiley and Camacho 1980) identifies seven to eight hours of nightly sleep as one of the most important predictors of good health and a long life. Any compromise of this time because of things you need to do will surely come back to haunt you. You will be more likely to get sick, miss valuable work time, function below par in your work, and feel emotionally down (Dahl 1999). Trust us, you will have greater net accomplishments in your life by getting a good night's sleep than by "burning the midnight oil."

Getting a good night's sleep can be a considerable challenge. Being in bed seven to eight hours may not be equivalent to sleeping seven to eight hours. Our suggestions will not solve problems of chronic insomnia, but they may help you fall asleep more easily and avoid extended periods of wakefulness during the night. Sleep experts (e.g., Weaver n.d.) recommend that individuals establish regular times for going to bed and rising, and that they stay within this time frame even on weekends. Regularity of your sleeping hours will help you set your internal biological clock, contributing to drowsiness at the designated bedtime and feeling rested when the time comes to arise. What you are attempting to do is normalize your sleep-wake rhythm.

Guidelines for Better Sleep

In his book *Maximizing the Quality of Your Sleep*, Weaver (n.d.) offers a number of suggestions that may help you experience a restful night's sleep:

- Spend at least thirty minutes outside during the day because daylight helps to regulate the circadian cycle;

- Avoid post-lunch caffeine in food (chocolate sweets), drinks (coffee, tea, and carbonated beverages), and medication (pain relievers, diuretics, and some cold remedies);

- Minimize daytime napping to avoid undermining your normal sleep-wakefulness pattern;

- Make sure your bedroom is free of lights, sounds, temperature levels, and touch sensations that will attract undue attention;

- Refrain from alcohol within two hours of bedtime because alcohol consumption near bedtime may increase wakefulness later in the night;

- Don't consume large meals within two hours of bedtime because heavy-duty gastrointestinal activity undermines the quality of sleep;

- Refrain from exercise within two hours of bedtime because exercise increases body temperature and stimulates the nervous system;

- Wind down for an hour or so before bedtime with low-arousal activities (e.g., listening to soft music, reading a pleasant book).

Even though you follow all the guidelines listed here, you may still have evenings when you lie in bed wide awake, unable to fall asleep or get back to sleep. When you are unable to sleep, conceal the clock from view so you aren't reminded of how morning is approaching without your being able to sleep. Most sleep experts recommend that you not continue to lie in bed wide awake. After ten to twenty minutes of being totally awake, get out of bed and leave the bedroom. Engage in a low-arousal activity (e.g., reading, watching television) in another room. Return to bed when you begin to feel a bit drowsy. Develop a calming ritual once you are in bed (e.g., breathing deeply, focusing on pleasant imagery). It is best not to use time in bed to review the day's work activities or to plan tomorrow's activities. If all of your strategies fail and you wind up getting a poor night's sleep, get up at the regular time rather than compensating by sleeping late. The next evening you should be ready for a good night's sleep.

Physical-Fitness Activity

Shifting our focus from rest to exercise may appear to be an abrupt transition, but the two topics are intimately connected. Perhaps you feel so tired when you finish your teaching day that you cannot even consider the possibility of physical activity. Paradoxically, you may be experiencing extreme tiredness because of too little physical activity. A physical-fitness program can prevent fatigue during the school day and give an immediate energy lift in the morning or evening. In addition, regular physical exercise is likely to enhance your self-image and sleep, while diminishing anxiety and depression (Raglin 1990). It is no wonder that teachers who have recovered from professional burnout often cite physical-fitness activity as part of their prescription for recovery.

In addition to raising your energy level, exercise will help you keep the events of teaching in a more balanced perspective. It is usually one's subjective interpretation of events rather than the objective reality of those events that poses the problem. A person who is physically tired is far more likely to attach ominous overtones to a problematic event than one who is energetic. Likewise, an individual who has a sedentary lifestyle outside the classroom may be more likely to have a pessimistic perspective on what happens in the classroom than one who has energizing experiences beyond the classroom. Few activities help one to feel more alive than vigorous physical activity.

A Time and Place for Exercise

What are the factors you need to change in your life to make physical activity a regular part of your personal time? First, view your involvement in exercise as an unconditional part of your schedule, not as something you do if everything else gets done first. Otherwise, other activities will often crowd out exercise. Second, identify the portion of the day that would be most compatible with exercise. Do not try to force exercise into the busiest part of the day, but neither relegate it to the last part of the day. In the latter case, fatigue may cause you to rationalize skipping your exercise for one day and then two days and so on until exercise completely disappears from your daily routine. We have personally found that shortly after completing the workday and near the midpoint of the evening hours are good times for incorporating exercise into our routine. However, other teachers like to get up very early and take care of exercise even before leaving for school.

Whether your preference is for morning or afternoon exercise, you should identify a regular time for exercise and then not allow other responsibilities to intrude on that exercise time. Time is at a

BIT BY BIT

If you have been wondering where you are going to find thirty minutes a day for exercise, you may be heartened by recommendations in Catherine Winters' article "Get Fit Bit by Bit" (1999). Her viewpoint is that you don't have to find your thirty minutes all at one time or all in one place. Five minutes here and five minutes there of moderate physical activity can soon add up to thirty minutes. Although we believe that thirty minutes of sustained physical activity has more conditioning value than thirty minutes of accumulated activity, the latter may be a good starting point in accelerating fitness activity in your life.

A physical activity becomes a passion.

More good news is that you don't have to go to a gym or even change clothes to exercise. In fact, you can accumulate some of your exercise time around school. Unless you are physically disabled or transporting audiovisual equipment, you can always take the stairs in going from one floor to the next in your building. During short breaks in your school day, you can go for a walk rather than finding the nearest easy chair. A short walk after lunch is especially helpful in getting you energized for the remainder of your school day. Plus, taking some brief stretching breaks with your students (simply standing and stretching your arms) can help everyone feel more alert.

In addition, there are some rather ordinary things you can do around home to accumulate exercise time: gardening, raking leaves, and washing windows. If you have a heavy housework schedule for the evening or the weekend, you can increase the exercise benefits by doing several tasks in succession. For example, you can gather up the laundry, change the bed coverings, vacuum the carpet, clear the table after dinner, and put the dishes in the dishwasher without stopping. If you're inclined to get bored with exercise, you can diversify your activity from day to day: mow the lawn one day, set out flowers the next day, and then go for a walk the following day. Instead of thinking of the conclusion of your work day or the weekend as a time to be sedentary, think of after-school hours as an opportunity to be physically active.

premium in establishing an exercise pattern. Although you might like to spend two hours each evening playing tennis, going to a dance class, canoeing, or mountain climbing, some of these activities will not be available to you on a daily basis and, even if they were, you would not have the time to pursue them. They might constitute excellent weekend excursions or biweekly outings, but you can hardly invest two hours a day in physical-fitness activity unless you are an experienced teacher and your workday is flawlessly organized. What is attainable for virtually all teachers is a physical-fitness routine that requires no more than thirty minutes a day and that is adaptable to varying weather conditions and locales.

Probably the most accessible and efficient physical-fitness activity for most teachers is vigorous walking. Thus, if more interesting forms of exercise are not convenient, walking is a perfectly effective and safe way to increase your physical fitness. If you have been a sedentary person for some time, your initial goal should not be thirty minutes of walking a day, but something far more modest, such as five minutes. You never need push yourself or go beyond what is comfortable to you. However, after a few five-minute walks at a relaxed pace, you may discover that you can easily walk a little longer or faster.

The Social Aspects of Exercise

Another consideration in establishing an exercise pattern is whether you exercise alone or

with others. For most individuals, exercising with others works better. The activity is usually more enjoyable because of the social stimulation involved; plus, you increase the likelihood of exercising because of mutual commitments. One of the biggest hurdles to exercise is getting started with the activity. Teachers often report that they enjoy exercise once they begin, but that they have difficulty getting prepared for the activity and getting to the exercise site. If you have made a commitment to a friend to join him or her at a particular time and place for an exercise activity, you are far less likely to set aside your exercise plans.

Making exercise a social experience entails two risks, however: socializing may become the focus of the exercise session, and other individuals may sometimes be unavailable to share exercise with you. For example, we have noted that in some fitness facilities and on some tennis courts, individuals spend as much time talking as working out or playing tennis. If you can talk while engaging in a fitness activity, fine. Otherwise, minimize talking until you have finished your workout.

Although many physical activities are more enjoyable when shared with others, you must be prepared to engage in some activities on an individual basis. Others' schedules may not conform to the time of day you need to exercise. You can certainly walk, swim, and bike alone. Even activities that require others' participation can be approximated on your own. You can practice your tennis serve and hit balls off a wall when no one is available for a match. Socializing can contribute to the enjoyment of exercise, but don't let preoccupation with socialization become an impediment to exercise.

Balance in Your Exercise Activities

As you establish a regular routine of exercise, you should work toward balance in your exercise activities. Just engaging in a variety of physical activities will contribute to balance, but nevertheless certain aspects of fitness can be underemphasized. A balanced exercise program includes activities that contribute to endurance, strength, and flexibility. Although some activities may contribute to all three of these outcomes, a particular activity most likely will be stronger in one of these areas than in the others. By far the most important of these outcomes is endurance, which contributes directly to the vitality of your respiratory and cardiovascular systems. To maximize endurance, you need to engage in activities that involve sustained movement of the large muscle groups (legs and arms) for at least thirty minutes. Walking, swimming, and biking are excellent prospects for endurance activities. At fitness centers treadmills, elliptical machines, and aerobics classes also are good choices for improving endurance.

Although neither flexibility nor strength-building activities contribute as extensively to overall fitness as endurance activities, each can make an indispensable contribution. Both minimize the likelihood of injuries in rapid-movement activities such as tennis and basketball. All muscle groups (e.g., chest, shoulders, arms, and legs) need flexibility or strength building, but the lower back and the midsection are especially important. Lower-back problems and weak midsections are among the most common contributors to reduced physical activity and painful injuries. The optimal combination is to do stretching exercises for the lower back and strength building for the midsection, which will provide support for the lower back. Enumerating particular stretching and strength-building activities is beyond the scope of this chapter, but virtually all teachers need to emphasize these activities as they progress from the young-adult to the midlife years (Adams 2003).

The Gift of Fitness

Obviously, fitness cannot be given from one person to another; it is always something the individual has to achieve by himself or herself. Your genetic endowment may contribute to good health, but genetics will not produce fitness. Only physical activity can do that. Therefore, no matter what your genetic heritage is or how much others may encourage you to be physically active, you won't be fit unless movement becomes a regular part of your life.

Your becoming and remaining physically fit is one of the greatest gifts you can give significant others (family and students). You are far less likely to become a burden on others or to be underpar in your attempts to help others if you are a fit person. Besides, presenting a healthy image to your students is likely to encourage them to emphasize fitness in their lives. Childhood obesity has become one of the major health problems of our society. Although owing in part to poor eating habits, obesity is more fundamentally attributable to a sedentary lifestyle. Students should know that you are physically active, how you became physically active, and how you benefit from physical activity.

Self-Assessment of Fitness and Fitness Activity

Now it is time for you to take stock of where you stand relative to fitness and fitness activity. Although fitness is not synonymous with health, being fit is likely to affect a variety of health indices (e.g., blood pressure, cholesterol level, blood sugar level, and pulmonary capacity). In the main, assessment of the latter indices requires medical equipment and personnel. However, two measures of fitness that can readily be assessed by anyone are resting pulse rate and recovery pulse rate. Also, many pharmacies have blood pressure equipment that can be used without medical assistance. Affirming the following statements shows that you are on the upward track with respect to your fitness:

1. My resting pulse rate is below sixty (man) or seventy (woman) beats per minute.

2. After one minute of continuously stepping up and down on the first rung of stairs, I can recover my resting pulse rate within one minute of inactivity.

3. I can walk at a pace of fifteen minutes per mile on a level surface without feeling short of breath.

4. I can walk up two flights of stairs and still be able to carry on a conversation at the top of the second flight.

5. When going from one floor to another in multilevel complexes, I usually take the stairs instead of the elevator.

6. Each day I have at least thirty minutes of sustained exercise at least equivalent to the pace of walking a fifteen-minute mile.

7. I include at least five minutes of stretching and ten minutes of strength-building exercises in my physical activity each day.

8. I have exercise options for all seasons of the year.

9. I do at least fifteen minutes of housework or yard work each day.

10. When given a choice between sedentary or exercise leisure options, I usually opt for the latter.

"SWEATING MAKES YOU SMARTER"

A recent article in a leading psychological journal made some rather striking claims regarding the impact of exercise on one's mental functioning (Jozefowicz 2004). First, the bad news. For virtually all human beings, the loss of brain tissue begins in their twenties and progressively increases in later decades. The good news is that regular, vigorous exercise can slow brain decline by solidifying old connections and promoting new ones. Recent research also indicates that exercise contributes to the production of a protein in the brain that improves cognitive functioning. The net result of exercise is that one is able to assimilate and store new information better than would be the case with a sedentary lifestyle. The bottom line is that a good workout may help your mind as much as your muscles.

The first four items relate to your fitness level and the last six to your fitness activity. Despite our "yes" or "no" response format, answers to these items can exist on a continuum from very high to very low. For example, a resting pulse rate of seventy is much better than one of ninety. The intent of the items is not necessarily for you to compute your total score on fitness level and fitness activity, but rather to pinpoint areas where you fitness might be improved.

Recreational Pursuits

For many individuals, sports involvement and recreational pursuits are practically synonymous. Enjoyment of sports activity is one of the surest ways to sustain exercise. However, there are some very good reasons for having some nonphysical recreational options. Perhaps the most notable reason is that physical illness and injury occasionally preclude exercise. Another possible disadvantage of focusing exclusively on exercise as your means of recreation is the inevitability of down periods in your exercise activity. You may grow bored with walking or swimming, and your tennis game may seem hopelessly off target. You may be continuing the activity, but not deriving much satisfaction from it. During such periods, in particular, the availability of other recreational possibilities can buoy your spirits.

Vacation Time for Teachers

One of the presumed benefits of teaching is the amount of vacation time it affords. Few professions permit as much time off during the Christmas season and the summer as does teaching. However, few teachers use most of this time for fun activities. They may have a part-time job, complete major projects around the home, take graduate courses, and prepare for the next school year. Although all of these options can bring satisfaction, or at least a diversion from the daily demands of teaching, they do not meet the classical definition of a vacation. Teachers truly need to take time off, do fun things, and travel to attractive destinations.

There are two kinds of vacations—the restful and the adventurous—with each having its distinct advantages. A trip to the beach where you have no demands on your time typifies the restful. Relaxation is the order of the day. Decisions involve only where to go today, which fun activity to do first, and where to dine tonight. You can linger as long as you like with an activity and do nothing more challenging than enjoy yourself. You can read, laugh, and engage in leisurely conversation with no time pressures.

The adventurous vacation involves more excitement than the restful, but it also entails more effort and uncertainty. This type of vacation involves traveling in a foreign country on your own or with another acquaintance. Now you have to worry about exchanging money,

traveling to different places, and arranging for accommodations possibly without proficiency in the native language or substantive knowledge of the local culture. You will learn a great deal and have priceless experiences, but you will have to work to achieve these outcomes.

A compromise between the restful and the adventurous is to travel in a foreign country with a group under the auspices of a travel agency. In fact, you may travel with a group of fellow educators who have the common goal of learning the native language or visiting schools around the country. Having most of the travel arrangements and accommodations planned by the travel agency relieves you of that potential stressor, and being with fellow educators (often from different schools) makes for bonding and communication with others who share your professional commitments.

Daily Recreation

Despite the restorative potential of vacation time, our analysis of "recreational options" does not target extended vacation ventures. Those experiences have a place and provide for much positive anticipation, but they may not be immediate enough to sustain you on Monday morning. What you need then is something to look forward to on Monday afternoon! Our goal is to infuse some vacation-like activity into each day.

What types of recreational activity can you include in your daily schedule? Reading, playing a musical instrument, listening to music, painting, working with crafts, gardening, collecting various items, and playing games are only a few possibilities. We strongly believe that among the fundamental purposes of life is the enjoyment of life. That seems to be the reason many give for working so hard—so they can enjoy life at some "later time." Our conviction is that those "later times" come too late and too infrequently for many people. A better approach is to include enjoyable activity in each day's schedule. In this way, you partake of life's fundamental purposes as you proceed through life.

Time for Recreation

Despite the multiple benefits of recreational activity, you may still have difficulty finding time for it. However, because such activity is inherently enjoyable, it can be included in your daily schedule when you might otherwise be fatigued or bored. Because recreational activity can recharge your spirits, you may wind up accomplishing more in the evening hours than if you had devoted the additional time to work. Instead of forcing yourself to work when you do not feel like it, why not involve yourself in an absorbing recreational activity for a few minutes? Or you may prefer to give yourself a list of work responsibilities

leading up to leisure-time activity (such as a night on the town or a weekend trip). The list should be sufficiently short so as to motivate rather than overpower. If the recreational activity is well within sight, you may breeze through your work in record time.

Decisions about the amount of time you invest each day in recreational activity obviously have to be made in the context of your other time commitments. Nonetheless, we encourage you to keep your recreational time at a modest level on weekdays, saving up for a double or triple dose on weekends. By "modest," we mean something on the order of thirty minutes to an hour a day. Greater time investment runs the risk of undermining other commitments, thus creating guilt feelings about work and interpersonal relationships. What should be a source of motivation and enrichment may become an albatross under those circumstances.

Time Well Spent

Perhaps you are concerned about the adverse effect that recreational activity may have on your professional productivity. If the recreational activity indeed does "recreate" and provide for renewal experiences, then infusing some recreational time in your nonteaching hours better prepares you to tackle your teaching day. Beyond personal renewal, recreational activities can provide for specific skills and information that contribute directly to teaching. For example, leisure reading can provide a wealth of examples to use in your teaching. An awareness of contemporary music can constitute a common ground for relating to many of your students. Your artwork can be used to embellish the atmosphere of your classroom. Playing a musical instrument can serve as entertainment and stimulation for your students. In fact, there is hardly any recreational activity that cannot contribute in direct ways to your teaching effectiveness.

Oral Consumption

This topic may seem like an odd inclusion in the current chapter and may even sound like a physical condition you don't want. Nonetheless, all of us engage in oral consumption every day and what goes in our mouths can be life sustaining or life threatening. Here we refer specifically to food, drink, and chemicals. Few actions more fundamentally affect the quality of your personal life and what you have to offer as a teacher than oral consumption.

Healthful Nutrition

Let's begin with food consumption, an action in which most of us engage every day and perhaps even several times each day. One might assume that teachers know how to eat well and consistently apply standards of healthful eating, but our public eating habits often belie that assumption. For instance, in the professional circles we have traveled, the favorite food items at morning meetings have often been pastries (frequently doughnuts). Whole-grain and soy products, fruits, and natural fruit juices would have been better options for sustaining our energy throughout the morning session and for promoting our long-term health.

Despite our less than superlative eating habits, most of us are concerned about over-consumption of food. This is a time when many adults, teachers not excluded, seem to be on some kind of diet. Perhaps there is good reason for this obsession with dieting, given that 65 percent of American adults are overweight and 23 percent qualify as obese (Patz 2003). Unfortunately, the succession of popular diets hasn't substantially lowered the rate of obesity in our country. Even the popular low-carbohydrate diets lack independent research evidence supporting their contribution to long-term health and weight management (Bravata et al. 2003). Although many individuals report weight loss with either a low-fat or low-carbohydrate diet, most have grievous difficulty maintaining that weight loss.

In assessing your diet, think primarily in terms of promoting good health rather than losing weight. A health-enhancing diet includes lots of whole grains, vegetables, and fruits, but minimal red meats, saturated fats, and starches. Regular consumption of vegetable oils, fish, and possibly poultry also contributes to good health. Fortunately, delicious soy products have been developed as alternatives to most meats. As long as you're sure that these

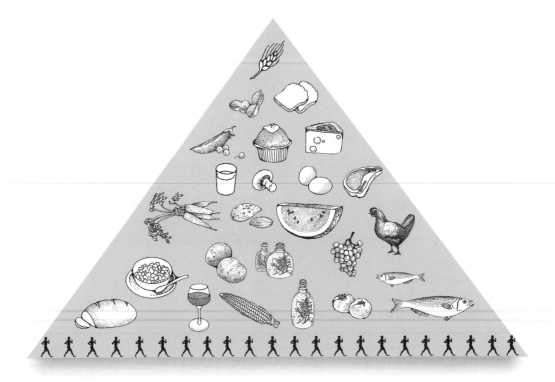

products contain no transfatty acids, substituting soy for all red meat and even for chicken can be a healthful trade-off. Also, an alcoholic drink or two a day may not hurt, although such beverages are heavy in calories. With respect to weight, the bottom line is still total calories. Too many calories from whatever source will contribute to weight gain. Keep your serving sizes small and eat slowly so you can experience satiation before you have overeaten. And you must exercise regularly to maintain weight loss at a healthful level, whatever your good food choices.

FOOD PYRAMIDS

In the early 1990s, the U.S. Department of Agriculture published the Food Pyramid, which came to be widely embraced in both nutritional and lay circles as reflecting the most valid guidelines for eating. Fat, especially saturated fat, was to be minimized, and complex carbohydrates (grains, potatoes, pasta) were to be maximized in one's diet. Animal protein, including red meat, could be consumed in moderation (two to three servings per day).

With the reemergence of the Atkins Diet, the pyramid was turned topsy-turvy. All carbohydrates, including both complex and simple, were to be minimized, whereas fats and proteins could be eaten freely. After substantial weight loss occurred, some carbohydrates could gradually be reintroduced into one's diet. The Atkins Diet appears not to have been widely embraced in the professional literature on nutrition, but millions tried it and lost substantial weight. Unfortunately, as individuals reintroduced carbohydrates into their diet, they regained much of the weight they had lost.

In 2003, a new food pyramid appeared in the nutritional research literature (Willett and Stampfer, 2003). In this new scheme, complex carbohydrates were divided into two categories:

whole grains and starches. Again, whole grains were to be eaten freely, but starches (e.g., white rice, white bread, and white potatoes) were to be greatly minimized. Although saturated fat also was to be minimized, plant oils (such as monounsaturated and polyunsaturated oils) joined whole grains at the base of the new food pyramid. Nuts, especially walnuts, were considered to be good sources of such oils. Daily consumption of fish and chicken was still considered permissible, but red meat was to be consumed sparingly, if at all. The major dietary models (the 1992 Department of Agriculture pyramid, the Atkins pyramid, and the 2003 pyramid) have all recommended a liberal consumption of vegetables and fruits in one's diet.

In April 2005, the USDA released a set of nutritional guidelines that can be individualized according to one's age, gender and activity level. In the main, these guidelines are consistent with the Willett and Stampfer pyramid, but the new USDA guidelines allow more liberal consumption of white complex carbohydrates than was the case in Willett and Stampfer's scheme.

For further information, refer to www.mypyramid.gov.

Smoking Cessation

Teachers, like professionals in all areas, consume some things they shouldn't. The most common daily offender in the larger society is smoking. We could find no research regarding the percentage of teachers who smoke compared to the percentage of individuals in other professions who smoke. If the incidence of smoking among teachers is consistent with that in the total U.S. adult population, probably around 22 percent of teachers are regular smokers. The personal costs of regular smoking are enormous. Smoking reduces both the longevity and quality of life, constituting the major preventable cause of death in our society and holding individuals hostage to one of the worst of all drug addictions.

In addition to the personal consequences of smoking, teachers who smoke set a terrible example of drug addiction for youngsters who may be tempted to experiment with drugs. Given that smoking is the most common gateway practice for using other drugs (Lai et al. 2000) youngsters who know their teacher smokes may be more inclined to smoke and perhaps subsequently to use other drugs. Think what a devastating, long-term effect you would have on your students' lives if you influence them to smoke.

Inasmuch as most schools do not provide smoking areas for either students or faculty, how would your students know if you smoke? They may occasionally see you smoking in settings away from school, and most assuredly they can smell cigarette smoke on your clothing and likely on your breath when you approach them. Also, if you grade student papers at home, they will likely smell cigarette smoke on the papers you return to them.

If you smoke, the only way you can maintain some credibility as an advocate of good health practices is to acknowledge that you smoke and to indicate you are trying to quit. No matter how many times you have tried to quit and failed, keep trying. The average number of attempts it takes to stop smoking permanently is between five and seven. In your repeated attempts to stop smoking, you need to identify physical and social cues that elicit smoking and replace them with cues for alternatives to smoking. Most important, you need to minimize time spent with smokers and maximize time spent with nonsmokers. If you have never smoked or have stopped smoking, we greatly applaud your health-enhancing choices. Perhaps you will find our antismoking guidelines informative in helping colleagues join you as a nonsmoker.

Social Relations

Another crucial facet of your nonteaching hours is relationships with significant others. Teachers who become deeply immersed in their profession have a tendency to let social relationships slide during heavy work periods. The requirements of teaching periodically become so great that spouse, family, and friends may be neglected. This pattern is likely to lead to profound problems in your personal life, which in turn will adversely affect your professional life. Others can tolerate neglect only so long without becoming resentful or beginning to withdraw from the relationship. You should make sure that your closest personal relationships get some of your best time and energy. Otherwise, what can be a source of your greatest support may become a source of your greatest distress.

Areas of Sharing

A good beginning point in staying intimately connected with a significant other is to share fun time. Each of you likely has an array of activities you enjoy, but you may participate separately in those activities. However, sharing mutually enjoyable activities should enhance the experiences for both you and your partner. Enjoying experiences together is among the most important contributors to enjoying each other. Shared good times are associated with good feelings about each other.

Another type of sharing is discussing some of the more positive occurrences of each person's day. It is unfortunate that sharing time with significant others is often problem oriented. By the time teachers finish "dumping" all of their classroom problems on their significant other, sharing may become an oppressive experience. Individuals typically like spending time with those who focus mainly on positive events in their lives. Besides, if you selectively attend to the positive aspects of each day, you are sure to feel better about the quality of your day.

For relationships to deepen and endure, there must also be times to share your deepest concerns with intimate others. If your sharing time is consumed in small talk, you may feel increasingly bland about the relationship. In contrast, if you share some of your deepest aspirations, anxieties, dilemmas, and perceptions of life, that sharing time will be invaluable. Others often long for that depth of communication and can provide you with vital support and feedback. Furthermore, if you share intimate aspects of your life with another, he or she is likely to share at an equally intimate level with you.

Communication Guidelines

We devoted an entire chapter (chapter two) to guidelines for communicating with members of your professional network. Unfortunately, teachers who exercise great care in communicating with students, parents, and colleagues may be quite negligent in how they respond to people at home who matter most to them. For instance, most successful teachers practice active listening in their interactions at school, but may be less inclined to listen so intently at home. Don't leave active listening at school when you return home in the afternoon. Remember, active listening demonstrates that you understand and appreciate others' experiences, something your intimates need to know.

Supportive comments are also just as important at home as at school. Taking others

"GET REAL"

Currently, you may be married or living with an intimate other. You also may have one or more children under your care during the evening hours. Our discussion about having fun together, sharing positive events from your day at school, and conversing in a deep and meaningful way may have sounded like a fantasy to you. In some teachers' homes, shouting and screaming at one another better characterize the evening homelife. Thus, our view of the American home as a place of civil, positive, supportive, and meaningful conversation may seem slightly out of touch with reality. We plead guilty. What we have described is perhaps more an ideal than the reality of the evening hours in many teachers' homes.

If your life at home in the evening is anything but serene, if you're trying to mediate fights among your children, and if you and your spouse are having one disagreement after another, don't despair. Some authorities (e.g., Lasswell 1985) contend that it is far better to air your disagreements than to maintain a facade of harmony. In fact, Lasswell proposes that disagreement often leads to marital growth rather than to marital failure. Superficial agreement allows sensitive areas to remain unconfronted and unresolved, with one or both parties paying the price later.

Although occasional open disagreement can be healthy, perpetual conflict presents problems. No one likes to live in a setting where individuals are constantly upset with one another. If your home life involves too much discord for your comfort level, where do you begin in improving the climate at home? Undoubtedly, you would like for your family to start treating you in a more civil and supportive manner. Given that you have much more control over your own behavior than that of your partner and even your children, the best place to begin is with your own responses to family members. If we teachers were to treat family members with the same level of courtesy and support that we do colleagues at school, perhaps the climate at home would become more civil. There are no guarantees with respect to your home life, but kinder treatment of family members may set in motion reciprocal actions that will make home life better for all.

for granted is a common tendency among those who have lived together for quite some time. Anything your partner does to make your life better should be acknowledged. Such contributions include preparing food, doing chores around the house, and paying the bills. Also, you should note anything your partner does to maintain or improve his or her health and appearance—for example, working out, eating better, and dressing nicely.

However, as emphasized in chapter four, praise can sometimes be interpreted as manipulation. To minimize that possibility, you should indicate simply that you have noticed a particular action and that you appreciate this action. You don't want to imply by the commendation that your partner has been doing badly in the past or must do better in the future to please you. For example, the comment "you look nice today" is sometimes interpreted as "you don't ordinarily look so attractive." Making your feedback precise and highlighting the benefits to your partner (e.g., "Your working out every day can really enhance your fitness") may reduce the likelihood of your compliment being interpreted as manipulative (e.g., "I've been keeping track of your working out recently, and you're doing just what I want you to do").

Domestic Responsibilities

Because few teachers are affluent enough to hire someone to take care of their home, some domestic activity is almost inevitable in the evening hours and on weekends. Domestic responsibilities can become extremely onerous and undermine pursuits in other areas discussed in this chapter. We are convinced that such an eventuality can usually be avoided. Three concepts useful in keeping domestic responsibilities at a manageable level are sharing equitably, balancing daily loads, and sequencing tasks.

Role Sharing

When teachers report that they are overwhelmed with domestic responsibilities in the evening hours, we usually find they have assumed a disproportionate share of the domestic tasks in their households. To avoid this imbalance, any person living in your household should assume his or her portion of the domestic responsibilities. You and your domestic partners might begin by listing all the work tasks to be done around the house. Do not forget those less-pleasant cleaning tasks (e.g., cleaning the oven, the top of the range, the bathroom fixtures, and the plastic shower curtains) to which most members of your household may be largely oblivious. You might attach a time estimate to each task to aid in the distribution of responsibilities.

You can then begin dividing work responsibilities on the basis of enjoyment and skill level. However, you may not be able to identify very many tasks that would be enjoyable to at least someone in your household. Many household chores are not particularly palatable to anyone. You may enjoy seeing a clean, attractively arranged house, but it is unlikely you will ever get much exhilaration from washing dishes or vacuuming the floor. At some point in your division of tasks, each person must be willing to share equitably those tasks no one likes to do.

Lack of skill in doing certain tasks is sometimes offered as an excuse for not assuming responsibility for those tasks. Certain members of the household may have meager knowledge of how to perform many domestic functions. However, if anyone in the home knows

Getting help with domestic tasks.

how to do a particular task, that person can teach others in the household to do the task. No aspect of domestic work is too difficult for a person of normal intelligence to master. Achieving a balanced distribution of tasks may require a great deal of in-service training for some members of your household.

Timely Attention to Tasks

An equitable distribution of domestic tasks should reduce each person's load to a manageable level. An extension of this concept is to distribute tasks across days. A few things may need to be done every day (e.g., preparing meals and washing dishes), but many things may need to be done only once or twice a week (e.g., washing clothes and vacuuming the house). Taking on only one or two major tasks each day should prevent you from feeling overwhelmed by what you have to do and will prevent domestic disarray from undermining other work and play possibilities. We estimate that given the sharing format we have proposed, no individual person needs to do more than an hour of actual housework each day.

Perhaps the most crucial dimension of this daily scheduling is the sequencing of tasks. The optimal time to shop for groceries is before the pantry is totally barren. The optimal time to wash clothes is before every stitch of clothing in your household is filthy. Develop a schedule that anticipates needs and prevents you from getting into domestic binds. Also, think in terms of how one task affects another. Task B may be considerably easier after doing task A. Look at the full gamut of domestic tasks to be done during the week. How can you best sequence those tasks not only to prevent difficult circumstances (no food in the house, no clean clothes to wear), but also to make subsequent tasks flow more easily? Such an approach can save hours of work and much psychological discomfort each week. It can also put you in control of a part of life that has a tendency to get out of control.

Self-Assessment of Domestic Management
Unless you have a tradition of being an outstanding homemaker, you may not have systematically analyzed how you can improve your household management. You simply have a sense that physical conditions within your home are not what you would like. Maybe the physical aspect of the household is messy and in some respects unclean. Dirty dishes, clutter on the floor, and clothing not put away may characterize your habitat. We list here some domestic practices that will serve you well over both the short run and the long run. They will make your living arrangement more pleasant and help you to be comfortable when company drops by unexpectedly. Can you identify any areas where your domestic management needs improvement?

> *Daily Tasks*
> Checking to see if you have clean clothes for tomorrow before you go to bed;
> Making up your bed before you leave for work in the morning;
> Putting away your clothes whenever you change clothes;
> Putting away items in your bathroom that detract from its appearance;
> Picking up clutter on the floor as soon as you notice it;
> Washing or putting breakfast dishes in the dishwasher before you leave for work;
> Preparing healthful food for your morning and evening meals.
>
> *Weekly Tasks*
> Shopping for a week's supply of healthful food items;
> Washing all your clothes for the week;
> Vacuuming the floors;

Dusting furniture;

Taking recyclable items to depositories if needed;

Cleaning windows (at least starting on the task) if needed.

Completing certain other tasks may be necessary to improve or maintain your comfort level with your domestic management. However, if you do all the things listed here, you will manage your household much more efficiently.

STRATEGIES FOR JUGGLING PROFESSIONAL AND FAMILY LIVES

One of our former graduate students, a single parent as well as a full-time teacher, developed some useful strategies for managing her life outside the classroom. Her suggestions bring together most facets of one's personal life discussed in this chapter.

1. Each Sunday evening review the week ahead and formulate your game plan. Jot down all family appointments and obligations, school-related activities and responsibilities, and social events. For the "light days," pencil in laundry, baking, grocery shopping, or miscellaneous household chores. For "heavy days," plan slow-cooker or microwave-oven dinners and the bare minimum of household maintenance.

2. Assign chores to everyone in the family; you cannot do it all! Children can be given monetary incentives or points to be traded at the end of the week for tickets to a movie or skating, for example.

3. No matter how busy you are, take a few minutes each day to talk to each child about the events of the day and to share a laugh, a game, or a snack.

4. Learn to say "no." Because you already have plenty to do, you need to learn the skill of assertive refusal when being pressured to help with the church bake sale, to take on another committee assignment, or the like. (You will be of little assistance to anyone if you spread yourself too thinly.)

5. Streamline your daily work as much as possible. Can you give a multiple-choice test rather than an essay test that will be more time-consuming to grade? Can students grade each others' papers instead of your carting them all home? Can you delegate other routine tasks?

6. Do something each day just for yourself to relax or "recharge your batteries." Take a walk, listen to music, take a relaxing bath, read a good short story, or phone a friend. You deserve it!

7. Plan a mini-vacation once a month—take the family to the lake or to an out-of-town ball game, for instance. Just getting away now and then from the usual environs refreshes everyone.

Academic Preparation

Academic responsibilities have a way of going beyond the school day and infringing on your personal time. Although many effective teachers do some school-related work at home, schoolwork does not dominate their evening hours and weekends. It is our conviction that the spillover into the evening hours is caused by teachers' trying to accomplish too much with students or mismanaging professional responsibilities during the school day. We prefer to operate from the premise that 80 to 90 percent of what the teacher does professionally should occur within the school day.

Several guidelines help keep most schoolwork at school for both teachers and students. As a teacher, do not make any assignments for which prompt, systematic feedback cannot be provided. Requiring work from students that is never carefully checked is absolutely taboo. If students are required to do the work, then it is your responsibility to see that the work is thoroughly checked. This guideline should temper any tendency you may have to give massive assignments.

Another guideline that may reduce your work load at home is to minimize repetition within assignments. Five problems related to a mathematical manipulation may serve as well as twenty problems related to the same manipulation. Repetition across many problems is likely to produce fatigue and boredom, conditions that are counter to the enjoyment of the activity. Make your assignments just long enough for the students to demonstrate comprehension of the concept or procedure under question. In general, give assignments that illustrate only one major concept or, at most, a few major concepts.

A third guideline for reducing schoolwork at home is to provide time at school for completing and checking assignments. Remember, the purpose of assignments is basically instructional, which requires that students be given prompt feedback and corrective instruction in areas of difficulty. To accomplish this requirement, you need to institute self-checking procedures and peer tutoring in your class. This arrangement permits students to determine many of their own deficiencies and allows those students who have mastered particular concepts to assist others who are having difficulty. It doesn't preclude the necessity of your feedback, but rather allows some improvement to occur in the student's work before you see it.

Giving students time at school to work on and correct assignments provides some planning time for you during the school day. The ideal is for planning, completion of assignments, feedback regarding assignments, and corrective instruction to occur within the time frame for a particular subject area. Consequently, when the reading period is over in the morning, both you and your students should be able to turn to other matters until the reading period the next day.

Concluding Comments

We readily admit that this chapter has taken a much broader perspective of the teacher's life than that advanced in most educational texts. However, we strongly contend that teachers' effectiveness in the classroom cannot be divorced from their lives outside the classroom. Inevitably, a troubled or sterile life outside the classroom will infringe on a teacher's productivity in the classroom.

We also admit that some recommendations run counter to established educational philosophy. Whoever heard of minimizing homework for both students and teachers? We believe that academe's infringement on the evening hours for both teachers and students operates much like a malignancy in the human body. A malignancy feeds on the body until it ultimately kills its own source of life. Extending work responsibilities long into the evening undermines the enjoyment and energy necessary for teaching and learning to occur most effectively during the school day.

Perhaps you have been keeping track of the time investment for the various activities recommended in this chapter. Have we gone beyond a twenty-four-hour day? Assuming a teacher spends about eight hours at school, has as much as an hour's travel time in getting to and from school each day, and sleeps for at least seven hours, that leaves exactly eight hours to do all the things we have recommended for the waking hours. Let's summarize how we have committed those eight hours: thirty minutes to an hour for exercise, thirty minutes to an hour a day for recreational activity other than exercise, one hour a day for quality socializing (which can sometimes be incorporated into other activities), one to two hours of domestic work (including meal preparation), one hour of schoolwork for you, and possibly one hour of assisting your children with homework.

Surely we have omitted some important categories in your personal life, and perhaps underestimated or overestimated the time involvement for some categories targeted in this chapter. Nevertheless, if we choose the upper end of our time ranges, seven out of your eight waking hours after school are largely committed (leaving all of one hour to do anything you want). You can adjust our time estimates to fit your particular situation. For example, if you have no children, you can reclaim the hour we designated for homework assistance. Be cautious about omitting other categories, however, even if you have to reduce the time we have projected for those categories. Most especially, don't omit the exercise and socializing categories. And, of course, get a good night's sleep.

References

Adams, R. (2003). *Strength Training: A Natural Prescription for Staying Healthy and Fit.* Teacher and Teacher Education Clearinghouse. British Columbia, Canada: ERIC ED481391.

Bravata, D. M., L. Sanders, J. Huang, H. M. Krumholz, I. Olkin, C. D. Gardner, and D. M. Bravata. (2003). Efficacy and safety of low-carbohydrate diets: A systematic review. *Journal of the American Medical Association* 289: 1837–850.

Dahl, R. E. (1999). The consequences of insufficient sleep for adolescents: Links between sleep and emotional regulation. *Phi Delta Kappan* (January): 354–59.

Jozefowicz, C. (2004). Sweating makes you smart. *Psychology Today* 37(3): 56–58.

Lai, S., H. Lai, J. Page, and C. McCoy (2000). The association between cigarette smoking and drug abuse in the United States. *Journal of Addictive Diseases*, 19(4): 11-24.

Lasswell, M. (1985). Illusions regarding marital happiness. *Medical Aspects of Human Sexuality* 19: 144-58.

Patz, A. (2003). 6 mindful ways to shed pounds. *Psychology Today* 36(1): 72–76.

Raglin, J. S. (1990). Exercise and mental health: Beneficial and detrimental effects. *Sports Medicine* 9: 323–29.

Weaver, D. B. (n.d.). Good sleep habits. In *Maximizing the Quality of Your Sleep: Advice for Overachievers in the New Millennium*. Retrieved July 9, 2004, from http://www.sleepmed.com/maxquality.html.

Wiley, J. A., and T. C. Camacho. (1980). Life-style and future health: Evidence from the Alameda County study. *Preventive Medicine* 9: 1–21.

Willett, W. C., and Stampfer, M. J. (2003). Rebuilding the food pyramid. *Scientific American*, 288 (1): 64–71.

Winters, C. (1999). Get fit bit by bit. *New Choices* (July–August): 24–26.

10

◄○►

Bringing It Together

A Brighter Day

Establishing effective classroom discipline is no simple matter. Many variables affect student behavior in the classroom, making it impossible to provide a single solution that fits every behavioral challenge. Teachers have to synchronize numerous variables to maintain productive behaviors from most students in most situations. For a particular behavioral problem in a particular situation, teachers have to identify the factors that are contributing to the problem in that situation and then alter those factors. Such an analysis can best be achieved by having a broad understanding of different disciplinary strategies and then integrating those strategies to form a coherent approach to classroom management.

This chapter looks at ways in which the ideas presented in previous chapters can be organized into a unified model of classroom management. We highlight a key concept from each of the first eight chapters, using the first letter of a term for the concept to form the acronym BRIGHTER. From chapter nine, we highlight DAY, using all the letters. A BRIGHTER DAY is presented as a model that synthesizes major concepts across chapters, allowing you to use those ideas in a cumulative fashion to manage different types of class-room management problems. We hope the use of the model will *brighten* your *day* as you attempt to meet the myriad challenges of classroom management. We apply the model first to two different classroom problems, and then we give you the opportunity to use the model in addressing a cross-section of other problems that occur in many classrooms.

General Review

Chapter one suggested that the **Beliefs** teachers hold about the nature of teaching can influence their effectiveness in managing a classroom. Teachers can maximize their effectiveness by recognizing their significant influence in the classroom, the good around them at school, the potential of their students, and the importance of principles to guide their daily actions. Chapter two then addressed ways teachers can improve their verbal and nonverbal skills to establish workable **Relationships** with students and other members of their school network.

Chapter three described how teachers can **Initiate** productive behavior by planning extensively, developing useful rules and procedures, assessing and using student interests as a framework for instructional activities, modeling behaviors that have enduring benefits to students, and prompting constructive behaviors that may otherwise not occur. Chapter four described how **"Good"** student behaviors (those that will help students perform better in school and prepare them for adulthood), once initiated, can be strengthened and maintained through favorable consequences.

Strategies presented in chapters three and four are best combined to promote good behaviors that either are absent or infrequently exhibited. For example, the strategies in these two chapters should be key elements in working with students who seldom complete assignments, interact minimally in class activities, attend school irregularly, or do not make good use of their learning opportunities. These strategies can be used in tandem to create a supportive learning environment for all students. Behaviors must occur at some level before reinforcing consequences can be applied, and prompted behaviors may be attenuated if not followed by reinforcement.

Although enhancing desired behaviors can do much to avert problems, it is not the total answer to classroom management. Teachers also need strategies for dealing with inappropriate behaviors that occasionally emerge even in the most effectively managed classrooms. Chapter five presented a variety of intervention strategies that have been used successfully in managing these behaviors. The emphasis throughout was on being **Helpful**—that is, replacing inappropriate behaviors, which are not in students' best interest, with constructive behaviors that will be helpful across time and situations. Thus, being truly helpful to your students in reorienting their behaviors in various situations necessitates combining methods for weakening inappropriate behavior with methods for teaching them what is appropriate. The strategies in chapter five are most applicable to problems such as disruptiveness, aggressiveness (bullying), defiance, and other tendencies that disrupt the teaching-learning process.

Classroom problems are frequently influenced by factors outside the classroom, with their solutions requiring cooperation between school personnel and the home. Having teachers and parents work **Together** for the benefit of students was discussed in chapter six. In the same spirit of working together, chapter seven emphasized how the laws related to working with students with disabilities underscore how important it is for teachers to work with the resource staff in their school to address the needs of **Everyone**, especially students with significant learning and conduct problems. In brief, chapters six and seven emphasized that no one can meet every challenge alone. Seeking assistance from parents and colleagues was presented as a sign of professional maturity—not of weakness.

Chapter eight dealt with the ultimate goal of all educational endeavors—having students take **Responsibility** for their own behaviors. Students, like most adults, want to feel they have a measure of control over what happens to them. Moreover, they are expected to manage their own lives after they finish their schooling. The emphasis in chapter eight was on developing work strategies that will give students more responsibility for directing their own learning, with the prospect of performing better in school and later in adulthood.

Finally, we concluded our journey through classroom management by putting the emphasis on **DAY**, underscoring teachers' needs to consider their own well-being each and every day. Teachers obviously spend most of their time addressing student needs, often neglecting their own personal needs. Everyone needs time to rejuvenate at day's end, if work is to be approached with energy and optimism the following day. Chapter nine offered suggestions for improving the quality of your life outside the classroom, resulting in a more productive career and a happier personal life—something everyone deserves. In sum, a *brighter day* necessitates considering your own needs as well as your students' needs.

Managing Problems

Our BRIGHTER DAY model is intended to serve as an overall guide for classroom management, eliminating the need for a different approach for each problem you encounter. Applying the model involves using each key term (e.g., *beliefs, relationships,* and so on) as a prompt for strategies that might help you manage a specific problem. You can repeat the approach with each problem you address. In brief, this problem-solving model includes the following steps:

B   1—Examining your *beliefs* to determine if they might be contributing to the problem or can be used in resolving the problem;

R   2—Using your communication skills to develop workable *relationships* with students and other members of your school family;

I   3—*Initiating* (i.e., prompting) appropriate student behaviors;

G   4—Strengthening *good* (i.e., constructive) student behaviors through application of rewarding consequences;

H   5—Using strategies to correct inappropriate behaviors that will *help* students learn to behave appropriately in a variety of situations;

T   6—Working *together* with parents to prevent and remedy the classroom-management problems connection to their children;

E   7—Working with other resource personnel to ensure that *everyone*, including students with any disability, is adequately served in your classroom;

R   8—Giving students opportunities to make choices and move towards greater levels of personal *responsibility* for their learning;

DAY   9—Recognizing and meeting your own personal needs each and every *day*.

Some problems involve greater emphasis on one or more of these steps than do other problems. For example, if you have determined that some students seldom complete assignments on time, you will need to rely heavily on determining whether you are appropriately communicating your expectations to them (chapter two) and whether assignments are consistent with your students' needs and interests (chapter three). You should also consider whether reinforcement is available for completing assignments in a timely and sufficient manner (chapter four). Furthermore, you want students to develop work habits consistent with completion of assignments (chapter eight). Given that completing assignments is something you want to strengthen, you would largely use positive rather than punitive strategies to accomplish the desired behavior change.

However, if the behavior in question is something you want to weaken, you should probably include at least some strategies presented in chapter five. This does not mean, of course, that you cannot use other steps in the model. Dealing with behaviors that need to be weakened can involve going through all the steps in the model. For instance, in dealing with bullying, you should examine your beliefs about the nature of bullying to ensure that all forms of the problem, including exclusion from a group, are being addressed. The way you communicate your concerns about bullying can also be part of the remedy. In potentially

explosive situations, you should be firm but respectful in what you say to students. You should also consult parents and other school personnel. With problems such as bullying, you should be sure that dealing with negative student behaviors does not undermine your own sense of well-being.

Using the model just described, let's look at how you might address two different problems: students' failure to interact well with all their classmates and students' defiance of teacher requests. We make suggestions from a number of chapters, using our model as a guide. You can use these suggestions in addressing similar problems in your classroom.

Achieving Greater Interaction Among All Students

Ms. Harris, a seventh-grade teacher, has a problem getting students to interact with one another. She is especially concerned that students separate themselves along racial lines whenever they have free-time activities or whenever they are permitted to choose peers with whom to work. Her students also tend to select seating arrangements that keep them with a particular group. Ms. Harris wants to have "one" class that interacts as a family, not separate cliques. What do you think can be done?

*Are there any **beliefs** the teacher holds about herself or students that can be altered to help resolve the problem?* Ms. Harris has already taken one step toward achieving cooperative interactions among her students—she believes they should function as a family rather than as separate subgroups. She needs to go a step further, though, and ensure that what she is expecting of students is realistic. For instance, is it realistic to expect students to have the same level of closeness with all their peers in the classroom? A more realistic expectation might be that students interact respectfully with everyone and exclude no one from any class activity, while still developing some special relationships with their peers. Functioning as a family does not preclude the possibility that some relationships are closer

than others. At the same time, respectful interaction across all members of one's class is both a reasonable and desirable expectation.

*How might the teacher use her communication skills to build better **relationships in the class?*** Ms. Harris must first examine how she is communicating her expectations to students. For example, does she communicate through her verbal and nonverbal behaviors that everyone is a capable and valued member of the class family? Students quickly pick up on any subtle signals that the teacher considers some students more important than others, and they may seek reaffirmation of their worth by isolating themselves into smaller groups. Ms. Harris may also need to teach listening skills to students, being certain they take turns, look at whoever is speaking, listen carefully to what others have to say, and respond respectfully to one another. Students who realize others are listening to them when they speak will likely be more attentive when their classmates are speaking. Moreover, if they see that their ideas are valued by the teacher and peers, they will feel more accepted within the class family. Functional families don't treat some members as more important than others, but rather communicate respect for each family member.

What behaviors can be initiated (i.e., prompted) to increase both the quantity and quality of interactions among all students? When students work in small groups, Ms. Harris has control over the makeup of the group. She can ensure there is diversity in each group and alter group membership so that students do not become accustomed to always working with the same individuals. One strategy for forming groups is to ensure that each group has a least one student who relates well to all students. That student can serve as a model for other students. Students are apt to imitate a student who has demonstrated interpersonal skills, especially when that student is popular among his or her peers.

Some groups, of course, may be formed on the basis of student interests. This does not mean, however, that students from any particular clique or racial background are going to have similar interests on every academic topic or even on most topics. As indicated in chapter three, teachers can conduct surveys to assess student interests and use data from those surveys to form interest groups. The teacher can maintain a record of who has been in a particular interest group and then form new groups to ensure that students have an opportunity to work with all class members. A different member of each group may also be given the role of providing a report of the group's progress, making a report to the class, or assuming the role of group leader or recorder. Students who have opportunities to get to know one another and form new friendships in small-group activities should be less "cliquish" when engaged in free-time activities or other non-academic pursuits. And sharing of responsibilities leads to everyone's having a sense of importance in the larger class family.

Another factor Ms. Harris has control over is the seating arrangement. Although it may initially be reinforcing for students to choose to whom they wish to sit near, the benefits of assigning students to seats or of having flexible arrangements (i.e., alternating seating arrangements from time to time) may far outweigh the benefits of letting students choose their own seats. Students will have opportunities when they are not doing seatwork to move about the room and speak with their closest friends. After all, school should not be a place where students are prohibited from speaking with others with whom they have close ties.

"Mrs. Harris"

How might "good" behaviors be strengthened? One important question Ms. Harris needs to address is, "What are the consequences for students of interacting constructively with classmates outside their primary social circle?" Heterogeneous groups can be formed to provide an opportunity for peer interactions, but these behaviors must be reinforced if they are to endure.

Ms. Harris cannot assume that peers will initially support those behaviors. In fact, interacting with peers they don't know may seem awkward to some students. Ms. Harris will need to identify ways that she can reinforce students when they interact positively with someone outside their primary peer group. This identification entails noticing and acknowledging such interactions whenever they occur. Given that cooperative interaction is a social behavior, it is appropriate to provide social acknowledgement rather than tangible rewards (e.g., trinkets, edibles). However, making a free-time social activity contingent on productive interaction within group work is also an appropriate social consequence for that interaction.

Ms. Harris can move about the room and offer appropriate comments. For example, she might note, "Everyone seems to be involved here," "I'm pleased to see you working so well together on this project," or "It's nice to see that everyone has a role in your group." Offering supportive statements not only provides needed reinforcement for behavior, but also models how students should be responding to one another.

Contingent reinforcement is essential for maintaining appropriate social interaction, but shaping (a procedure introduced in chapter four) may be needed for students who

Teacher and students researching a geography project together.

seldom interact with peers. Some students may be uncomfortable participating even in small-group discussions. With shaping, these students might initially be reinforced simply for listening to others. Once listening is well established, the student might simply be asked if he or she agrees with something that has been said. A nod of agreement by the student might be reinforced with a smile from the teacher. The student might also be given a role, such as recorder, that makes him or her feel more important in the group. Ms. Harris can privately

offer positive comments about the student's performance. If the size of the group is currently six to eight students, she might try forming smaller groups, with only four or five members. It is often easier for someone to speak up when the group is relatively small. The goal is to make whatever modifications are needed to move the student gradually toward being an active group member.

What teacher actions can ***help*** *students replace counterproductive behaviors with constructive behaviors?* Because getting students to interact cooperatively with all their peers is something Ms. Harris wants to strengthen, reprimands and other forms of punishment would not be appropriate in the behavioral strategy. On occasion, she may need to challenge students' use of sarcasm in responding to peers, but her major objective is to increase supportive interaction among students. As you may recall from chapter five, punishment decreases the behavior it follows, but it does not teach students what they are to do. Therefore, an alternative to punishing students for counterproductive behaviors is to strengthen behaviors that compete with negative behaviors. Students can't ignore or exclude others if they are interacting cooperatively with them. Ms. Harris primarily needs to reinforce behaviors incompatible with ignoring, excluding, or criticizing certain peers.

Another strategy mentioned in chapter five that Ms. Harris might consider is the use of logical consequences. For example, an applied logical consequence for excluding

someone from a group or for ignoring others in a group is to lose temporarily the privilege of being in a preferred interest group. However, before retracting group privileges, Ms. Harris needs to explore the usefulness of prompting (through small-group activities) constructive interaction and then reinforcing that interaction. Remaining in a group requires that one make an effort to interact effectively with other group members; however, one cannot learn to interact effectively unless one has the opportunity to function in a group.

*How might Ms. Harris and parents work **together** to help improve the situation?* Ms. Harris may want to consider various types of parental assistance with classroom activities. She might be able to use some parents as tutors, aides, or supervisors of small-group interaction. Parents can provide another set of eyes to ensure that all students are being included in group interaction. When parents from all the ethnic and socioeconomic groups represented among students have a role in the classroom, students are more apt to embrace the notion of the class as a family and want to interact with everyone in that family.

Parents need to be kept well informed about what is happening in the classroom, especially with their child, and must be provided with a comfortable mechanism for asking about assignments, classroom activities, and their child's progress and conduct. For example, teachers can identify specific afternoon hours when they will be available for phone calls from parents. The teacher also can solicit feedback from parents and make needed changes based on their suggestions. Parents want their children to be treated with respect by both teachers and peers. If invited to do so, they can offer useful suggestions for helping their children feel more a part of the class family.

How can the well-being of everyone, including those with special needs, be considered in promoting peer interaction? By applying some of the techniques described earlier, Ms. Harris can probably improve interactions among her students without consultation with other specialists. Nonetheless, school specialists such as the school psychologist, school counselor, or school social worker can provide assistance if needed. School counselors, for example, can be especially helpful in providing in-class fun activities to build interpersonal rapport. School psychologists can help teachers involve students with disabilities in group activities by identifying roles they can play and the assistance they will need from peers in the group.

Although the statement of Ms. Harris' problem does not include reference to students with special needs, students with learning disabilities or behavioral disorders may not readily be accepted by their class peers. Some may even be ostracized or teased. Every child, irrespective of his or her needs, should be integrated in some fashion in class activities. It is the teacher's responsibility to make sure that this happens and that each child is treated with respect by other children. How the teacher treats the child sets the tone for how other students respond to that child. If the teacher needs help in integrating a student with exceptional needs into group activities, resource personnel are available to assist with this process.

How might the teacher move students to higher levels of personal responsibility for improving interpersonal relationships in the classroom? Having students participate in planned group activities is a good starting point, but Ms. Harris shouldn't overlook student ideas for improving peer relationships. Even very young students can offer possible answers to the general question, "What would make a good classroom?" But Ms. Harris needs to be more specific in soliciting student ideas for promoting more positive interactions among students. Certain questions provide many clues as to what both the teacher and students can do to enhance classroom interactions: "What does it mean to be a productive member of a team?" "What does it take to be someone's friend?" "What can we do to get to know one another better?" or "How can we show respect for all our classmates?"

The ultimate endeavor of any educational goal is to move students to higher levels of self-responsibility for their behavior, especially how they treat others. We want students to interact with others when they leave the classroom not just because it is a classroom policy, but because they view interpersonal interaction as a way to enhance their own lives and others' lives. Giving students a role in planning classroom activities can be a step toward their becoming more responsible members of the class family, showing concern for all members of that family.

*Can Ms. Harris change any aspect of her after-school **day** to help her promote better relationships among her students?* As noted earlier, how Ms. Harris responds to her students is a powerful model of how they should treat each other. If she consistently blends tact, kindness, patience, and firmness in her responses to students, they will have a clearer conception of how to respond with civility to one another. However, such supportive conduct may be difficult for Ms. Harris to maintain across the ups and downs of each school day. Teachers see and experience interpersonal treatment that is inconsiderate and obnoxious. Their ability to keep those episodes in perspective (i.e., the student doesn't always behave that way, and the student is clearly capable of better behavior) depends a great deal on the good things teachers experience both in the classroom and outside the classroom. The more frequently they engage in activities that cause them to feel good about themselves, the more capable they will be to overcome bad treatment with good treatment.

Just as students need support to strengthen appropriate interaction, teachers need support from others to maintain their high interpersonal standards. Associating with others who are optimistic and encouraging can have an impact on their outlook and on their desire to be helpful to students. Teachers can be proactive by sharing their avocational skills (e.g., music, art, tennis) with those likely to appreciate those skills. Also, when they have a tendency to feel sorry for themselves (who doesn't, occasionally?), they might think of someone who can benefit from a phone call (e.g., a sick friend or an acquaintance with job problems). Even a kind act toward a student who is giving the teacher problems may make both parties feel better. Doing something to help others is one of the most powerful ways for teachers to feel better about themselves. In short, teachers who respect themselves are more likely to model humane treatment in their many interactions with students.

Reducing Student Defiance

Mr. Johansen, a first-year high school teacher, had been experiencing increasing difficulties with several of his math students. Early in the year he had related well with them, and they had worked hard in class. They appeared eager to please him. As time passed, however, he noticed that some students were becoming less compliant with his requests. They would murmur among themselves, snicker at his requests, and delay responding to the requests. Sometimes they would ignore him, acting as if they didn't hear what he said.

Mr. Johansen initially avoided taking any action about student resistance to his requests, hoping the situation would improve. He was also afraid that if confronting students about their defiance proved unsuccessful, he would earn a reputation of being inept in managing his classes. However, he realized something had to be done when one of his students made an obscene gesture after being asked to stop talking. What would you suggest that Mr. Johansen do to reduce student defiance of his requests?

Examining Beliefs. Although Mr. Johansen should not tolerate open defiance from students, would you agree that it might be unrealistic for him to expect unquestioned compliance with everything he "tells" students to do? Most students, especially in high school, like to feel they have some say in what happens to them rather than constantly being told what they must do. Thus, Mr. Johansen needs to examine his beliefs about students' legitimate role in determining classroom procedures. Does the teacher always know best, or do students sometimes have valuable input about what they need to learn and how they can best learn it? If what Mr. Johansen is asking them to do is truly busy work, would it be legitimate for them to grumble about the assignment?

Would it be acceptable for students to question how an assignment is to be done and why it is important to do? If you allow students to question the rationale for your request, perhaps students will see the request as more legitimate and be more willing to comply with it. If it turns out that student questioning uncovers flaws in your rationale, would it be appropriate for you to amend your request? When students have been involved in suggesting, questioning, or refining classroom procedures, they are more likely to comply with teacher requests. It appears Mr. Johansen has been relying more on his personal appeal to manage the class than on involving students in the establishment and revision of class procedures.

Mr. Johansen's fears about getting a bad reputation also suggest he may subscribe to the view that "good teachers don't have problems." All teachers encounter some classroom-management problems, but effective classroom managers don't ignore their problems. As you may recall from earlier discussions, problems such as defiance that are not confronted may spread rather than spontaneously disappear. The problem with defiance is sometimes more one of style than substance. A student in one of our classes objected to an established classroom procedure, calling it the "stupidest thing I ever heard of." Although we had a number of reasons for the procedure (mainly not giving some students preferential treatment over others), the wording of the student's objection largely negated any chance of our bending the procedure for this student. Thus, it may be valuable to coach your students in framing their reservations about your requests so that they increase the likelihood of a favorable response to those reservations.

Building Workable Relationships. Regardless of whether the problem is getting students to perform a desired task or to refrain from misconduct, teachers should assess whether their actions demonstrate concern for students. Perhaps a change in the way Mr. Johansen communicates his requests to students would affect the way those requests are received. Instead of issuing incessant "do this" and "do that" commands, he might frame his requests in less-autocratic terms (e.g., "Now that you have finished reading the first section of the chapter, please turn to page 100 in the text. There you will find questions about what you have just read. Let's see how many of those questions we can answer"). In assessing his approach to making requests and dealing with student responses to those requests, Mr. Johansen might ask himself the following questions:

1. Am I responsive to student difficulty with the work I have asked them to do? For example, do I ask questions to determine whether anything about class assignments is creating frustration? (Students who can't do the work requested are more apt to resist undertaking a task.)

2. When students are off-task, have I tried asking what they think they should be doing rather than telling them what they should be doing?

3. Do I have something positive to say to each of my students, at least on a weekly basis?

4. Have students been involved in discussions about appropriate and inappropriate ways to express dissatisfaction with others' requests?

5. Do I respond calmly to challenges from the students? (Harsh reactions are apt to intensify problems.)

6. Do I put past indiscretions in the past as opposed to bringing up those offenses whenever a new problem arises?

7. Am I willing to admit mistakes and make adjustments in requested procedures? (As opposed to giving students the impression I must always be right.)

Initiating Appropriate Behavior. Students obviously cannot simultaneously cooperate with and defy the teacher. Thus, one key to dealing with defiance is to prompt and reinforce cooperative actions. A good starting point in prompting cooperative actions is to examine the seating arrangement to determine if different groupings might result in more productive behaviors. Separating students who reinforce one another's inappropriate behaviors might be one issue to consider when assigning seats or giving students choices about where they may sit. Using texts appropriate for the students' skill levels and closely monitoring their activities will also let students know the teacher is concerned about their progress and is aware of their actions.

Certain approaches might prove helpful to Mr. Johansen in prompting and reinforcing positive behaviors to compete with defiant behavior:

1. Attempt to notice when students cooperate and then verbally praise this behavior. The praise can be offered in a private manner consistent with the suggestions in chapter four.

2. Make sure students understand that praise and rewards are tied to cooperative behavior. Immediately acknowledge how student cooperation is helpful to both you and all students.

3. When a student seldom cooperates, shape cooperative behavior by reinforcing behavior that increasingly approximates the goal of full cooperation (e.g., first thanking students for passively complying with a request—you can see from their nonverbal behavior they aren't happy about the request, but they comply anyway—and later explaining your rationale for a request when a student has tactfully questioned the purpose of the request).

4. Model compliant behavior. That is, tell students why you yourself are following certain policies and demonstrate how you comply with those procedures.

5. Avoid giving commands that you have no authority to enforce or that you would be unable to enforce if resisted by students. It is better to ask students what they should be doing than to tell them what they are going to do.

Being Helpful. Many of the preceding strategies involve establishing reciprocal respect between teacher and students. In working toward this mutual respect, Mr. Johansen might first try to understand better why students are defying his requests. The best time to do this would be in a private conversation. In opening channels of communication with students, he should focus on the student's feelings and reasons for the defiance rather than just on the overt behavior itself. For example, Mr. Johansen might say, "You believe I should not have asked you to stop talking when I did," or "You feel I have been unfair with you today." If the student responds positively to the teacher's expression of empathy, the door may be open for talking about how to resolve the problem. Showing respect for the student's feelings may prompt the student to be more respectful of the teacher's perspective.

Building on his attempt to communicate understanding of the student's perspective, Mr. Johansen may need to be more assertive in requesting a change in student behavior. Assertive behavior does not involve the delivery of ultimatums, but rather explicitly pinpoints the student behavior that needs to be changed and how both the teacher and the student would benefit from that change. Mr. Johansen can indicate how he is being affected by the student's behavior. Suppose a student responds to one of the teacher's requests with the retort, "What you are asking us to do is *stupid.*" A potential assertive response to the student's comment might include the following elements: "Your comment is disrespectful, and I want you to avoid using the word stupid in responding to any of my future requests. You may question what I ask you to do, but you always need to do so in a tactful manner, which will get you far more concessions than will the use of offensive language."

When a teacher's authority is challenged in front of other students, as appeared to be the case between Mr. Johansen and one of his students, others in the class are likely to be emotionally affected by both the student's comment and the teacher's response to it. To avoid possibly reinforcing defiance by directing attention to the problem, the teacher may need to refocus student attention on assignments. For example, Mr. Johansen might say, "We have work to do; this incident is between (student's name) and me. He and I will talk after class." The teacher wants to avoid engaging the whole class in a problem that is restricted to a single student. When others are involved or appear inclined to become involved in the problem, a group meeting can be held at a later time to discuss how to respond appropriately to one another's requests.

Working Together with Parents. Repeated rudeness or defiance of an extreme form (e.g., cursing, using obscene gestures) necessitates parental involvement. Conferences with parents, however, should not focus solely on a student's inappropriate behavior. Mr. Johansen can also talk about what the student is doing right and demonstrate a genuine desire that the student learn to respond in ways that will get positive results. Beginning on a positive note will set a more productive tone for the conference than immediately highlighting the student's misbehavior. When Mr. Johansen describes the student's misbehavior to the parents, he can ask for their suggestions and assistance in altering the behavioral tendency. If he has already had contact with the parents regarding positive experiences with the student, they should be more receptive in working with him in resolving the problem.

Despite their positive input to parents, teachers should not be surprised if some parents initially blame the teacher for what has happened (e.g., "Your request was unreasonable," "You expect too much."). Mr. Johansen will need to avoid becoming defensive at this point and instead stress his desire to work effectively with their child. He can emphasize what positive approaches have been taken thus far and indicate what yet might need to be done if the misbehavior continues. The follow-up will likely involve asking the parents to have a conversation with their child about his or her misconduct and possibly make home-based privileges contingent on improving his or her conduct. If the parents and Mr. Johansen cannot come to any agreement, he can suggest that he and the parents meet together with the principal to see if a compromise can be reached.

Working to Meet Everyone's Needs. In addition to the principal's involvement, other school professionals may need to be involved if the child has been suspected or identified as having special educational needs. A few students exhibit extreme oppositional behavior, showing great emotional arousal (such as rage or physical aggression). The school psychologist is typically the resource professional who can offer suggestions for working with students who have emotional problems. These suggestions will not only help the student respond more appropriately, but also help the teacher manage his or her stress in dealing with the problem.

If a student has a specific disability, the student's defiant behavior may need to be interpreted in light of that disability. In that case, the teacher needs to review the student's

IEP to determine what strategies would be appropriate in minimizing oppositional behavior. If no functional behavior assessment has been done to determine what might be triggering and reinforcing the child's defiant behavior, the teacher should consult with the IEP team and ask for such an assessment. It may well be that events preceding the child's behavior, such as working on a difficult task, may have precipitated the behavior, or that certain consequences, such as teacher acquiescence to the child's defiant demands, may have served as reinforcement for defiant and abusive behaviors. In any event, a plan needs to be provided to identify how to deemphasize triggering events for defiant actions, to withhold reinforcers for those actions, and to provide reinforcement for cooperative behavior.

Students' defiant behavior in Mr. Johansen's class appeared more widespread than the conduct of one individual who might have a special problem such as emotional disturbance. The problem described resembles a breakdown in classroom management rather than an isolated problem involving a single student. The school counselor or school psychologist should be willing to conduct observations in the classroom to determine how

widespread the problem is and to offer helpful suggestions about replacing triggering events and reinforcers for defiant behavior with triggers and reinforcers for cooperative behaviors.

Moving Students toward Greater Personal Responsibility. One of the primary strategies for helping students behave more responsibly is to teach them to think before they act. For example, students can be taught cognitive strategies to help them reflect on the likely consequences of their reactions to teacher requests. Before responding to a request from the teacher (or others), they can ask themselves, "What is likely to happen if I cooperate, and what is likely to happen if I refuse?" Teachers can help students understand the relationship between what they do and the outcomes that follow those actions by ensuring that positive outcomes (e.g., supportive comments) follow cooperative behaviors and by trying not to reinforce offensive behavior.

Discussions in which students analyze how appropriate and inappropriate behaviors lead to different outcomes might also help students understand the control they can exercise over their lives. In brief, students can discuss how different behaviors lead either to conflicts with others or to better relationships. The teacher might also employ behavioral contracts, clearly spelling out the positive and negative consequences for cooperative and uncooperative actions. If a routine has been established for beginning work on assignments, putting away material, handing in assignments, or completing other classroom activities, students can monitor their own behavior by using a teacher-prepared checklist to note which actions they have taken in complying with teacher directions. Such self-monitoring would reduce problems associated with the teacher's repeatedly telling students what they should be doing.

Considering the Teacher's Daily Needs. Perhaps nothing is more stressful to teachers than open conflicts with students. Having outlets to reduce the stress of dealing with defiant behaviors, therefore, is critical to teachers' well-being. How they respond on the job cannot be separated from what they do after school to relieve stress. Tension carried over from one day to the next will likely worsen rather than lessen conflicts at school. Teachers should get today's tension out of their system as much as they can or at least gain perspective on troubling events before returning to class the next school day.

Teachers differ in how they find relief from accumulating stress. Some may feel better after vigorous physical activity, whereas

Stress relief

others may find relief through more passive activity such as listening to soft music or engaging in meditation. Whatever your personal preferences for stress-reducing activity, be sure to choose activities that don't create additional stress (such as smoking and drinking) and build in time for stress-reducing activities soon after the school day ends. Such events may help you gain a more balanced perspective of what happened at school that day.

On Your Own

Given that our text has presented a variety of techniques for addressing a variety of classroom problems, you may wonder how to choose the best techniques for dealing with a particular problem. For instance, when a problem behavior must be stopped immediately, which technique should be used—a soft reprimand, a time-out, or a response-cost approach? The answer depends on your students' level of maturity, the nature of the offense, and the conditions that might have triggered or reinforced the behavior. For instance, your students' age might preclude frequent use of certain techniques (such as time-out). Also, your experience with a student may reveal that one technique will be far more productive than another.

Although you may favor certain techniques over others, you will probably need to use most of the recommended techniques with different students at different times. For this reason, we have provided here some examples of classroom problems to give you practice in identifying strategies likely to be effective with those problems. We have organized the problems in terms of student behaviors that *primarily* need to be strengthened (deficit behaviors), student behaviors that need to be weakened (excessive behaviors), and problems requiring changes in teacher behaviors.

Just as we did with the problems of inadequate peer interaction and defiance of teacher requests, we suggest you peruse chapters one through nine in selecting the techniques you believe most appropriate for each problem. You may want to work with a small group of colleagues in identifying the most workable solutions for each problem. You can use a BRIGHTER DAY as your guide. Remember to include the following elements in your solutions:

1. Examination of your **beliefs** about students and the problems they present,

2. Communication patterns to build workable **relationships**,

3. Strategies for **initiating** appropriate student behaviors,

4. Ways to reinforce **good** student behaviors,

5. Means of **helping** your students replace maladaptive behaviors with constructive actions,

6. Channels for working **together** with parents,

7. Assistance from school-resource personnel in promoting learning for **everyone**,

8. A framework for moving students toward greater personal **responsibility**,

9. Consideration of your own quality of life each **day**.

Problems Involving Deficit Behaviors

Ms. Edwards, a seventh-grade math-science teacher, has a problem "motivating" her students to complete homework assignments, which she estimates should take about an hour each night. Watching television, surfing the Internet, and playing video games seem to be higher priorities than schoolwork. "I know they're busy, but too many fail to complete their homework" is how Ms. Edwards describes her class. What

might Ms. Edwards do to use the activities competing with homework so that they serve as an aid rather than as an impediment to homework?

Mr. Herman frequently has his students work in small groups to do special projects or to discuss current events related to topics in the course. He says that students "take forever completing their group tasks." When Mr. Herman checks in with each group, he notices they often are off task and discussing personal issues. What factors might be triggering and reinforcing off-task behavior in group work, and how can Mr. Herman change those factors to help his students be more productive in their group work?

Mr. Harrison's eleventh-grade U.S. history students seem interested in class activities and do well on in-class and homework assignments. Many students, however, do below average on unit exams given each month. Mr. Harrison worries that students will perform poorly on the systemwide exam at the end of the school year because of their poor performance on his exams. What factors might be contributing to their below-average exam performance, and how can Mr. Harrison change those factors to improve students' test performance?

Ms. Workman's fourth-grade students often don't have materials needed to complete class work. Some forget to bring paper and pencils. Others take books home to study and fail to bring them back the next day. Some don't have a copy of the assignment distributed the previous day. What factors might be contributing to this pattern of apparent forgetfulness? What can Ms. Workman do to ensure that students will have all the materials they need to complete their in-class assignments in a timely fashion?

One of Ms. Triplett's ninth graders, Jay, is absent from school more frequently than he is present. She is concerned about his truant behavior. What factors might be contributing to Jay's high absenteeism? What can Ms. Triplett do to alter any or all of these factors?

Christy is a very quiet, shy, and withdrawn fifth grader. Her teacher reports that Christy is a loner in class, does not approach other students, and is not approached by them. She seems to be an unhappy child. What factors might contribute to the isolation of children like Christy? What might the teacher do to begin building connections between Christy and her peers?

Two of Mr. Branson's tenth-grade girls are consistently tardy to English class. They give one excuse and then another for being late. Mr. Branson wants to give them the benefit of the doubt, but he is convinced that their excuses are invalid. What can be done to reduce tardiness? (*Note:* This problem deals with both a deficit—being on time—and an excessive behavior—invalid excuses.)

Problems Involving Excessive Behaviors

Ms. Phillips is concerned about "cute" remarks and "off-color" comments students are making in class discussions. She thinks some of the remarks are imitative of what her students are hearing on situation comedies they watch on television. What can she do to eliminate these comments in class discussions?

Several of Mr. Jones's fourth-grade boys are loud and boisterous during lunch. Their table manners are usually poor, and some days are worse than others. For example, they throw bread and swap food, sometimes overloading their plates. The students' behavior disrupts Mr. Jones's own lunch. How can he create a calmer, more enjoyable lunch period for both himself and his students?

Andrea and Deborah are close friends. During class periods, they continually whisper and pass notes. Some of the other students complain that they cannot concentrate on their work because the whispering disturbs them. How can their teacher curtail inappropriate talking during class activities?

Several students report to their teacher that their school supplies and personal clothing have been stolen at school. Problems with stealing appear to be increasing at school. What are some things teachers can do to reduce thefts around school?

George and Randy run to tell their teacher that two of their fifth-grade classmates are fighting on the playground. This is not the first time that these classmates have fought during recess. What can the teacher do to deal immediately with the behavior, and how can he or she prevent fights in the future?

Phillip is a fifth-grade student who frequently has temper outbursts. The problem occurs most often during his physical education class. For example, when the students play softball, he argues vehemently when things don't go his way. During one game, when he was called "out" at first base, he kicked the ground, jumped up and down, and yelled that "he was robbed." Phillip also throws things (his hat or his glove) when his side loses and will pout for some time when returning from P.E. What might the P.E. teacher and his regular teacher do to help Phillip become a more constructive participant in his P.E. activity?

Scott tends to assume a threatening posture and be verbally aggressive toward other seventh-grade males. In particular, he engages in name-calling and brags about beating up other boys if they bother him. How can his aggressive conduct be diminished?

Ms. Crawford's seventh-grade male students are afraid to go to the restroom because they have been subjected to "wedgies" from eighth-grade students who think this practice is fun. What might be done to alleviate this problem?

Ms. Veltzy's students often play soccer, touch football, or softball during her P.E. class. She initially had let the students choose sides, but she noticed several of the students were always chosen last. She then decided to select who would be on each team, but students complained, "We'll never win with him on our team." How might Ms. Veltzy reduce such derogatory comments toward the less-skilled students?

Mr. Hardy's students tend to engage in disruptive behaviors any time they are walking down the hallway to lunch or going to recess. They jump up to touch the top of doors and often race to get where they are going. In addition to being unsafe, their behaviors are disruptive of other classes. What can Mr. Hardy do to eliminate this problem?

Problems Involving Needed Changes in Teacher Behavior

Mr. Wilson is an eighth-grade language arts teacher who believes praise is the most effective strategy a teacher can use to motivate students to do their schoolwork. He is lavish in offering praise for almost any appropriate social behavior and for any good academic work he sees. His approach to misbehavior is to ignore it. Things are not going well, however. Many students are not doing high-level work and are not achieving their potential. Student misbehavior is also on the rise. What factors might be accounting for student reactions to Mr. Wilson's well-intentioned approach? What changes can he make in his approach to get better results?

Mr. Carson believes his students need to be more attentive to his directions regarding in-class and homework assignments. Sometimes students say they didn't do their work because they didn't understand what they were to do. Others sometimes complete their work, but not in the way he wanted it to be done. What might Mr. Carson do to facilitate better student work on their homework assignments?

Mr. Glass, a young teacher, is having difficulties with several of his eighth-grade girls. They follow him around, want to talk with him in private, pass notes to him, and in general let him know that they like him very much. Mr. Glass wants to be friendly, but he realizes that he must establish clear and proper limits with these girls. What limits should he set on his interactions with them, and how can he enforce those limits?

Ms. Hernandez is in her third year of teaching but is thinking of quitting at the end of the school year. She likes working with students and believes that teachers can make

an important contribution to society, but she comes home exhausted from what she describes as "a mound of paperwork." Ms. Hernandez spends most of her planning time at school grading papers and brings additional student work home each day. Much of her evening time is spent grading more student papers and planning for the next day. Her husband works nine to five and does not bring work home with him, so the two are spending less and less time interacting. She says, "I am about at the end of my rope." What factors do you think are contributing to this problem of too much schoolwork at home? Can Ms. Hernandez change these factors sufficiently to improve the quality of her home life without reducing the quality of student learning in her classroom?

Concluding Comments

Some classroom-management problems are a given. That will remain the case even if a teacher applies all the classroom-management strategies described in this book. Some problems are simply the natural result of teachers and students' working closely together for several hours day after day. However, we believe our strategies will reduce both the frequency and intensity of classroom-management problems. We have seen a number of teachers apply these strategies in difficult urban schools, thereby reducing classroom-management problems to a minimum. In these classrooms, the emphasis was largely on prevention rather than on suppression of problematic behaviors. Nonetheless, despite the best preventive strategies, some bad behaviors will occur, and teachers in all classrooms must be prepared to respond to these behaviors thoughtfully and decisively.

We believe that virtually all teachers can make their classroom experiences more enjoyable for themselves and their students. Our goal in this book has been to increase your knowledge of classroom-management techniques that will help your students learn appropriate social and academic skills. Your task now is to apply what has been presented to the variety of challenges you currently face or will face in the classroom. Of course, you should take good care of yourself in the process. Only the combination of productive activity at school and renewal experiences after school can bring *brighter days* for both you and your students.

◄○►

Appendix

Not in Their Best Interest—
Corporal Punishment

T he indiscriminate use of any behavior-change strategy is unlikely to be helpful to students. For example, in chapter four we noted concerns about the misuse of teacher praise. Problems with teacher praise range from embarrassing some students with public accolades to creating the impression that pleasing the teacher is the most important reason for good behavior. Private and specific praise that invites students to value their own efforts is more acceptable. Negative techniques also have their liabilities, however, and at least one negative strategy—corporal punishment—is subject to both ethical and legal concerns.

Ethical Concerns Related to Corporal Punishment

Although some school districts allow corporal punishment, we question whether teachers have a right to inflict physical pain and humiliation on students. Certainly, most teachers would refrain from doing so to another adult. In the case of a child, however, corporal punishment is justified by such platitudes as "that child will learn to behave" or "spare the rod and spoil the child." We have even heard college students justify spankings on the grounds that it never did them any harm. A "spanking" from a loving parent might admittedly be interpreted differently from a spanking at the hands of a teacher. Nevertheless, any adult who spanks or paddles is modeling aggressive behavior for children. Furthermore, corporal punishment may engender strong emotional problems in children (e.g., anxiety, fear, depression, and resentment).

There are many ethical questions regarding the use of corporal punishment, including the following: (1) What are children being taught when they are hit or observe others being hit by the teacher or principal? (2) Will children actually refrain from misconduct as a result of physical punishment, or will they learn they can do as they please when they are big enough to exert power over others? (3) What are the negative emotional effects of being paddled? (4) Will children who are paddled develop a dislike for teachers, the school, and academics? An additional consideration is that physical punishment does not teach children what they should be doing. The bottom-line message of physical punishment may be that a teacher is upset or out of control, not a particularly instructive message for students.

Legal Issues Related to Corporal Punishment

The use of corporal punishment in the schools can be traced back to the Puritan settlement of the Massachusetts Bay Colony (Piele 1978). Religious views no doubt played a major role in its early use and still do. However, considerable societal concern about the use of corporal punishment in schools has prompted the courts to establish precedents regarding its use. The foundation of current corporal punishment policies is the 1977 Supreme Court case *Ingraham v. Wright* (430 U. S. 65 [1977]) (see Hinchey 2003).

The *Ingraham v. Wright* case was first brought to the attention of the courts when Ingraham and several fellow students at Drew Junior High School in Dade County, Florida, charged they had been the victims of beatings from teachers that resulted in injuries ranging from a hematoma to a badly disfigured hand. A class-action claim also sought relief from the use of corporal punishment in the Dade County school system. Following appeals through the lower courts, the case was heard by the U.S. Supreme Court. The Court held that the cruel and unusual punishment clause of the Eighth Amendment does not apply to corporal punishment used as a disciplinary measure. It further held that the due process clause of the Fourteenth Amendment does not require notice and hearing be given prior to the imposition of corporal punishment, inasmuch as corporal punishment in school is limited and authorized by common law (Englander 1978).

In writing the majority opinion, Justice Lewis Powell noted that schools are essentially open institutions where support of family and friends is available. He reasoned that students have little need of protection offered by the Eighth Amendment and further noted that students' interests were adequately protected by state law. The first type of safeguard was prescribed by Florida statute and required the teacher to confer with the principal before using corporal punishment with any student; the second safeguard resulted from the teacher's liability for civil damages in tort when corporal punishment was deemed unreasonable for the circumstances; and the third safeguard hinged on the teacher's liability for the crime of assault and battery if he or she physically harmed a child.

The issue of corporal punishment remains controversial. The vote on the 1977 *Ingraham v. Wright* Supreme Court ruling was close (five to four), with the minority opinion taking issue with the arguments offered in the majority opinion. The debate on the use of corporal punishment did not end with the *Ingraham v. Wright* decision. Although the Supreme Court of the United States has not prohibited the use of corporal punishment in the schools, twenty-seven states and the District of Columbia have laws banning the use of corporal punishment (Center for Effective Discipline 2003). Other states have pending legislation regarding the prohibition of corporal punishment in the schools. Even in states where corporal punishment is not explicitly prohibited by state law, local ordinances and school board directives may prohibit its use.

Remember, too, that although physical punishment may be permitted, it cannot be used indiscriminately. Essex (2002) outlines a number of ways school officials may risk lawsuits, one of which is failing to try less-aggressive means of controlling disruptive and offensive behavior. The Center for Effective Discipline (2003) reports that physical

INSTANCES OF CORPORAL PUNISHMENT

Data compiled by the National Coalition to Abolish Corporal Punishment in Schools indicate that 342,038 students were subjected to corporal punishment in the 1999–2000 school year in the United States, with most corporal punishment occurring in southern states (Center for Effective Discipline 2003). A *USA Today* article ("States Too Slow" 2002) reports that in elementary and middle schools paddling is usually done by teachers, although some schools permit only school administrators to paddle students. The article further reports that parents can often withhold permission to use corporal punishment. However, school personnel may not always solicit parental consent, and some parents may not understand their rights or realize the adverse effects of having their child physically punished. Moreover, depending on the state or school district, parental consent is not always necessary. More information about banning corporal punishment in schools can be obtained from http://www. stophitting.com, which offers a listing of professional groups and organizations that oppose corporal punishment in school.

punishment can be used only as a last resort. The center also reports that bruises and injuries are relatively common. Psychiatrists warn that in extreme cases physical punishment can be the equivalent of child abuse (Boser 2001). In brief, corporal punishment puts children in peril and poses legal risks for those who use it.

Legal concerns over corporal punishment are not restricted to how the punishment has been applied, what behaviors warrant physical punishment, and what harm it might have caused. Another legal issue is what children are the recipients of corporal punishment. Data indicate that corporal punishment is used disproportionately with minority children, poor children, and children with disabilities (Center for Effective Discipline 2003). It is also used more often with male students than with female students. A legitimate question is why certain groups are subjected more often to corporal punishment than are other groups? Educators have a responsibility to ensure the fair treatment of all students. Relying on alternatives to corporal punishment for all students provides greater assurance that no one's rights are abridged.

References

Boser, U. (2001). The unsparing rod. *U.S. News and World Report* 130 (24): 43–44.

Center for Effective Discipline. (2003). *Discipline at School (National Coalition to Abolish Corporal Punishment in Schools)*. Columbus, Oh.: National Center Against Corporal Punishment in Schools. Retrieved May 24, 2004, from http://www.stophitting.com.

Englander, M. E. (1978). The court's corporal punishment mandate to parents, local authorities, and the profession. *Phi Delta Kappan* 59(8): 529–32.

Essex, N. L. (2002). Ten costly mistakes in disciplining disruptive students. *Education and the Law* 14(3): 167–72.

Hinchey, P. H. (2003). Corporal punishment legalities, realities, and implications. *Clearing House* 76(3): 127–34.

Ingraham v. Wright, 430 U. S. 65 (1977).

Piele, P. K. (1978). Neither corporal punishment nor due process due: The United States Supreme Court's decision in *Ingraham v. Wright. Journal of Law and Education* 7: 1–19.

States too slow to spare the child, part with the rod. (2002). *USA Today*, August 23, 12a.

Index